70 YEARS OF
CHAMPIONSHIP FOOTBALL

JOHN STEINBREDER

Bruce D. Corey
Coordinating Consultant

Jack Smith
Publisher & Director, Fine Books

Tony Seidl / TD Media, Inc.
Packager

Frank Coffey
Editor

Robert Engle and Roger Greiner
Design and Art Direction

Production Assistance by Wanda Mellody, Michael Zahn
Dust Jacket Design by Robert Engle
Dust Jacket, Endsheet and Interior Art by Robert Sullivan
Contributing Photographers: Robert Riger, Jerry Pinkus, Fred Roe, Joe McKenna, Gus Boyd, and Dan Rubin
Remaining photos courtesy of New York Football Giants, Inc., Pro Football Hall of Fame

Published by Taylor Publishing Company,
Dallas, Texas

ISBN: 0-87833-092-5 (General)
ISBN: 0-87833-093-3 (Limited)
ISBN: 0-87833-094-1 (Collectors)

For Exa,

who has shown me
there is no greater joy
than the love of a child

ABOUT THE AUTHOR

Andrée McAdam

JOHN STEINBREDER has been writing professionally for the past 15 years. After attending Franklin College in Lugano, Switzerland and the University of Nairobi, he graduated with a B.A. degree in journalism from the University of Oregon. He worked for two New England newspapers before joining Time Inc. in 1982. Steinbreder spent five years as a reporter at *Fortune* magazine and then moved to *Sports Illustrated*, for which he covered a wide variety of subjects as a writer/reporter. He left the staff of *SI* in 1991 to go out on his own, though he continues to do work for the magazine as a special contributor. He has also written for the *New York Times Magazine*, the *Wall Street Journal*, *Forbes FYI*, *Sports Afield*, *People*, *Met Golfer* and *Sporting Classics*. He lives in Easton, Ct. with his three-year-old daughter Exa and their Black Labrador Retriever Timber.

CONTENTS

ACKNOWLEDGEMENTS

viii

FOREWORD   BY WELLINGTON MARA

xi

INTRODUCTION

xiii

CHAPTER ONE   THE DUKE OF WELLINGTON

1

CHAPTER TWO   "I'M GOING TO TRY TO PUT FOOTBALL OVER IN NEW YORK"...1925–1955

17

CHAPTER THREE   BEASTS OF THE EAST...1956–1963

37

CHAPTER FOUR   THE WILDERNESS YEARS...1964–1978

115

CHAPTER FIVE   GEORGE AND BILL; LAWRENCE AND PHIL...1979–1990

133

CHAPTER SIX   A DANDY FUTURE...1991–PRESENT

201

CHAPTER SEVEN   STATISTICS AND RECORDS

222

ACKNOWLEDGEMENTS

No one said that writing a book would be easy. And no one said I wouldn't need a lot of help pulling it together. This project began in the spring of 1993, and any excitement I felt after signing my contract quickly dissipated when I realized how little time I actually had to complete the task. But thanks to some extremely helpful people, I was able to get it done. Ahead of schedule, I might add.

First off, I owe a tremendous debt of gratitude to Rusty Hawley, the Giants' director of marketing. It was over a nice lunch in New York City last winter that we first talked about this book, and I am eternally grateful for his support in making me a part of the project and then helping me execute it. Once I got started, my main man around the Giants' offices was Aaron Salkin, the assistant director of public relations. Many times I interrupted Aaron's busy days with inane questions about obscure players, long-forgotten games, hard-to-find documents and temperamental copying machines, and he cheerfully came through for me every time. Ed "Boomer" Olivari guided me in my search through the team's archives, and PR director Pat Hanlon made sure I got whatever else I needed. Wellington Mara was extraordinarily generous with his time and gave me a wonderful sense of what his family and his football team are all about. George Young graciously answered my many questions as did Dan Reeves.

I'm also thankful for the help I received from a number of former Giants. Bill Parcells, Allie Sherman, Andy Robustelli, Tom Landry, Pat Summerall, Harry Carson and Alex Webster all took time from their schedules to tell me about their days with the team. I also appreciated the insights Pete Rozelle shared.

Nothing makes a project like this easier than a good editor, and I was fortunate to have Frank Coffey. Not only is he a deft wordsmith, but he also treats a writer with respect, understanding and compassion, a rare commodity these days. I'm also happy to have worked with Frank's partner Tony Siedl, of T.D. Media, and the folks from Taylor Publishing, Jack Smith and Bruce Corey. Kudos, also, to photographers Robert Riger and Jerry Pinkus whose fine work brought this book to life. Thanks as well to the designers Robert Engle, Roger Greiner, and Lorenz Skeeter of Robert Engle Design for making this such an attractive package.

I used a number of different books and periodical sources throughout the project, and none was more helpful than Richard Whittingham's book, "The Giants," which came out after the team's first Super Bowl win. It contains a wealth of good information, and I'm glad I had a copy by my desk. I am also appreciative of the extensive coverage the New York and New Jersey newspapers have given the Giants over the years; their stories proved to be an invaluable resource as well.

On a personal note, I have several people I'd like to thank for their help and support. My daughter Exa is only three years old, but her bright smile and big hugs kept me going on even the toughest days. My mother Cynthia has long known my dream of writing a book, and she always took the time to call and see how I was doing. A crossword puzzle fanatic, she also helped me find the right word on a couple of occasions when I was too tired to figure it out for myself. My sisters Sissy, Gillett and Sarah frequently telephoned in their support, even though two of them are rabid 49ers fans and like to hang up on me whenever I mention Leonard Marshall's hit on Joe Montana in the 1990 playoffs. I'm only sorry that my father Sandy, a lovely man who died much too young in 1985, and my godfather John Fistere, who passed away shortly thereafter, can't see this. (Well, maybe they can.)

New York Times reporter Bill Wallace is an old family friend, and he took the time to chat with me about his years covering the team and was nice enough to lend me an armful of books. Strat Sherman, Geoff Colvin and Steve Malley never saw this manuscript, but they have been enormous helps in other parts of my writing career, and I appreciate their friendship and their willingness to listen and advise. John Bryan, too, listens well, and I would not have survived this past winter and spring without our talks on the phone and in the duck blind. Nor could I have made it through those months without the Hemingwayesque dinners Mike Dailey and I enjoyed in some of New York's finest steak houses. Thanks for the help, Mike; I promise I'll buy my first office building from you.

Writing a book about a team I have rooted for all my life made me think a lot about the people with whom I have shared so many Giants games. So here's to Nat Foote, Peter Dunn, Tucker Crolius and Scott Miller, great fans and great friends. I'd also like to thank Richard Kent for helping me keep my daughter in town; Brian Waldron for fixing my back in the middle of chapter three; Arvid and Pam for being such good neighbors; Brenda for her Godivas; Kylie, Alex and Elise for their friendship; and Andrée McAdam, whose love, patience and under-standing have been a terrific source of comfort and inspiration—so far.

John Steinbreder
Easton, Ct.
July 1994

FOREWORD

I can't remember when The Giants were not an important part of my life. I was nine years old when my father started the team and fourteen when my brother Jack and I became co-owners. I began working full time for the team after graduating from Fordham University in 1938. Jack ran the business operation and I was responsible for personnel. I spent all of my time with the coaches and players and was the first one to take motion pictures of our games. The Giants have won 14 Divisional Championships and 6 NFL Championships. 25 members of our organization are in The Pro Football Hall of Fame.

I take pride in The Giants' accomplishments and tradition which have been so well captured by the book you now hold in your hands. I've enjoyed reliving The Giants seventy years of championship football and I'm sure you will too.

Wellington Mara

INTRODUCTION

There is something special about the New York Giants, and as a lifelong fan, I recognized that from the first time I saw them play. It was in 1963, when the team held its training camp at Fairfield University in my hometown of Fairfield, Ct., and Bill Wallace, a family friend who was covering the Giants for the *New York Times*, brought me there to watch them scrimmage. I remember meeting several of the players after practice one day—Jack Stroud, Alex Webster and Andy Robustelli to name a few—and being awed by their size and strength. I was only seven years old, and they seemed as big as polar bears. They were also a friendly bunch who happily took the time to chat with a young fan and sign their autographs.

The Giants were still competing for championships back then, and they seemed to captivate the metropolitan New York area like no other sports franchise before them. Fans packed Yankee Stadium week after week to see their games, and sportswriters waxed eloquent about the team's stellar play. There was a certain glamour about players like Frank Gifford, Sam Huff and Pat Summerall, and many of them were employed by the television networks as announcers and commentators or used by advertising executives on Madison Avenue to sell everything from shoes to automobiles. Members of the team were treated as heroes wherever they went, and as Summerall recalls: "I don't remember ever having to pay for a drink or a dinner in all my time with the Giants."

Even when the Giants struggled in later years, the team retained much of its luster. Fans kept showing up for games, and they never gave up their dreams of seeing their team rise again. And when the Giants did come back, when they began winning in the early 1980s and finally snagged that elusive NFL title in 1986, all of metropolitan New York erupted in an outpouring of affection and adoration rarely seen among the famously cynical fans of that region. As one sportswriter stated after that Super Bowl win: "No team owns New York like the Football Giants."

It wasn't always that way, however. New York sports fans hardly noticed the Giants when the team started out in 1925. Baseball, college football and boxing were far bigger attractions in those days, and that was so apparent to Timothy J. Mara, the team's founder, that he named his ball club after the baseball Giants in hopes of kindling interest in his new venture. Sure, Mara was able to draw some 70,000 spectators to a game that opening season, but that was only because the opposing Chicago Bears team had Red Grange, the most famous runner in football. And though the Giants later boasted stars such as Mel Hein and Ken Strong, though they had a great coach in Steve Owen, though they won NFL Championships in 1934 and 1938, they played second fiddle, maybe even third or fourth, in the great arena of New York sports.

But all that began to change in 1956 when the Giants beat the Bears 47-7 for the NFL Championship. There had been a harmonic convergence of talent for the team that year, and the Giants featured a remarkably skilled squad of players. Frank Gifford, Kyle Rote, Charlie Conerly, Alex Webster and Rosey Brown led a potent offense while Andy Robustelli, Dick Modzewelski, Sam Huff, Jimmy Patton, Emlen Tunnell, Rosey Grier, Harland Svare and Jim Katcavage anchored a smart and brutally tough defense. Head coach Jim Lee Howell also had an All-Pro roster of assistants that included Vince Lombardi and Tom Landry. And to anyone who watched the fans fill Yankee Stadium each Sunday, to anyone who heard them cheer, who listened to their chants of "DEE-FENSE, DEE-FENSE" echoing in the rafters of that grand ball park, it was clear there was something special about that team.

That became even more apparent in 1958 when the Giants beat the formidable Cleveland Browns twice at the end of the season and then faced off against the Baltimore Colts for the league title. CBS had begun televising NFL games the year before, and the title match-up was being seen by hundreds of thousands of people across the country. Those who witnessed it were treated to a stirring overtime victory by the Colts in a contest that would become known as "the greatest game ever played" and be credited with starting America's love affair with professional football. It also help cement the Giants' standing in the New York sports scene and hastened their emergence as one of the best-known and most popular sports franchises in the entire country.

What exactly makes the Giants so special? "Heritage," says former head coach Allie Sherman. "The team has one of the richest histories of any club in professional football, and to be a part of the Giants is to be a part of that heritage." Harry Carson concurs. "I didn't really know much about the Giants until I got here, but I could feel the tradition and history of the team as soon as I arrived," says the former inside linebacker. "I met guys like Sam Huff and Dick Modzewelski, and people were constantly telling me about greats like Y.A. Tittle, Charlie Conerly and Rosey Grier. You become part of that tradition and history when you join the team, and you feel an obligation to play a little better as a result of that."

Wellington Mara thinks it is the fans who give his team its distinctive character. "We have had the same fans coming to our games year in and year out," he says. "Tickets have been passed down from grandfather to father to son, from grandmother to mother to daughter, and so has their love and knowledge of the team." Adds George Young: "Many of the fans go back a long way, and rooting for the Giants has become something of a religion to them. And their fervor has grown over the years." (Indeed it has. There is currently a 20-year waiting list for season tickets.)

Andy Robustelli, who retired as a player nearly 20 years ago, is amazed at how people still react to the Giants teams on which he played. "I'm looking at five letters I received yesterday," he said one day from his travel agency in Stamford, Ct., "and I'm sure that when I open them, each one will be about the Giants. Just the other day I was at the headquarters of a Fortune 500 company, waiting in the lobby for an appointment, and some guy came up to me and asked, 'Aren't you Andy Robustelli?' Almost 30 years since I first came to the Giants, and people still recognize me."

It also helps that the Giants play in the media and advertising capital of the world. "When I was with Dallas, Tom Landry used to talk about the immensity of competing in New York, of playing in the biggest city in the country," says head coach Dan Reeves. "He used to tell us that we wouldn't be considered a great team if we didn't do well in New York. And he said that if a New York team succeeds, its accomplishments are just magnified." Former NFL commissioner Pete Rozelle agrees. "I think being in New York only enhanced the team's image and stature in the league," he says. "I remember that up until the sudden death game in 1958, the NFL had very little in the way of national endorsements for any of its players. But after that game, several players started appearing in advertising campaigns, and most of them were New York Giants."

My hope is that this book, which chronicles the 70-year history of the New York Football Giants, will help people appreciate this team's heritage even more and understand why it is such a special franchise. I know it has for me. Before I started working on this project, I considered myself fairly well-versed in Giants lore. But after spending a couple of weeks at the teams' offices at Giants Stadium, I was shocked at how little I really knew about the franchise. I relished the stories I read about the team's first year, how it struggled at the gate and barely survived the Great Depression. I couldn't believe that Wellington Mara was only 14 years old when he became a part-owner, or that he and Vince Lombardi were classmates at Fordham University. I knew that the Giants used sneakers to beat the Bears in the fabled 1934 championship game, but I had no idea that the players were being served whisky during timeouts to keep them warm.

Each day I spent pouring over old clippings was full of discovery. Mel Hein had retired after the 1942 season, for example, to take the head coaching job and to teach physical education at Union College in Schenectady, N.Y. But because of World War II, the school decided to disband its team for the 1944 season. When Steve Owen heard of that, he phoned Hein and talked him into playing for the Giants on weekends. So Hein, who was 35 years old, taught classes all week, then rode the train down to Manhattan on Friday nights to practice with the Giants on Saturdays and play for them—both ways, a full 60 minutes—on Sunday. One of my other favorite stories was of Giants running back Ward Cuff playing against Chicago Bears fullback Bronco Nagurski one Sunday afternoon at the Polo Grounds and then watching the future Hall-of-Famer wrestle for the world championship at Madison Square Garden that night.

The fascination didn't end as I worked my way into the early 1960s, when I started rooting for the team. I knew a lot about Tittle and Shofner, Robustelli and Huff. But I had no idea about how Pat Summerall got his first broadcasting job or why Tom Landry left for his home state of Texas after the 1959 season. I loved reading the clips about my first Giants game—a 31-3 loss to the Eagles in Yankee Stadium in 1966. It was in the middle of a dismal 1-12-1 season, and I can still hear the crowd singing "Goodbye Allie" as the Eagles piled on the points. I enjoyed the stories of the 1970 season-ending loss to the Rams, mainly because I had been in Europe at the time and never got to read an account of that game. I cringed when I read again and again about "the fumble" in 1978, the plane flying over Giants Stadium later that year, the fans burning tickets. And I was delighted to review the team's resurgence under George Young, Ray Perkins and Bill Parcells, culminating in two glorious Super Bowl wins and a return to greatness.

Much as I enjoyed the reading, the best part of researching this book was speaking with people like Wellington Mara. I'm a bit of a history buff, and I was always sorry when our meetings ended because I could have gone on for so much longer. I had some wonderful conversations with George Young, Bill Parcells and Dan Reeves, and I remember thinking to myself on a couple of occasions how lucky I was to be trading football talk about my favorite team with such men. And getting paid to do it as well.

When I was finished writing, I went back over my notes, and I was struck again with what Harry Carson had said about feeling the history and tradition of this team when one becomes associated with it. I now know exactly what he was talking about. My hope is that after reading this book, you will, too.

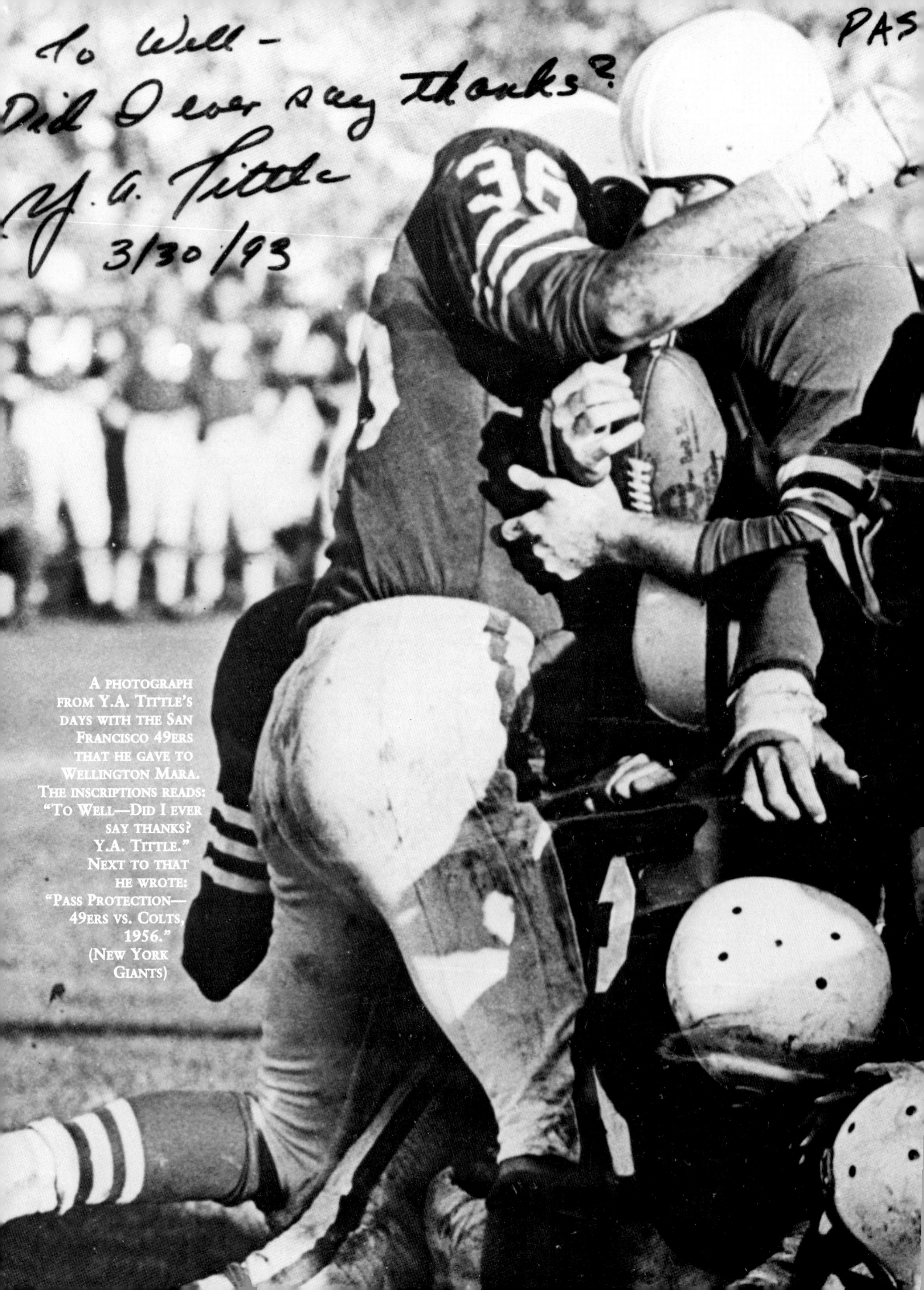

To Well —
Did I ever say thanks?
Y.A. Tittle
3/30/93

PAS

A PHOTOGRAPH
FROM Y.A. TITTLE'S
DAYS WITH THE SAN
FRANCISCO 49ERS
THAT HE GAVE TO
WELLINGTON MARA.
THE INSCRIPTIONS READS:
"TO WELL—DID I EVER
SAY THANKS?
Y.A. TITTLE."
NEXT TO THAT
HE WROTE:
"PASS PROTECTION—
49ERS VS. COLTS,
1956."
(NEW YORK
GIANTS)

CHAPTER 1

THE DUKE OF WELLINGTON

There were only six minutes left in Super Bowl XXI, and the Giants were leading 33-13. But Wellington Mara still could not relax. An official from the National Football League had walked into his private box at the Rose Bowl in Pasadena, Ca. and asked the Giants owner to follow him down to the locker room for the presentation of the Lombardi Trophy. But Mara was not budging. "It's too early," he said. "I saw what Elway did to get his Broncos here. I remember what Johnny Unitas did to us."

Mara went back to watching the game as the league official shuffled nervously by the door. The Giants had just recovered an onside kick attempt by the Denver Broncos and were driving again. Lee Rouson scampered for 18 yards, and then Phil Simms ran a 22-yard bootleg. Only when Ottis Anderson bulled in from the two-yard line and put his team up 39-13

did Mara feel comfortable enough to leave. He turned to his escort and said, "Let's go." And then he began the long walk to the Giants' locker room, the locker room of the new Super Bowl Champions.

The Rose Bowl was jammed with more than 100,000 spectators and buzzed with excitement, but 70-year-old Wellington Mara hardly noticed the people or the noise as he made his way downstairs. He was thinking, instead, of his many years in football, of all he had experienced in the NFL, of the great victories and frustrating losses and the 30 long years he had been waiting for his team to be crowned champions again.

He thought back to the fall of 1925, when he was a nine year old boy attending mass with his family at Our Lady of Esperanza Roman Catholic Church on 156th St. between Broadway and Riverside Drive in Manhattan. His father, Timothy J. Mara, was a bookmaker (a legal occupation at the time), and after the service he was telling some friends about a football franchise he had just purchased for $500. "I'm going to try to put pro football over in New York today," he said. And when he was done socializing in front of church, he took his wife and two sons—Jack, who was 17, and Wellington—to the Polo Grounds, which stood just across the Harlem River from newly-built Yankee Stadium, for the home opener of the New York Football Giants.

should move the Giants bench to the sunny side of the field, where it was warmer. He did that for the next game, and it's been that way ever since."

Mara had so many memories of the opening season. After losing its first three games, the team went on to defeat its next seven opponents in a row. Then it came time to face Red Grange and the Chicago Bears. The Galloping Ghost had just finished an illustrious career at the University of Illinois, where he dazzled football fans throughout the Midwest,

> "We lost the last game of the season in 1937 to the Redskins and finished second, and the next year we beat them 36-0 on the last day to win our division. In the second game of the season in 1939 we played to a scoreless tie, and a few games later we battled them at home. We won 9-7 when their kicker, Bo Russell, missed a field goal in the final seconds. In those years, the Redskins marching band sat in the center field area of the Polo Grounds, and half of them cheered when the kick went up, thinking it was good, while the other half moaned, thinking it was bad. George Preston Marshall, who owned the Redskins, believed the half that cheered. The referee was a Providence, R.I. postmaster, and as soon as Marshall got back to Washington, he tried to get him fired."
>
> **Wellington Mara**

That squad, which featured an aging Jim Thorpe at running back, had already played, and lost, two road games. Nonetheless, some 25,000 fans came to see this spectacle of pro football for themselves, and more than a few of them were disappointed when the Giants fell 14-0 to the Frankford (Pa.) Yellow Jackets.

Obviously, young Wellington wasn't happy with the end result either, but loss or no loss, he was immediately hooked on the sport. He had started watching the game from the stands with his mother while his brother worked the sideline markers. But by the second half he had talked his way down to a seat on the bench. "I remember hearing the coach, Bob Folwell, sending a player, Paul Jappe, into the game, saying, 'Go and give them hell,'" Wellington recalls, "and thinking to myself what a rough game this must be."

The youngster, a trim boy with sandy hair, loved sitting on the bench, but his mother was not at all happy. It had been a chilly day, the Giants bench was in the shade and she worried that her boys would catch cold. "She talked to my father about it after the game," Wellington says, "and told him that he

and this game would mark his first appearance as a player in the Northeast. More than 70,000 people filled the Polo Grounds that day, by far the largest crowd in pro football history. And though his Giants lost 19-7, Tim Mara considered the game a success: sports fans has responded to pro football and the gate receipts he took in from the contest allowed him to wipe out a $40,000 deficit and actually report a profit of $18,000 for the year. The Football Giants would be back in 1926.

Wellington smiled when he thought of how much a part of his life football had become. He had barely turned fourteen and was attending Loyola High School, a Jesuit institution across from his family's apartment at 83rd Street and Park Avenue, when his father made him and his brother titular owners of the Giants, mostly to protect the franchise from financial problems Tim Mara was having with some of his other business holdings in the wake of the stock market crash of 1929. Even in the best of times pro football would have been a tough sell; it was a relatively unknown sport and a poor second cousin to college football and baseball. Fans were hard to come by, and the Giants tried everything to

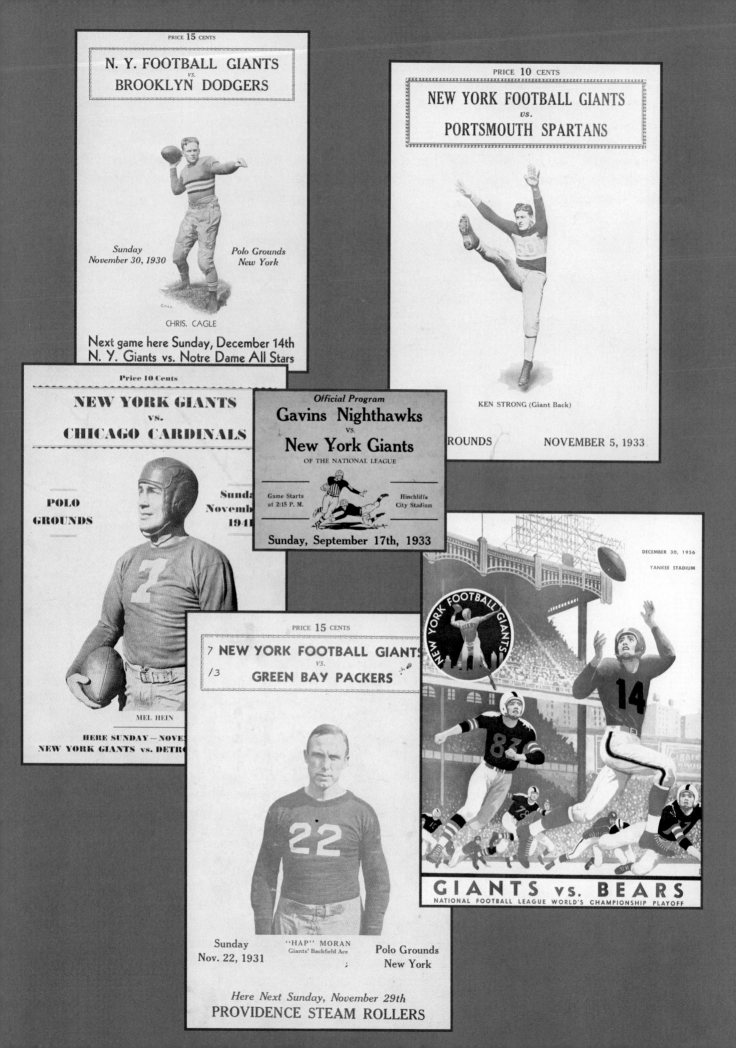

fill seats. Games were advertised in the local news-papers, and Wellington passed out free tickets to his friends at school. It wasn't unusual for as many as half the spectators at any given contest to be using complimentary tickets. Even the big match-ups didn't always bring in the crowds. When the Giants played the Bears in 1927 for the league championship—a game they won 13-7—less than 100 people showed up.

and when his father gave the go-ahead, 19-year-old Wellington wired the player to let him know he was coming to Washington D.C. with a contract. They met a few days later, and Leemans was shocked to see someone that young handling such an important job. In fact, the story goes, Leemans felt so bad for the boy that he hardly bargained at all, and the Giants got the future Hall of Famer for close to their asking price.

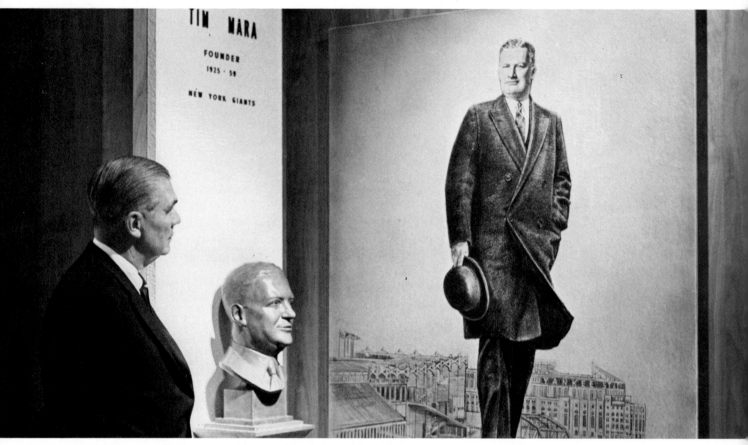

Four years after becoming the youngest owner in pro football histo-ry, Wellington Mara enrolled in col-lege. He went to Fordham University in the Bronx, where one of his class-mates was Vince Lombardi, who would become one of the Rams' famous Seven Blocks of Granite and later an assis-tant coach for the Giants. Mara studied hard, but he never let college get in the way of his duties for the Giants. He became the team's chief talent scout and while he was in school compiled information on hundreds of college athletes that the Giants used when it came time to sign new players. One of Wellington's finds was Tuffy Leemans, a relatively obscure running back from George Washington University. He urged the Giants to sign Leemans,

TIM MARA
CONSIDERED BUYING A
PIECE OF BOXER
GENE TUNNEY BUT
PUT HIS MONEY
INTO THE NEW YORK
GIANTS INSTEAD.
(NEW YORK GIANTS)

When he wasn't scouting players or haggling over contracts, Wellington was going to games. One of his best memories was of the famous "sneak-ers" game that took place at the Polo Grounds in 1934. The temperature was nine degrees, the field was frozen, and the Giants were about to face off against the Bears for the NFL Championship. Before the start of the contest, Coach Steve Owen sent clubhouse man Abe Cohen up to Manhattan College to fetch some sneakers in hopes they'd provide better trac-tion for his players. When Cohen returned at half-time, the Bears were leading 13-3. But with their new footwear, the Giants were able to outrun and outmaneuver the burly Bears in the second half, and they took control of the game, scoring 27 points in the fourth quarter to win 30-13 and capture their first NFL Championship.

Mara graduated from Fordham in 1937 and went to work for the Giants full-time. "My father wanted me to go to law school," he recalls, "but the only thing I was interested in was pro football." Wellington scouted players and negotiated salaries. He arranged transportation for the team and bought equipment. He ran pass patterns during practice and participated in kick coverage drills. He took movies of the team's games with a 16 mm. camera his parents had given him for Christmas one year and ran the projector during team meetings.

He also remembered how most players held jobs during the week in the early days and could only practice after work or on Saturdays. One Sunday evening after a bruising battle with the Bears, his roomie Wade Cuff went to see a world championship wrestling match at Madison Square Garden. And there on the main card was Bears Hall of Fame fullback Bronco Nagurski. Nagurski saw Cuff sitting ringside and said to him in a stage whisper before his bout, "This isn't going to be nearly as tough as playing against you guys this afternoon."

The fields didn't have hash marks in that era, and if a player was tackled one yard from the sideline,

WELLINGTON MARA WELCOMED BOB TISCH AS CO-OWNER SHORTLY AFTER THE GIANTS' SECOND SUPER BOWL WIN. (JERRY PINKUS)

He knew every offensive and defensive assignment.

How different things were in those days, Wellington thought as he approached the Giants locker room at the Rose Bowl. Back then, he was the same age as most of the players, and he considered many of them to be his friends. The team stayed at the Whitehall Hotel on upper Broadway, where Coach Owen had a penthouse, and Mara roomed for a time with Ward Cuff, the star running back. It was those same players who nicknamed him "Duke" because they knew he had been named after the Duke of Wellington, a man Tim Mara called "the fightingest of all Irishmen."

that's where the ball was marked. The Giants had a tailback from Georgetown in the late 1920s named Tony Plansky, a terrific athlete who also drop-kicked. He normally kicked with his right foot, but in one game the ball was spotted just a few yards from the left sideline. So he drop-kicked a 40-yarder with his left foot for the win.

Wellington couldn't believe how much he missed football when he served overseas in the Navy during World War II. (A lieutenant commander when he got out, he served on aircraft carriers in both the Atlantic and Pacific theaters.) Perhaps it was that longing that energized him so when he returned to

WHEN BILL PARCELLS SPOKE,
WELLINGTON MARA LISTENED—
WITH GOOD REASON. THE
GIANTS HAD GONE 30 YEARS
WITHOUT A NFL CHAMPIONSHIP
WHEN PARCELLS TOOK THE TEAM
TO THE TOP IN 1986. AND
WHEN HE REPEATED THE FEAT IN
1990, PARCELLS BECAME ONLY
THE SECOND GIANTS COACH—
AND THE FIRST SINCE STEVE
OWEN IN THE 1930s—TO WIN
TWO LEAGUE TITLES.
(JERRY PINKUS)

FOR MANY YEARS THE NFL'S OFFICIAL FOOT-BALL WAS CALLED THE DUKE, AFTER THE YOUNGEST SON OF GIANTS FOUNDER TIM MARA. (ROBERT RIGER)

the Giants in 1946. The team got to the NFL Championship game again that year but lost to Sid Luckman and the Chicago Bears. The Giants slumped over the next few years, but then Wellington began revamping the team through trades. He acquired Andy Robustelli and Dick Modzelewski, Pat Summerall and Del Shofner, Dick Lynch and Erich Barnes, Harland Svare and Y.A. Tittle, Joe Walton and Charlie Conerly. He drafted Sam Huff, Kyle Rote and Frank Gifford. And when he was done he had built one of the strongest teams in NFL history. They were a close-knit, hard-hitting group of men who developed a style of playing so uniquely ferocious that it came to be simply known as Giants football.

Those were great ball clubs. The 1956 squad was coached by Jim Lee Howell, and after going 8-3-1 during the regular season, defeated the rival Bears 47-7 for the NFL Title. After going 5-3 in 1958, the Giants reeled off five consecutive wins, including two in a row against Jim Brown and the Cleveland Browns, to get to the Championship game. It was in that contest that Johnny Unitas led his Colts down the field for the tying field goal at the end of regulation and then for the winning touchdown in overtime. Wellington knew the game was important for the future of pro football, but he never liked hearing it called the greatest ever played. "How could it be the greatest when our team lost?" he asked. (Two months after that game, Wellington suffered an even worse loss: his father died. The 1958 Championship game was the last one the Giants founder ever attended.)

If pressed to select the greatest Giants game he ever saw—and he has seen all but a handful—Wellington points to the first Cleveland game that year, which took place on the snow-covered Polo Grounds field the last day of the season. With time running out, Pat Summeral booted a 49-yard field goal to win it 13-10 and set up a play-off game with the Browns the following week. "No one knew how long that really was because the yard markers were covered with snow," Mara says. "But it was some kick."

It was a glorious era for the Giants, they were truly the toast of New York. Fans flocked to games, chants of "DEE-FENSE" echoed from the upper deck at Yankee Stadium as the crowd urged the team to shut down an opponent. It had been more than 30 years since he had started with the team, and Wellington was still in charge of the day-to-day football operations while his brother Jack ran the business side. And he still worked out with the team, only it was Y.A. Tittle and not Ed Danowski who was throwing him passes at practice.

The Giants made it to the NFL Championship Game three years in a row—1961, 1962 and 1963—but lost each time: twice to Vince Lombardi and his Green Bay Packers and then to the Bears at frigid Wrigley Field. Wellington was disappointed with those defeats, but he still felt he had a winning team. It was an aging team, but a winning one just the same, and he was confident about the future.

But it turned out to be a dismal time. The 1964 team fell to 2-10-2, and fans became so disenchanted with the Giants and their coach Allie Sherman that instead of chanting "DEE-FENSE" from their seats in Yankee Stadium they began singing "Goodbye Allie." Sam Huff and Dick Modzelewski were traded. Gifford and Tittle retired. Years later, Wellington Mara explained to Sports Illustrated what he thought had happened. "Through 1956 to 1963 we won the Eastern Championship six times," he says, "and the two years we didn't win we were the team to beat. We did that basically with the same team—Conerly, Rote, Huff, Gifford. They perpetuated themselves; they never wanted to come out of a game, and we almost never developed a younger player. Every game was important to us, and our great tendency was to use what I call a patch-up system: you trade for a Tittle, a Shofner."

"I remember about 1962 I talked to Tex Schramm in Dallas about a trade," he continued. "And I said, 'Tex, when we go, we'll go with a bang.' But I thought it was worth trying to stay on top rather than to provide for the future five years ahead, and so we would trade a first draft choice for a player who would give us two years."

> *"I coached for the Giants from 1955 to 1970, and Wellington and I used to sit up in the stands together during games. We were in the front row of the upper deck at Yankee Stadium, and we'd take pictures of the offensive and defensive formations with one of those instant cameras, then stuff the photos inside a sock weighted with football cleats and toss them down to our bench. It's the same sort of thing they do today, only with a much better communication system."*
>
> **Ken Kavanaugh, Giants scout**

Unfortunately, that system didn't always work. The 1966 squad posted a 1-12-1 record and gave up a then record 501 points, and while the Giants managed to finish second in their division the next three years in a row, it was a far cry from the championship football the team and its fans had known. In 1969 Mara replaced Sherman as head coach with former running back star Alex Webster, but he had only uneven success. Then in 1974 he brought in Andy Robustelli, who had built a successful travel business in his hometown of Stamford, Ct., to serve as director of football operations and hired Bill Arnsparger as coach. The team moved to a sumptuous new home situated in the New Jersey Meadowlands, but it still floundered.

Arnsparger, who had been the architect of the vaunted Miami Dolphins defenses of the early 1970s, lasted only two and a half seasons before giving way to John McVay.

McVay, who would go on to become director of football operations for San Francisco's 49ers during the Bill Walsh/ Joe Montana era, did not fare much better.

The Giants recorded a 5-9 mark in 1977, his first year, and were standing at 5-6 the following season when they met the Philadelphia Eagles at Giants Stadium. This was one of the most pivotal games in Giants history, not for the quality of play or the significance of the meeting, but because with 31 seconds left in the game and a 17-12 lead, the Giants called a running play instead of simply having quarterback Joe Pisarcik fall on the ball. Pisarcik lost control of the snap, and the ball squirted free. The Eagles' Herman Edwards scooped it up and ran 26 yards for the winning touchdown.

That blunder unleashed a wave of resentment

THE MARA KIDS CAN STILL BE
FOUND WHEREVER THE GIANTS
PLAY AND PRACTICE; JOINING
MIAMI DOLPHINS' HEAD COACH
DON SHULA AND WELLINGTON
MARA ON THE FIELD OF JOE
ROBBIE STADIUM IS DANNY
MARA, ONE OF WELLINGTON'S 26
GRANDCHILDREN. (JERRY PINKUS)

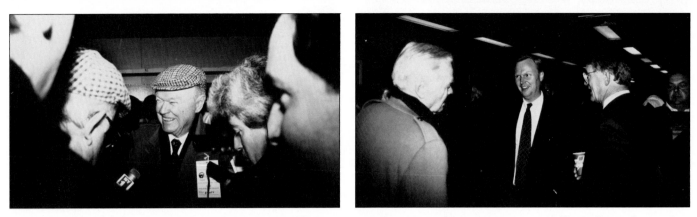

and frustration in the New York area. Fans gathered before a game two weeks later to publicly burn tickets. The next Sunday a group that called itself the "Committee Against Mara Insensitivity to Giants Fans" sent a small plane over the stadium during the season's final home game with a banner that read, "15 Years of Lousy Football...We've Had Enough!" Mara was accused of being too cheap to field a good team and too aloof to really care if the Giants won as long as they were selling out. Those charges pained Wellington Mara, for he loved nothing more than his Giants and took losing as hard as any of his players or fans.

> "I used to pass out free tickets at school when I was a kid, and once a snowstorm cancelled a game against the Bears at the Polo Grounds in the late 1920s. I was up in the stadium offices when I looked out to the field and saw some kid walking in the snow. It turned out to be my buddy Bill Colihan writing his name in the snow to prove to me he had been there."
>
> Wellington Mara

Now eighteen years later, Mara again thought back to that time. He didn't feel as close to his players as he once had, and one day in the mid-1970s he called Bob Lurtsema, a defensive end and the team's player representative, into his office and asked him what kind of rapport he had with the players and what they thought of the Giants family image. Dutifully, Lurtsema went to the players one by one and then reported to Mara that none of them felt they had a rapport with the owner and that the Giants family image was not there. The man who had once been affectionately called Duke by his charges was crushed, and after asking Lurtsema a couple of questions, shook his hand and said, "At least I know you gave me an honest answer."

Mara was hurt by the revelation because he was a man who had always had a strong sense of family. Devoutly Catholic, he had married a woman, Ann, whom he had met at mass at St Ignatius Loyola in New York City when they had gone to help an elderly woman who had fainted. Together, they had 11 children, and the kids could often be found running around the offices or out at the Giants practices.

Wellington always tried to treat his team the same way he treated his family, with great care and understanding. When Vince Lombardi wanted to take the head coaching job at Green Bay in 1959, Mara let him go, even though he had hoped Lombardi would take over his team one day. He brought Alex Webster and Andy Robustelli to the organization largely because they were Giants and he felt a special loyalty to those who had been part of his organization. When players such as Doug

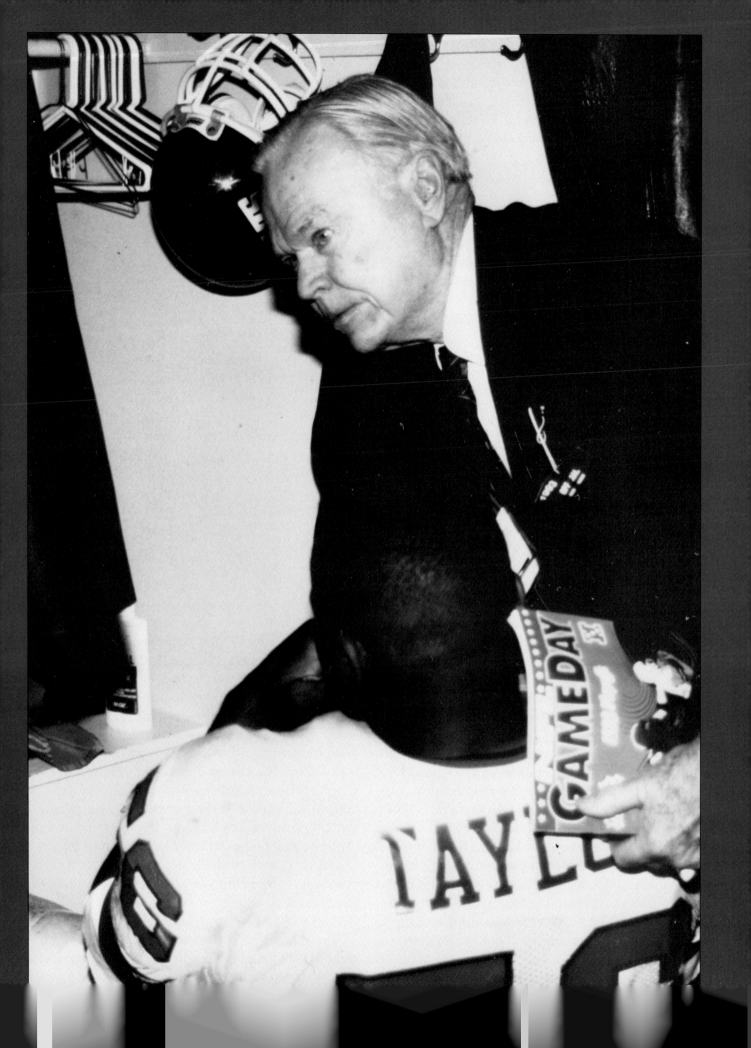

Kotar, Karl Nelson, Dan Lloyd and John Tuggle fell ill to cancer, Mara made sure the team picked up their medical bills and lent any other financial support they might have needed.

The Maras also extended his largess to the NFL family. It was Wellington's brother Jack who pushed for the league to share television revenues equally so that the smaller markets like Green Bay would receive the same amount of network money as the Giants. They did it because they felt it was the right thing to do for the league, and therefore the right thing for their team.

It just wasn't his players who were less than happy; fans frequently wrote Wellington to express their feelings and concerns. He remembered one letter from an 11-year-old girl who called him "a mean old man" for trading Fran Tarkenton back to the Minnesota Vikings in 1972. The Giants owner replied, giving his reasons for the trade and noting that although he had been called mean before, no one had ever called him an old man. Several days later, the girl wrote back to apologize. My father says, she wrote, that anyone who would answer her letter certainly was not mean.

But good things came out of the disastrous end to the 1978 season. When he and his nephew Tim Mara, who had acquired control of half the franchise when his father Jack died in 1965, could not agree on a replacement for departed head of football operations Andy Robustelli, NFL Commissioner Pete Rozelle recommended George Young, a former high school teacher who had served as an executive with the Baltimore Colts and the Miami Dolphins. The Giants signed him, and soon the team was standing tall again. Young's first move was to hire Ray Perkins as head coach and next he drafted a relatively unknown quarterback named Phil Simms from Moorehead State in Kentucky in the first round. Two years later the

team drafted Lawrence Taylor out of the University of North Carolina, and at the end of that season made the playoffs for the first time since 1963. They stumbled again in 1982 and 1983, but were back in postseason play the following year. The march to the Super Bowl was on.

Wellington Mara still hung around the practice field in those years, wearing his rumpled golf hat to protect his fair skin from the sun as he watched from the sidelines. He no longer ran pass patterns for the team and none of his players called him Duke anymore. And he let Young, Perkins and later Bill Parcells run the team pretty much as they saw fit. But he was still there, like he had been so many years before. And he was enjoying it again, enjoying the winning that had been so much a part of the Giants tradition.

Now he stood outside the Giants locker room at the Rose Bowl and took a deep breath before he walking inside. It was pure pandemonium, players and coaches hooting and hollering, television cameras and microphones everywhere. As had been his custom for so many years, he began walking around the room shaking hands with his players: Simms and Lawrence Taylor, Phil McConkey and Mark Bavaro, Joe Morris and Lionel Manuel. Then he stepped up onto the platform with his old friend Pete Rozelle and accepted the Lombardi Trophy for his team's super win.

Mara squinted into the cameras and did a number of radio and television interviews. Charlie Conerly, the tough Southerner who had led the Giants to so many title games, came up to his former boss, hugged him heartily and with tears in his eyes told him how happy he was that the Giants had finally won. Then Harry Carson, the All-Pro linebacker from South Carolina State who had been plugging holes and pouring Gatorade all season, approached him.

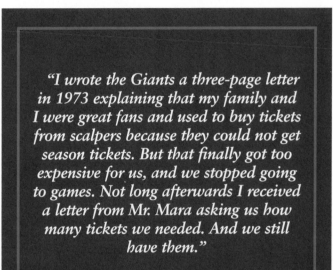

"I wrote the Giants a three-page letter in 1973 explaining that my family and I were great fans and used to buy tickets from scalpers because they could not get season tickets. But that finally got too expensive for us, and we stopped going to games. Not long afterwards I received a letter from Mr. Mara asking us how many tickets we needed. And we still have them."

Michelle Walsh, Giants fan

Carson remembers the moment well. "We didn't have any champagne in the locker room," he says, "just things like Diet Coke, and you can't go around pouring that on people. So we thought we'd employ another tradition."

"In the old days, players used to toss a coach or an owner into the shower after winning a championship," Carson says, "and that seemed liked something we should do for Mr. Mara. He had taken a lot of abuse over the years, especially when the team wasn't doing well but was still selling out Giants Stadium. Some people said Mr. Mara didn't care about winning, that he was cheap, but the players all knew that wasn't true. This was a man who cared deeply about us, who cared about winning. And when we won the Super Bowl that year, I honestly felt more excited for Mr. Mara than I did for myself. He didn't play the game, but the victory was as much his as it was ours."

"So after he received the Lombardi Trophy," Carson says, "a bunch of us pulled him into the shower and got him a little damp. For that moment, we were all kids, and he was just the biggest one."

After his shower, Wellington Mara started walking around the locker room again, his blue suit dripping wet and a smile locked across his face, the biggest and proudest Giant of them all.

I'M GOING TO TRY TO PUT FOOTBALL OVER IN NEW YORK

B ill Findley was a football fan, but he had a hard time satisfying his craving for the game. A letter carrier who worked out of the U.S. Post Office at 102nd Street in Manhattan in the mid-1920s, he occasionally watched high school and sandlot teams play. But he could never get tickets to the big college match-ups, and the only pro football teams in the country at the time were based in the Midwest. There was, obviously, no television, so all Findley could do was read accounts of pro and college games and dream of getting a chance to see some for himself.

He liked to talk football, and in his daily rounds he frequently found people who were just as interested in the sport as he was. One such fellow was a New

TIM MARA'S TEAM IS ONE OF THE OLDEST FRANCHISES IN THE NFL AND HAS ITS OWN SPOT IN CANTON. (ROBERT RIGER)

York physician named Harry A. March, and whenever Findley delivered mail to his office, the two men took a few minutes to chat about the game. "Why don't you or somebody else give those of us who can't get tickets for a college game but who like football just the same a chance?" he asked March. "If professional football will go over in the Midwest, it should certainly go over here."

The idea intrigued March. A native of Canton, Oh., he had been associated with the professional football team in that town, and the more he thought of Findley's words, the more he became convinced that New York City needed and wanted a team of its own. So he applied for a franchise in the

17

fledgling National Football League. And when he received it, he went out looking for financial help.

First he went to boxing promoter Tex Rickard, but Rickard was in the midst of building Madison Square Garden and didn't have the money to help out. He liked the idea, however, and suggested March meet with Billy Gibson, manager of heavyweight boxer Gene Tunney. In turn, Gibson introduced the doctor to Timothy

> *In the second half of the Giants' first season, Tim Mara hit on an idea to draw more fans to the Polo Grounds: he would go out to Illinois and sign the immensely popular and talented Red Grange. The owner felt this would save his franchise, and he promptly booked a drawing room on the 20th Century Limited train to Chicago. And from there he would go down to Champaign to meet with the Galloping Ghost.*
>
> *"We were all very excited about the prospect of getting Grange," son Wellington recalls, "and a few days after my father left we received a telegram:*
> *'Partially successful,' it read. 'Returning on train tomorrow. Will explain.' We couldn't figure out what partially successful meant. But when my father returned, he told us, 'Grange will be playing in the Polo Grounds this year,' he said. 'Only he'll be playing for the Bears.' It seems that George Halas had gotten to him before my father."*

J. Mara, who had been talking to Gibson about buying a piece of Tunney. Mara asked how much the franchise would cost. The price was $500, and he immediately decided to pass on the boxer and take a stab a football. "Any franchise in New York is worth that amount of money," Mara said. "An empty store with chairs in it is worth that much." (To put that figure in perspective, the New York Yankees baseball team had been sold ten years earlier for $460,000, and that was before it had ever won a pennant.)

Mara was excited about his new venture. He had never seen a football game before, but he loved sports. The son of a New York City police-

NINETEEN-YEAR-OLD WELLINGTON MARA WENT DOWN TO WASHINGTON D.C. TO PERSONALLY SIGN RUNNING BACK TUFFY LEEMANS IN 1936; IT PROVED TO BE A GOOD MOVE FOR THE FORMER GEORGE WASHINGTON UNIVERSITY STAR RUSHED HIS WAY INTO THE HALL OF FAME. (PRO FOOTBALL HALL OF FAME)

MEL HEIN DIDN'T MISS A GAME IN HIS 15 YEARS WITH THE GIANTS.
(NEW YORK GIANTS)

man who died before he was born, Tim grew up on the Lower East Side in Manhattan. He left school when he was 13 to run bets for bookmakers and soon was acting as a "beard" or betting agent for a gambler named Chicago O'Brien. Tim prospered by betting his own money on O'Brien's selections and then went into bookmaking on his own, eventually setting up a stand at Belmont Park before the advent of mutuel machines.

Thanks mostly to money he made at the track, Mara was able to put up the franchise fee for his new team and then lay out $25,000 for players, coaches, equipment, transportation and other necessities. He found a home for his ball club when Charles A. Stoneham, owner of the New York Baseball Giants and the Polo Grounds in upper Manhattan, said that Mara's football team was welcome to play at his stadium. The baseball Giants had taken their name from the giant buildings that made up the city of New York, and they had won the last four National League pennants in a row. Since they were the pride of professional baseball and extremely popular in the area, Mara decided to give his football squad the same name. He figured it would strike a chord with people in the city and help nurture interest in his football club.

Mara asked Dr. March to be secretary, and the

two of them set out to build the team. Their first hire was head coach Bob Folwell, who had been working at the Naval Academy. Next, they began filling their roster. Tim wanted a name player to give his team instant recognition, and after searching around, settled on Jim Thorpe, who had played the year before on the Rock Island (Ill.) Independents. Thorpe was 37 years old at the time, out of shape and a mere shadow of his former self, but Mara thought he would sell tickets and signed him to a unique deal: $200 "per half game," because it was clear Thorpe could not play an entire 60 minutes. The rest of the squad was filled with former college players—Century Milstead, Dowie Tomlin, Hinkey Haines to name just a few—who were paid on average from $50 to $150 a game.

The football Giants opened on the road in 1925, losing first to the Providence (R.I.) Steam

"This will give you an idea about how much loose money there is around. Along with most everybody else, Tim Mara is finding it hard to get help these days. So last week before the Bears-Giants game, when his ticket seller was out of the office, Tim took over the window himself. He hadn't been there long when a young man came along who wanted 25 box seats. Tim counted out the tickets and the buyer proffered a $100 bill. Tim made change but was taken aback when the young fellow shoved a $10 bill back through the window, saying 'Stick this in your kick.' 'Oh no,' said Mara, returning the bill. 'You mean, you don't want ten dollars?' said the ticket buyer. 'Not as a tip,' Mara said. 'You see, I happen to be the owner of the Giants.' 'Well, keep it anyhow,' said the surprised buyer. 'It's worth that to meet you.'

From Bill Corum's column
in the
New York Journal-American, 1943.

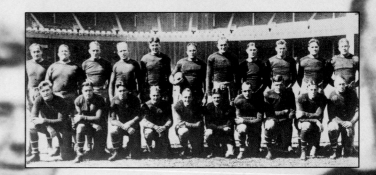

THE GIANTS STARTING OFFENSE AT THE BEGINNING OF THE 1925 SEASON; JIM THORPE IS STANDING SECOND FROM THE LEFT. (NEW YORK GIANTS)

THE 1941 GIANTS WERE PLAYING THE BROOKLYN DODGERS AT THE POLO GROUNDS WHEN THE JAPANESE ATTACKED U.S. FORCES AT PEARL HARBOR. (NEW YORK GIANTS)

THE GIANTS WON NFL TITLES WITH THESE PLAYERS IN 1934 (ABOVE) AND 1938 (RIGHT). (NEW YORK GIANTS)

THE 1939 SQUAD FINISHED COMPILED A 9-1-1 RECORD
BUT CAME UP SHORT AGAIN IN THE NFL CHAMPIONSHIP
GAME TO THE PACK. (NEW YORK GIANTS)

WELLINGTON MARA (SECOND FROM LEFT, TOP ROW)
POSED WITH HIS 1947 SQUAD. (NEW YORK GIANTS)

BRIDESMAIDS AGAIN, THE 1946 GIANTS FELL TO THE
CHICAGO BEARS IN THE TITLE GAME, 24-14.
(NEW YORK GIANTS)

THE 1950 TEAM WENT 10-2 AND FINISHED IN A FIRST-PLACE
TIE WITH THE CLEVELAND BROWNS IN THE AMERICAN
CONFERENCE. (NEW YORK GIANTS)

THE 1944 GIANTS GAVE UP ONLY 75 POINTS DURING THE
REGULAR SEASON AND FINISHED ATOP THE EASTERN DIVISION;
THEY LOST, HOWEVER, TO THE PACKERS IN THE NFL
CHAMPIONSHIP GAME. (NEW YORK GIANTS)

"As a child, I sat in one of the field boxes that were set up directly behind the Giants' bench in the Polo Grounds. One could actually reach out and touch the players. When old Doc Sweeney started swearing as he stitched a finger or taped a knee, Grandma Mara would make me cover my ears."

"When the Giants took the trains to games in Philadelphia and Washington, I had meals with the players in the dining car. The thrill of sitting across from Eddie Price as he tore off the wrapper from his ice cream bar remains with me still."

"I remember training camps at Bear Mountain and Wisconsin Dells, and one plane ride to Cleveland when the team charter lost an engine. Bobby Gaiters, a diminutive running back, came rushing through the cabin shouting, 'Captain says some of you big guys will have to jump.' "

Maura Mara Concannon, daughter of Jack Mara and granddaughter of team founder Tim.

THE GIANTS PLAYED AT THE POLO GROUNDS (ABOVE & BACKGROUND) IN UPPER MANHATTAN FROM THEIR FOUNDING IN 1925 THROUGH THE 1955 SEASON; THE NEXT YEAR THEY MOVED ACROSS THE HARLEM RIVER (OPPOSITE PAGE) TO THE HOUSE THAT RUTH BUILT. (NEW YORK GIANTS)

Roller 14-0 and then to the Frankford (Pa.) Yellowjackets 5-3. Their first home game was against the same Yellowjackets the next day. Hampered by an injured knee, Thorpe was unable to complete even a half of play for the Giants, and they fell to Frankford 14-0 before some 25,000 spectators. (It has been told that when Frankford scored its first touchdown and many in the crowd jumped up, Tim Mara nudged his son Jack and asked "What's a touchdown?") Thorpe collected his $200, but was released after the game and returned to the Independents for the remainder of the season.

The Giants played their next seven games at the Polo Grounds, and they won each one, including four by shutout. But as successful as they were on the field, they had problems at the gate, and by the time the Chicago Bears came to town in early December, Mara was already some $40,000 in debt. Help was on the way, however. A week earlier, the Bears had signed Red Grange to his first professional football contract, and he would be accompanying the team to New York. In the 1920s, Grange was one of the best-known athletes in the country, on a par with Babe Ruth and Jack Dempsey, and Mara was counting on him to draw a big crowd for the game. "I remember that it rained all week before the game," his son Wellington recalled years later, "and my father was really worried. Then about two o'clock the morn-

OVER THE BRONX: YANKEE STADIUM WITH THE HARLEM RIVER, THE POLO GROUNDS, THE HUDSON RIVER AND NEW JERSEY'S PALISADES IN THE DISTANCE.

ing of the game, one of his friends called and told him to look out the window. The stars were out, and it turned out to be a pretty nice day."

So nice, in fact, that some 70,000 fans jammed the stadium. The Bears beat the Giants 19-7, with Grange, who was said to be working off a percentage of the gate, rushing for 53 yards, catching one pass for 23 yards and returning an interception for a touchdown. Tim Mara was disappointed with the loss, but the tremendous crowd convinced him that pro football could make it in New York. And it enabled him to turn a small profit for the year. He couldn't wait for the 1926 season to start.

But 1926 was a tough year. Red Grange's agent, a brash promoter named C.C. (Cash & Carry) Pyle, had just completed a barnstorming tour with his top property and felt so confident of his drawing power that he decided to launch a competing league—dubbed the American Football League—and put franchises in The Bronx (at Yankee Stadium), Brooklyn and Newark. To make matters even worse, Pyle assigned Grange to play for the Bronx team, which was called the New York Yankees. The Giants lost thousands that season, but so did the new league, and it folded after one year.

The following season, the Giants won their first league championship with a record of 11-1-1. Their defense posted ten shutouts and gave up only 20 points the entire season. One of their star players was a stout Oklahoma lineman by the name of Steve Owen, who worked at a fuel depot in Harlem in his spare time and would later go on to become head coach of the team.

> "We were playing the Bears one time, in the years before facemasks, and just as I snapped the ball, George Musso, a 260-pound nose tackle for the Bears, slugged me in the face. I told him not to do that again, but on the next play he did the same thing. So on the following snap, I was ready. I hiked the ball with one hand and with the other I hit Musso with an uppercut square in the face. I could tell he really felt it, and he left me alone for the rest of the game."
>
> Mel Hein, former Giants center and member of the Pro Football Hall of Fame

The Giants played miserably in 1928, compiling a 4-7-2 mark. Tim Mara was so dismayed with the results that he decided to clean house. Head coach Earl Potteiger and most of the players were let go, and the only starter to return for the 1929 season was Steve Owen. Mara went to extremes to build a new team. He desperately wanted a 5'8", 170 lbs. quarterback by the name of Benny Friedman, a player Red Grange would later call the best of that era. Problem was, Friedman was under contract with the NFL Detroit Wolverines. The only way Mara could get his man was buy the entire franchise, and since Detroit was in dire financial straits, he was able to arrange a deal: he purchased the

team, then folded it and kept Friedman and several of Detroit's best players. It was a deft move. Friedman threw for a record 19 touchdown passes that year—at a time when most quarterbacks were tossing five or six for a season—and the Giants won 13 games and lost only one, finishing second to the undefeated Green Bay Packers. It was also a good year financially; the team turned a profit of $8,500, their first since their maiden season in 1925.

The 1930s didn't start out so well. The Great Depression was setting in across the country, and no one was sure if football fans would be able to keep springing for game tickets. And Tim Mara was having financial problems of his own. He had lost big when the stock market crashed and was also embroiled in a nasty lawsuit with his old friend Billy Gibson. Fearing that his financial setbacks and legal problems might threaten his football team, he turned ownership of the Giants over to his sons Jack, then 22, and Wellington, 14.

There were other concerns as well. The Giants had wanted desperately to sign an All-American from New York University named Ken Strong, but lost out in a bidding war to a local rival, the Staten Island Stapletons. Benny Friedman, their star passer, had taken an assistant coaching job at Yale University and was noticeably fatigued during the season from his daily round-trip commutes between New Haven and New York. Even so, the Giants posted a 13-4 record and finished second again to the Packers.

Though the season was over, the Giants still had another game to play. That fall, Tim Mara had approached his good friend Jimmy Walker, then mayor of New York, about having a fundraiser to help the unemployed. He proposed holding an exhibition between the Giants and an All-Star team from Notre Dame coached by Knute Rockne, with all the proceeds going to the New York

Unemployment Fund. The game was held in December, and more than 55,000 fans showed up on a bitterly cold day to watch the Giants beat a smaller, less-experienced Notre Dame squad 22-0. Charles Stoneham provided the stadium free of charge and more than $115,000 went toward the unemployment fund. Sadly, the game was the last one Rockne ever coached; he died the next year in a plane crash.

The Giants struggled in 1931, finishing fifth with a 5-6-1 record. But some good things did occur during that season. Former player Steve Owen was named head coach, a position he would hold for the next 23 seasons. And the team signed Mel Hein.

A rangy 6'3" center and defensive lineman from Washington State, Hein was a consensus All-American who had led his team to a Rose Bowl victory the year before. Good as he was, however, he had to write to three NFL clubs to get a try-out. The Rhode Island Steamrollers initially offered him $125 a game. That seemed like a lot of money at the time, so Hein inked the contract and mailed it back. But then the Giants came up with a better deal: $150 a game plus a $100 advance to pay for his travel expenses. Hein told the team it was too late, but Giants captain Ray Flaherty suggested he try and get the Providence, R.I. postmaster to intercept his Steamrollers contract and tear it up. Hein managed to do just that, and then signed on with the Giants.

It was the beginning of a beautiful relationship. Hein would go on to play 15 years with the team

and never miss a game. He was named All-Pro eight consecutive seasons and in 1938 was voted the league's first Most Valuable Player, the only offensive lineman ever so honored. He was also a fierce defensive player, so good in fact that he was probably the first Giant to make fans aware of the importance of defense. Upon his retirement, Hein was inducted into the Pro Football Hall of Fame and had his number 7 retired.

The 1932 squad did not fare much better then the '31 team, ending up with a 4-6-2 mark and in sixth place. The 1933 season, however, would be different. To begin with, the NFL instituted a number of rule changes. The ball was reduced slightly in size, making it easier to pass and harder to drop-kick. Hash marks were added to the fields, and the goalposts were moved from the endline to the goal line. In addition, the league decided to divide itself into two divisions and schedule a championship game at the end of the season to determine the best team.

The Giants were also busy in the offseason. The Stapletons folded, and Tim Mara was finally able to get Ken Strong into a Giants' uniform. And it was then that he learned why he hadn't been able to sign Strong right out of college. "My father shook Ken's hand after they agreed on a contract and said, 'Well, Ken, you are three years too late,' " Wellington Mara recalls. " 'I never understood why you went over there for less money than we offered you.' Ken didn't know what he was talking about. 'We offered you $10,000 a year,' my father said. But Ken said he had only been offered $5,000. It seems the man we

The Spalding J5-V was the official football of the NFL from 1920 to 1940, and in the 1930s the company named the ball "The Duke" after Giants owner Wellington Mara. Wilson Sporting Goods began manufacturing NFL balls in 1941, and they carried on the Duke name until 1969, when it was retired. "I don't know how it came to be name that," Mara says, "but I'm pretty sure my father had something to do with it."

Wellington Mara

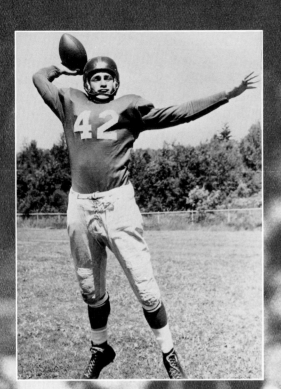

CHARLIE CONERLY HAD STARRED AT MISSISSIPPI BEFORE COMING TO THE GIANTS IN 1948.
(INSET—NEW YORK GIANTS).

HE BECAME AN INSTANT SUCCESS; THAT FIRST YEAR HE COMPLETED 162 PASSES FOR MORE THAN 2,000 YARDS AND 22 TOUCHDOWNS.
(ROBERT RIGER)

had sent to sign Ken was going to pocket the extra money, or save the club some money and make some points for himself. Either way, it kept us from having Ken Strong until 1933."

But the important thing was, Strong was now a

"Harry Newman assumed the position of a T formation quarterback behind Hein. The player who was to Mel's left shifted into the backfield as one of our backs moved up to the right side of the line. That made Mel eligible to receive a forward

Charlie Conerly had been battered during his first six years with the Giants, and when Steve Owen left as coach, he decided to retire. But incoming coach Jim Lee Howell liked Conerly as a quarterback, and he wanted to bring him back.

"I tracked Charlie down somewhere in Missouri or Iowa. He was working on a farm, putting down fertilizer and wearing those high rubber farm boots. When I asked him about returning, he told me he didn't want to be hurt anymore. I told him I would get him a line to protect him, that that would be the first order of business. And Charlie said okay, he'd come back."

Jim Lee Howell, Giants head coach 1954-60.

Giant, and with his sure running, tough blocking and tremendous kicking, he led the team to the Eastern Division crown. The Championship game was held at Wrigley Field, and the Giants lost a hard-fought thriller 23-21. With only seconds remaining, Giants quarterback Harry Newman completed a pass to Red Badgro, who was to lateral the ball to a trailing Dale Burnett. All that stood between Badgro and a touchdown was Red Grange. But Grange sensed what the Giants were trying to do, and he tackled Badgro high so he could not get the ball to Burnett.

It was not the only trick play the Giants attempted that day. "Earlier in the game we went into a spread formation, with all but one player lined up to the right of our center Mel Hein," Wellington Mara reminiscences fondly.

pass. He snapped the ball to Newman, who then gave it back to Mel. Newman rolled out to the right, pretending he had the ball while Mel remained crouched over with the ball hidden. He looked up, saw that everybody's attention was focused on Newman and then started walking toward the goal line."

"We had told Mel before the play to keep walking until he was sure he could outrun everybody," Mara continues. "But after ten yards, he couldn't stand it anymore and started running. The Bears safety saw Mel and tackled him after he had gained 15 yards. Who knows, if Mel had been able to restrain himself, we might have had a touchdown."

The two teams would meet again for the title the following year, this time at the Polo Grounds, in what would become

FRANK GIFFORD AND CHARLIE CONERLY TALKING TO EACH OTHER ON THE GIANTS BENCH DURING THE 1955 SEASON, THE TEAM'S LAST YEAR IN THE POLO GROUNDS. (ROBERT RIGER)

the storied "Sneakers" game. The temperature at game time was nine degrees, the wind was howling and the field was frozen. Ray Flaherty, who had played at Gonzaga University in Spokane, Wa., remembered using sneakers on an icy field there one time, and he suggested the Giants try the same thing. Jack Mara called A.G. Spalding's and Alex Taylor's, the two biggest sporting goods stores in New York, to see if he could buy some sneakers, but it was Sunday and both stores were closed.

All was not lost, however. The Giants had an assistant clubhouse man named Abe Cohen. A tailor who also worked part-time for the athletic department at Manhattan College, he had a set of keys to the locker room there. Just before game time, he rode a cab up to the school and rounded up the largest pairs of sneakers he could find.

CONERLY WAS A SINGLE WING TAILBACK AT OLE MISS AND KNEW LITTLE ABOUT THE T FORMATION WHEN HE STARTED PLAYING IN THE PROS; TO MAKE THE TRANSITION EASIER, HEAD COACH STEVE OWEN HIRED ALLIE SHERMAN, A FORMER BACK-UP QUARTERBACK WITH THE PHILADELPHIA EAGLES WHO WAS SEVERAL YEARS YOUNGER THAN THE GIANTS QB, TO SCHOOL CONERLY. (ROBERT RIGER)

Cohen arrived back at the Polo Grounds at half-time, with the Giants sliding around on their cleats and losing 13-3. But with their new footwear, they began overpowering the Bears and went on to score 27 unanswered points for a 30-13 victory and the NFL Championship.

A less publicized source of help that day came from trainer Gus Mauch. He noticed that the players were having a hard time staying warm, so he went to Jack Mara and asked for some whisky. Mara fetched him a bottle, and Mauch began handing out paper cups of the liquor to various players. On the play after the first batch was consumed, Ken Strong ran a reverse and took the ball in for a

AFTER SERVING AS AN ASSISTANT COACH FOR THREE YEARS, JIM LEE HOWELL BECAME HEAD COACH IN 1954 AND LED THE GIANTS TO A 53-27-4 RECORD AND ONE NFL CHAMPIONSHIP OVER SEVEN SEASONS. (ROBERT RIGER)

touchdown. Mara produced a second bottle, and Mauch set out another tray of paper cups. But this time, most of the players waved him off, worried that the booze would make them drunk.

The Giants made it back to the Championship Game in 1935 but lost to Detroit 26-7. The following year the NFL instituted its first college draft, and the Giants unveiled their rookie sensation Tuffy Leemans, who ran 45 yards for a touchdown on his first play from scrimmage and went on to lead the league in rushing. But the team finished at 5-6-1.

The next year wasn't much better. With 17 rookies on the squad and new blue jerseys, the Giants posted a 6-3-2 mark. They won the Eastern Division in 1938 but fell to Green Bay in the title game. The team captured their division again in

1939, besting the Redskins 9-7 on the final game of the season. It was a dramatic contest. Shortly after arriving in New York, Redskins owner George Preston Marshall led an impromptu parade up the city streets with the team's marching band and some 12,000 'Skins fans in tow. The contest ended when the referee ruled that a last-second kick had gone wide. Spectators and players gathered on the field after the game, and a small riot broke out as some of the Redskins accosted the referee who had made the controversial call. But order was restored, and the Giants went on to Green Bay, where they lost yet another title contest to the Pack.

The loss discouraged Tim Mara, but all in all, it was a good ten years of football for his Giants. They had won five Division titles and two championships and played in more championship games than any other NFL team.

The 1940s started out much like the previous decade had, with the world in turmoil and football people wondering whether the NFL would survive. The problem this time was World War II. It didn't have much of an effect on either the Giants or the NFL in 1940, when the team finished third in the East with a 6-4-1- record. But during the team's last regular season game in 1941, an announcement came over the loudspeaker informing all military servicemen to report to their posts. It was December 7th, and that day the Japanese had attacked Pearl Harbor. And nothing in the league would be the same for several years.

More than 630 NFL players went overseas to fight in Europe and Asia during World War II, and though the league decided to continue operations, there were grave doubts about whether it would make it through. Many of the players who stayed behind were battered veterans past their prime.

Attendance plummeted, and some teams were forced to fold.

Attempting to dealing with common financial problems led to a merger of The Philadelphia Eagles and Pittsburgh Steelers for a time. They called themselves the Steagles.

Fifty-two Giants (including Wellington Mara) fought in World War II, and two players lost their lives: Al Blozis, a tackle from Georgetown, died in his first combat mission in France about six weeks after playing in the 1944 Championship game, and Jack Lummus, an end on the 1941 team, was killed in the battle for Iwo Jima. But

"I was 20 years old when I left Brooklyn College and joined the Philadelphia Eagles as a back-up quarterback. Our second game in 1943 was against the Giants at the Polo Grounds, and though many thought they were the better team, we were beating them 24-14 near the end of the game. One of our players intercepted a pass deep in their territory, and our coach, Greasy Neale, sent me in. 'Listen kid,' he barked. 'Don't throw any passes. Just send your plays in the line and run out the clock.' I went out to the field, and I figured the safest way to use up time was to run a quarterback sneak. No hand-offs, no fumbles, right? Besides, it was my first NFL game, and I was nervous. So I took the ball and just plunged ahead, all 160 lbs. of me. I kept churning my legs, and the next thing you know it, I'm in the end zone. My first play as a pro, and I score a touchdown."

"I headed for the North Philadelphia station after the game to catch a train home to Brooklyn, and when I got there I found a group of big men coming toward me. It was some of the Giants. I recognized Steve Owen, Mel Hein and Ward Cuff, but it was a cinch that none of them knew who I was. And Owen was chewing them out. 'What a disgrace,' he thundered, 'to lose to a bunch of humpty-dumpties like that. You guys were so lousy that you even let that little squirt from Brooklyn score on you.'

"I smiled and walked to my train."

Allie Sherman, Giants head coach 1961-68.

29

KYLE ROTE JOINED THE GIANTS IN 1951 AND PLAYED FOR
ELEVEN SEASONS. (NEW YORK GIANTS)

despite those tragedies and their depleted rosters, the Giants managed to keep on winning. They made it to the title game in 1941, only to lose to the Bears 37-9 before a crowd of only 13,341. After a third-place finish in 1942, the Giants rebounded to captured the Eastern Division in 1943 (when the league was down to nine teams) and 1944, only to lose the title game each time. But the team slumped again in 1945, going 3-6-1. Part of the problem was age; Ken Strong was 39, Mel Hein 36, Arnie Herber 35 and Ward Cuff 32. The Giants bounced back in '46, however, and won the East again with a 7-3-1 mark. But they fell to their old nemesis, the Bears, in the championship game, 24-14.

It was a contest marred by controversy. On the day before the game, Tim Mara received a call from New York Mayor William O'Dwyer, who asked that he and Coach Steve Owen meet him and NFL Commissioner Bert Bell at Gracie Mansion to discuss a problem. A gambler named Alvin Paris had been accused of offering bribes to Giants quarterback Frank Filchock and fullback Merle Hapes to throw the big game. After examining the evidence, Bell, who was in only his first year as commissioner, decided to suspend Hapes for not reporting the bribe

attempt, but allowed Filchock to play when the quarterback said he had never been approached by the gambler. Filchock performed valiantly, tossing two touchdown passes after he had broken his nose early in the contest. But it wasn't enough to beat back the Bears. And when it was revealed afterwards that Filchock had known more about the bribe attempt than he had let on, Bell suspended him as well.

By this time, Tim Mara had passed on control of much of the football team to his two sons. "Jack ran the business side, I ran the football operations, and our father ran us," Wellington says with a smile.

The war may have ended in 1945, but the Giants and the NFL faced a different sort of battle the next season. The New York Yankees and Brooklyn Dodgers had switched over to a new league called the All-American Football Conference (AAFC). For three years, the AAFC sapped talent and money from the established NFL teams and threatened their very existence. But in 1949 it agreed to suspend operations; three of its franchises—the Cleveland Browns, the San Francisco 49ers and the Baltimore Colts—joined the NFL, and the rest closed up shop.

The Giants struggled on the field through the remainder of the 1940s, but the seeds for the great

KYLE ROTE AND JOURNALIST CHRIS SCHENKEL
CHAT BEFORE A GAME. (ROBERT RIGER)

teams of the 1950s were being sown. In 1948 the team acquired Charlie Conerly from the Redskins, and later signed its first black player, Emlen Tunnell. Tunnell simply walked into the Giants' offices one day and asked Jack Mara for a tryout. He had played for a year at the University of Toledo, and then after a stint in the Coast Guard had gone to the University of Iowa. Mara gave Tunnell his tryout, and the defensive back and punt return specialist went on to make the team. He played through the 1958 season, and nine years later was voted into Pro Football's Hall of Fame.

Conerly, a former single wing tailback from Mississippi, became an instant success. In his first year with the team he completed 162 passes for more than 2,000 yards and 22 touchdowns. Against the Steelers that season, he completed 35 passes in one game, a record that would stand for nearly 20 years. In 1949, Steve Owen switched from the A formation to the T and brought in Allie Sherman, a former Philadelphia Eagles quarterback, to help Conerly make the conversion. "The Giants were the last NFL team to go over to the T," Sherman recalls. "The Bears had started it, and they were kicking the hell out of everybody. Stanford University was also using the T, and they were doing the same thing to college teams. So, as always happens when something good comes along, everybody in the league jumped on board and started using it themselves. Charlie had been a single wing tailback at Ole Miss, so he needed a little guidance in switching over. But he picked it up pretty fast and become a terrific quarterback." Indeed he did. Conerly had another good year in 1949, again passing for more than 2,000 yards. It was a sign of things to come.

The Giants began the 1950 season by adding several orphans from the defunct AAFC to its roster, mostly notably a defensive halfback from Texas named Tom Landry, whom the team had drafted but been unable to sign the year before.

Vince Lombardi was a Giants assistant coach from 1954 to 1958. (Robert Riger)

"Right after we hired Jim Lee Howell as our head coach, we contacted Vince Lombardi about running our offense. Vince was excited about the prospects of coming to work for the Giants, and we suggested that he go down to Arkansas for an interview with Jim Lee. Howell lived on a farm or ranch in the offseason there, and he interviewed Vince while they were both standing in a cattle corral. Lombardi later told me that he spent as much time dodging piles of cow dung as he did talking football. He said it was the strangest interview he ever had."

Wellington Mara

the ends would drop back in coverage while the backs—Emlen Tunnell, Tom Landry, Otto Schnellbacher and Harmon Rowe—formed a sort of umbrella in the backfield, with the two halfbacks shallow and wide and the two safeties deep and tight. Steve used it for the first time in the Browns game, and it worked beautifully. We shut them out 6-0."

The team had a good season, finishing in a tie with the Browns with a 10-2 record. They faced off in a play-off game for the Division title, and the Browns won 8-3.

The next year began on a positive note when the Giants won the right to select the first player in the college draft and picked Kyle Rote, the All-American tailback from Southern Methodist University and a runner-up for the Heisman Trophy. Alas, Rote hurt his knee in an exhibition game and was lost for much of the season. Charlie Conerly was also troubled by injury, in his case a sore throwing shoulder, and he missed several games as well. But the Giants managed to compile a 9-2-1 record, though they finished second again to the Browns.

The team had another good draft in 1952, and their number one pick was USC halfback Frank Gifford. But

The Giants beat Pittsburgh the first game of the season, and then faced the formidable Browns in Cleveland the following week. "They were a tough squad," Wellington Mara remembers. "They had annihilated the defending champion Eagles the week before 35-10 and had a very good offense. But Steve Owen had a plan. He had developed a new defense that he called the umbrella, in which

they had a tough year on the field, going 7-5 and coming in second again. One game they lost 63-7 to the Steelers. Conerly reinjured his shoulder in that contest and was replaced with a rookie, Fred Benners. But Benners was quickly knocked out of the game, so Steve Owen sent Tom Landry in to play quarterback.

Things got even worse in '53, and after the Giants

BIG ROSEY BROWN WAS A FORCE ON THE GIANTS'
OFFENSIVE LINE FOR 13 SEASONS; HE WAS ELECTED TO THE
PRO FOOTBALL HALL OF FAME IN 1975. (NEW YORK GIANTS)

money, Howell had also been serving as head football coach at Wagner College.) He accepted his new post with the Giants, said good-bye to Wagner and then began assembling a staff, naming Vince Lombardi as offensive coordinator and Tom Landry head of the defense. "I had started to do a little coaching when Steve Owen was in charge," Landry says. "Jim Lee knew what I had been doing and told Wellington he would take the head coaching job if I could handle the defense."

The Giants also made a number of good player personnel moves before the 1954 season, drafting defensive halfback Dick Nolan, signing running back Alex Webster from the CFL and trading for Bill Svoboda from the Chicago Cardinals. That

BEFORE HE BECAME A FULL-TIME COACH, TOM LANDRY
PLAYED SIX SEASONS FOR THE GIANTS. A DEFENSIVE HALFBACK,
HE ALSO SERVED AS THE TEAM'S PUNTER. (NEW YORK GIANTS)

dropped to 3-9, the Maras fired Steve Owen as coach. It was not an easy decision. Owen had played for the team from 1926 to 1936 and had begun coaching in 1931. He was considered a defensive genius and in all his years with the Giants he had never signed a contract; he operated the entire time under a handshake agreement with the Maras. But the family felt like it was time for a change.

There was lots of activity in the offseason. To begin with, the team named Jim Lee Howell head coach. An ex-Marine who had played nine seasons with the Giants in the 1930s and 40s, Howell was working as the team's receivers coach when he was offered the top job. (To earn some extra

VINCE LOMBARDI RAN THE GIANTS OFFENSE DURING HIS YEARS WITH THE TEAM; HERE HE IS CHATTING WITH FRANK GIFFORD.
(ROBERT RIGER)

year, the team won seven games and finished third.

The 1955 season didn't turn out much better record-wise—the Giants posted a 6-5-1 mark—but they had beefed up their team by drafting Rosey Grier, Jimmy Patton and Mel Tripplet and trading for Harland Svare. It was their last year in the Polo Grounds; the Maras had signed a deal to begin playing across the Harlem River in Yankee Stadium.

Wellington Mara recalls how the move came about. "My father and brother met me in my apartment before our fourth game in the 1955 season, and my father said he had an offer for the team for $1 million, which was all the money in the world then. But the deal was contingent on our moving to Yankee Stadium from the Polo Grounds. 'If we're worth $1 million in Yankee Stadium and nothing in the Polo Grounds, then we had better look into this,' he said, and shortly thereafter he began negotiating with the Yankees. And we were able to cut a deal. It's a good thing, too, because after we finalized everything with the Yankees, we learned about the baseball Giants impending move to San Francisco. We realized then that we might have been left with a vacant stadium."

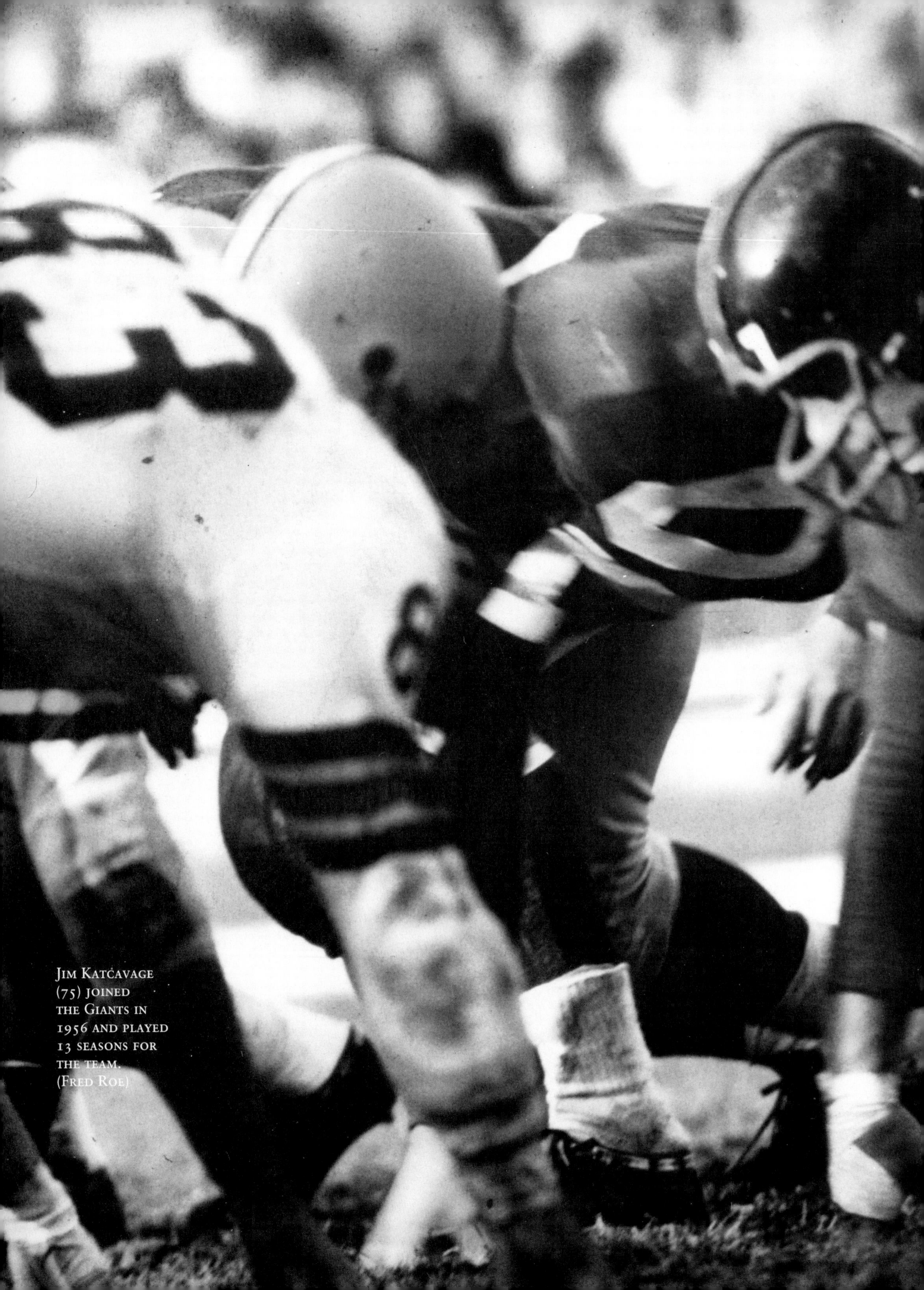

JIM KATCAVAGE
(75) JOINED
THE GIANTS IN
1956 AND PLAYED
13 SEASONS FOR
THE TEAM.
(FRED ROE)

BEASTS
OF THE EAST

Relocating to Yankee Stadium wasn't the only move the Giants made before the 1956 season began. The team acquired a slew of new players through the college draft, including Sam Huff, a 21-year-old offensive and defensive lineman from the coal-mining region of West Virginia; Jim Katcavage, a defensive end from Dayton; and Don Chandler, a punter, place kicker and occasional halfback from Florida. And just before training camp the Maras traded for two men who would go on to anchor their defensive line for the next several years.

First to arrive was Andy Robustelli. A native of Stamford, Ct. and a lifelong Giants fan, he had played at little-known Arnold College in Milford, Ct. after serving a hitch in the U.S. Navy. He was 25 years old when he was drafted by the Los Angeles Rams in the spring of 1951. "I liked the Rams, but I hated commuting between the coasts," he recalls. "I never wanted to live in L.A., so I'd go out there for the season and then come back to Connecticut when I was done. Sid Gillman took over the team in 1955, and he was one of those guys

who wanted you to lay everything out. Two weeks before training camp the next year, I asked if I could report a few days late. My wife had just given birth to our third child, and she needed me around for a little bit. But Gillman wouldn't hear of it. He told me that if I wasn't in camp on time he was going to trade me. And true to his word, that's what he did."

Not long after Robustelli appeared at the Giants camp, Wellington Mara engineered a deal for Dick Modzelewski of the Pittsburgh Steelers. A 260-pounder who was called "Little Mo" only because he had an older brother, Ed, who played fullback for the Browns, Modzelewski went up to Head Coach Jim Lee Howell after he arrived and predicted a championship. "Last year, you know, Brown (Paul, coach of the Cleveland Browns) made a trade for my brother and won the championship. This year it's your turn."

That was news to most New York sportswriters, for none of them were picking the Giants to win it all. But few would argue that the Maras hadn't assembled a talented team. The offense

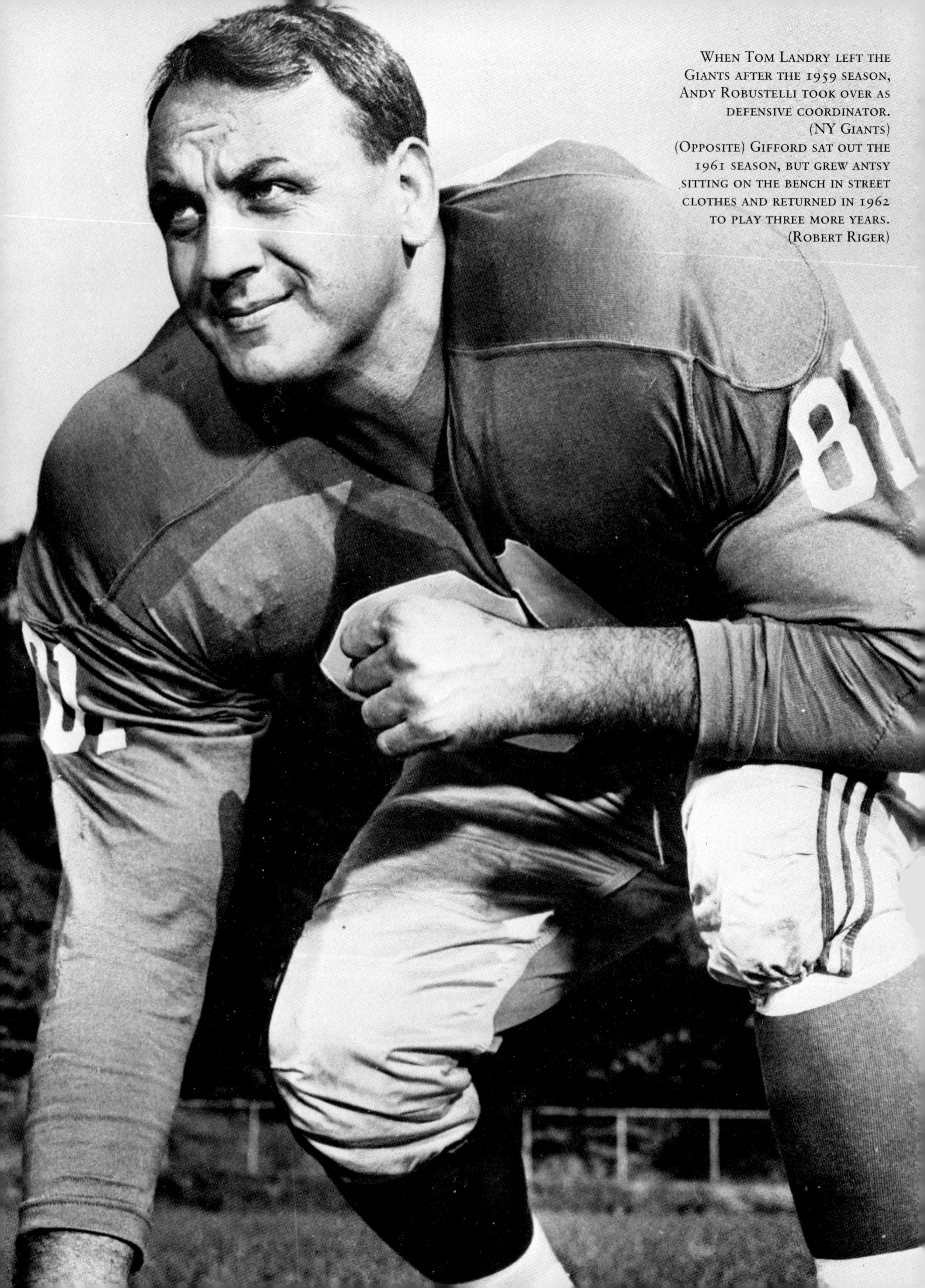

WHEN TOM LANDRY LEFT THE
GIANTS AFTER THE 1959 SEASON,
ANDY ROBUSTELLI TOOK OVER AS
DEFENSIVE COORDINATOR.
(NY GIANTS)
(OPPOSITE) GIFFORD SAT OUT THE
1961 SEASON, BUT GREW ANTSY
SITTING ON THE BENCH IN STREET
CLOTHES AND RETURNED IN 1962
TO PLAY THREE MORE YEARS.
(ROBERT RIGER)

featured Frank Gifford, Charlie Conerly, Kyle Rote and Alex Webster as well as linemen Jack Stroud and Rosey Brown. And the defense was chocked full of fine players, including Emlen Tunnell, Dick Nolan, Jimmy Patton, Harland Svare, Rosey Grier and Bill Svoboda.

Training camp was held in Winooski, Vt. that year, and the newcomers made quite an impression. Rookie Huff, who had taken the number 70 because he had been projected to fill in on the offensive line, was switched to middle linebacker when Ray Beck went down with an injury, with terrific results. Modzewelski and Robustelli brought great verve and power to an already formidable defense, and Katcavage showed remarkable progress for a first-year man.

To accommodate the Yankees, who were working their way to yet another World Series title, the Giants played their first three games of the 1956 campaign on the road. They thumped the 49ers 38-21, but then lost to the Chicago Cardinals 35-27. A win at Cleveland the following week was the beginning of a hot streak, and the team reeled off five victories in a row.

By mid-November, all of New York—and most of the NFL—was talking about the Football Giants. To be sure, they were a skilled club. But more importantly, they had developed a unique chemistry and played as a team better than any other squad in the league. "We all got along so well," remembers Alex Webster. "Most of

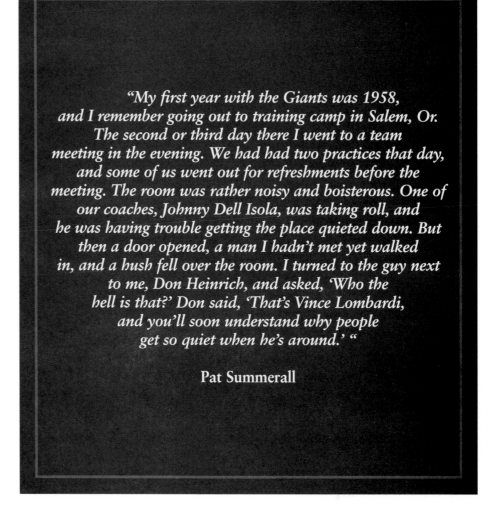

"My first year with the Giants was 1958, and I remember going out to training camp in Salem, Or. The second or third day there I went to a team meeting in the evening. We had had two practices that day, and some of us went out for refreshments before the meeting. The room was rather noisy and boisterous. One of our coaches, Johnny Dell Isola, was taking roll, and he was having trouble getting the place quieted down. But then a door opened, a man I hadn't met yet walked in, and a hush fell over the room. I turned to the guy next to me, Don Heinrich, and asked, 'Who the hell is that?' Don said, 'That's Vince Lombardi, and you'll soon understand why people get so quiet when he's around.' "

Pat Summerall

the players lived in the Grand Concourse Hotel up from Yankee Stadium, and we spent a lot of time together off the field. On the field, there was a sensational feeling of unselfishness, of doing what was best for the team. I can't say exactly why, but we kind of knitted together as the year went on, and got better and better."

Another reason for the team's success was, of course, the coaching. Jim Lee Howell had assembled a Hall-of-Fame staff, with Vince Lombardi running the offense and Tom Landry, who had retired as a player at the end of the previous season, heading up the defense. "All I have to do with these guys around is check curfews and pump up footballs," Howell often said. "Tom and Vince take care of the rest."

Indeed they did. The offense thrived under Lombardi, and when the season was over it had racked up 264 points, more than any other squad in the Eastern Conference. But it was Landry's defense that defined the Giants teams of this era. While most other teams were using a five-man

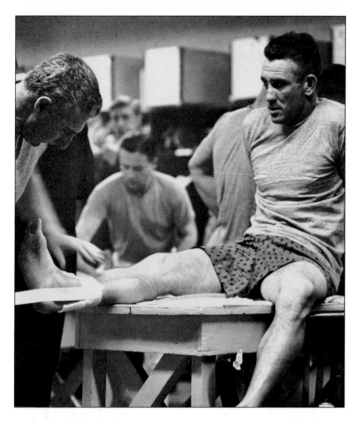

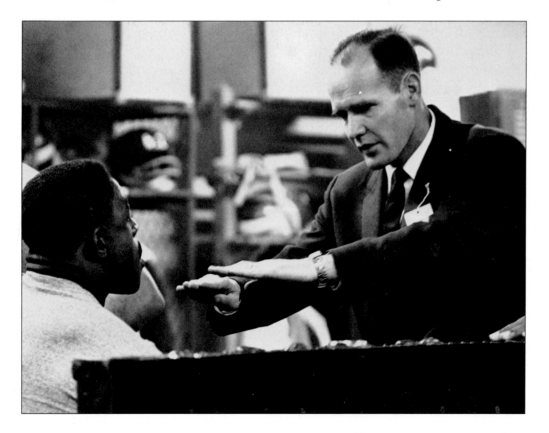

(above) Conerly gets his ankles taped before the 1958 NFL Championship Game. (Robert Riger)
(below) Tom Landry helped to make the Giants defense of the 1950s one of the league's best. (Robert Riger)
(opposite top) Dick Lynch defending Del Shofner in a 1963 practice at Yankee Stadium. (Robert Riger)
(opposite bottom) Dick Modzelewski and Sam Huff dwarf Cowboys quarterback Eddie LeBaron (14). (Robert Riger)

front, Landry developed what would become known as the 4-3 defense, dropping the lineman over the center in favor of a middle linebacker. It was a system perfectly suited to the players the Giants had acquired. During their five-game winning streak in 1956, for example, they gave up only 46 points, an average of less than 10 points a game, and for the first time in league history, fans began focusing on the defensive team. Chants of "DEE-FENSE, DEE-FENSE" began echoing from the upper decks of Yankee Stadium whenever Landry's squad took the field or braced itself for an important series. They were so good, in fact, and so popular that the Giants began introducing their defense to the crowd before the game instead of their offense.

The team's drive for the play-offs stalled somewhat when they lost big to the Redskins and then tied the Chicago Bears a week later. But the Giants rebounded to beat the 'Skins the following Sunday, and Lombardi was heard to remark in practice the week after, "I'm beginning to smell something." That something was a championship.

As history would prove out, Lombardi had the nose of a bird dog. The Giants finished the 1956 regular season on top the Eastern Conference with an 8-3-1 mark and hosted the Bears for the championship game on December 30th. As was the case with their postseason encounter in 1934, this one, too, was held on a treacherously icy field. Both teams wore sneakers, but thanks to some quick thinking by Robustelli —who ran a sporting goods store in Cos Cob, Ct. and brought four dozen pairs of new sneakers to the locker room the day of the game—the Giants enjoyed better traction. "The Bears were playing with older sneakers they had been using in practice," Robustelli says, "and they were sliding all over the place. But we had figured out during the week that new sneakers gave us much better footing than our old ones. So a couple of days before the game I put a call into the U.S. Keds sales representative, and he went up to the factory, which was in Naugatuck, Ct., and picked up 48 pairs of new sneakers for us. And they made all the difference."

Gene Filipski took the opening kickoff 53 yards, and the romp was on. The Giants went into the half leading 34-7 and would add 13 more points in the second half for a final of 47-7. Coach Jim Lee Howell called it "the closest thing to a perfect game I have ever seen," and the Giants had their first championship since 1938.

Several Giants were rewarded with individual honors after the season ended. Huff was named Rookie of the Year, and five Giants were selected All-Pro: Frank Gifford, Rosey Grier, Emlen Tunnell, Andy Robustelli and Rosey Brown.

Big things were expected the following year, and nine games into the season, it looked as if the Giants might be on their way again. Even though they were playing without Rosey Grier, who was fulfilling his military obligations with the U.S. Army at Fort Dix, N.J., the Giants won seven of their first nine games and were second only to the mighty Browns as they readied themselves for their last three games. The Browns were the class of the league that year, with rookie star Jim Brown running wild, and 1957 marked the beginning of a series of epic battles between the former Syracuse back and Giants middle linebacker Sam Huff. In an effort to neutralize Brown, Coach Landry had Huff key on the bruising runner. But not even Huff could pull the Giants out of the slump they fell into at the end of 1957. The team lost its last three games, including a 34-28 contest to the Browns on the last day of the season, and finished second in the Eastern Conference.

Though the Giants had faltered in their final games, Wellington Mara didn't think major changes were needed the following year. But he did tinker a bit in the offseason, acquiring end and place kicker Pat Summerall from the Chicago Cardinals and drafting running back Phil King out of Vanderbilt. The team welcomed Rosey Grier

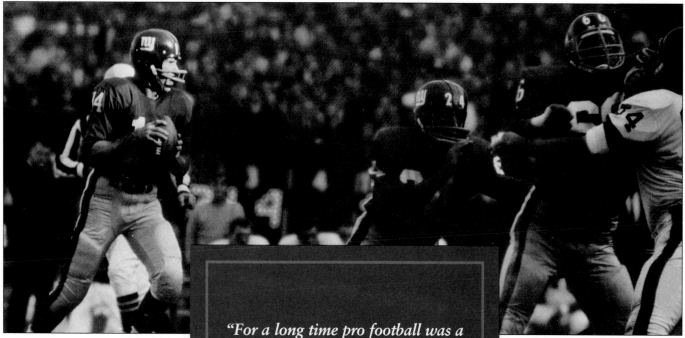

back from the Army and went into the preseason full of optimism. But those feelings faded in the wake of a 1-5 exhibition season, and no one in New York, including the players and coaches themselves, were sure how good this Giants team really was.

Again, the Giants opened up on the road. They beat the Cards 37-7 and then split the next four games. Their record stood at 3-2 when they went into Cleveland to face the undefeated Browns. More than 78,000 fans filled cavernous Municipal Stadium, and they were as shocked as anyone in the league when the Giants prevailed 21-17.

The Colts traveled to New York the following week. They had just pummeled the Green Bay

"For a long time pro football was a part-time job for both the players and coaches. I remember Vince Lombardi, for example, working several different jobs in the offseason while he was with us. Actually, the year he decided to go to Green Bay, he had taken a position with a local banker. In fact, the day the Packers signed Vince, his picture appeared in the financial section of the New York Times underneath a a small story announcing his new job as vice president of a New York bank.

Wellington Mara

Packers 56-0 and featured one of the most formidable teams in the league. Yankee Stadium was packed with some 71,000 spectators—the largest crowd to see a Giants game since Red Grange came to town in 1925—and they were treated to an exciting 24-21 win, with Pat Summerall kicking the deciding field goal with just over two minutes remaining.

The Giants seemed emotionally spent after their big wins over the Browns and Colts, and they lost the next Sunday to the Pittsburgh Steelers. But they would go on to take the three following games, including a stunning 19-17 triumph in Detroit on a blocked field goal. All that stood between them and another shot at the Eastern crown was a rematch with the Browns.

The Browns came to New York with a 9-2 record; the Giants were 8-3 and needed to beat Paul Brown's squad to force a playoff. A tie would do them no good. It was a blustery December day, and the field was covered with snow. Jim Brown

(opposite) DEL SHOFNER AND FRANK GIFFORD WATCH THE GIANTS DEFENSE PLAY. (ROBERT RIGER)
(above) Y.A TITTLE LED THE LEAGUE IN TOUCHDOWN PASSES HIS FIRST TWO YEARS WITH THE GIANTS; IN THIS SHOT HE IS GETTING READY TO THROW AGAINST THE CLEVELAND BROWNS. (ROBERT RIGER)

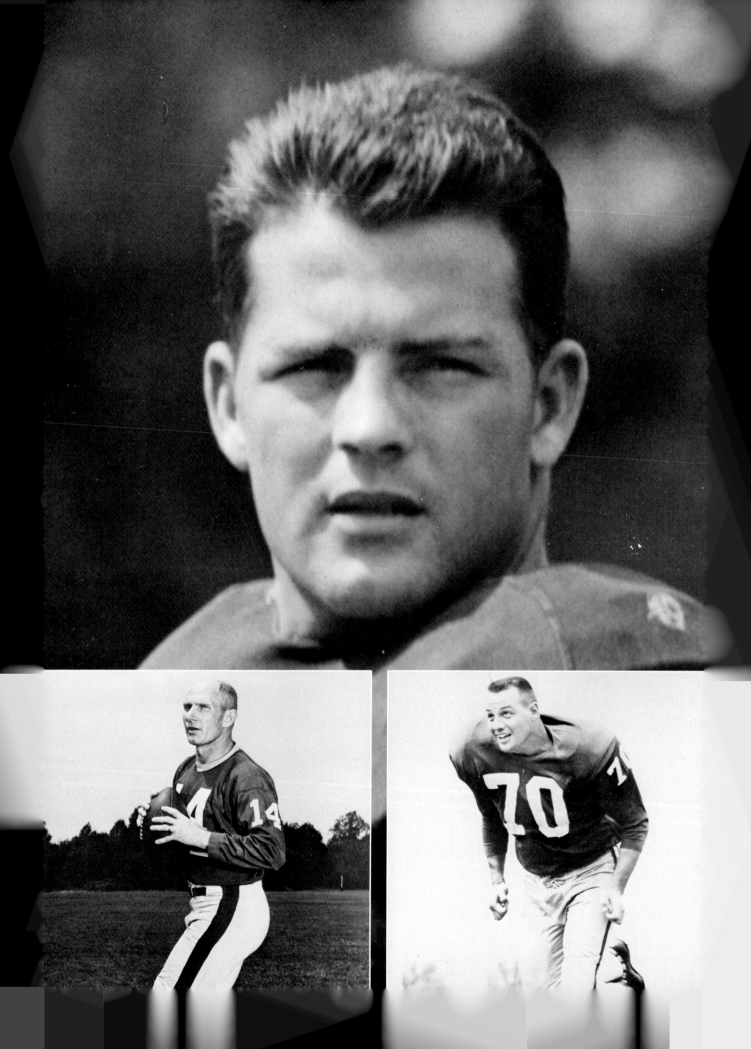

(background) GIFFORD WAS ENSHRINED IN THE PRO FOOTBALL HALL OF FAME IN 1977. HE IS FOURTH AMONG ALL-TIME GIANTS RUSHERS AND SECOND IN RECEPTIONS. (PRO FOOTBALL HALL OF FAME)

(bottom left) ALEX WEBSTER RAN FOR OVER 4,600 YARDS AS A GIANT AND CAUGHT 240 PASSES. (NEW YORK GIANTS)

(bottom right) THE THINGS THE GIANTS' PUBLICITY PEOPLE MADE FRANK GIFFORD DO...(NEW YORK GIANTS)

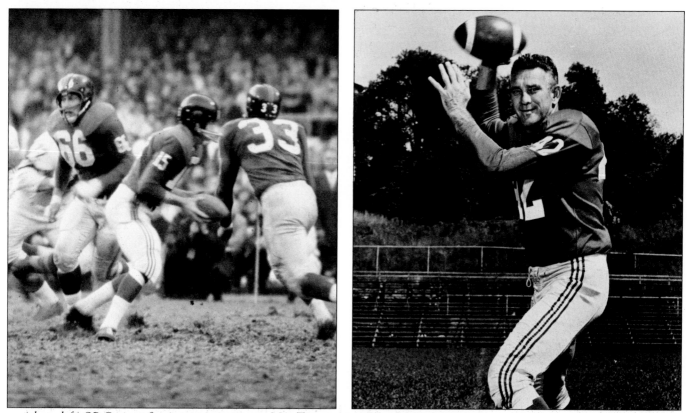

(above left) QB George Shaw handing off to Mel Tripplett as Jack Stroud looks for someone to block. (Fred Roe)

(above right) An All-American from Ole Miss, Charlie Conerley originally played tailback for the Giants when he joined the team in 1948 and was named league MVP in 1959. When he retired after the 1961 season, only Sammy Baugh, Bobby Layne and Norm Van Brocklin had thrown more TD passes. (New York Giants)

(opposite) The 1959 Giants, who lost to the Colts in the title game that year. Defensive coach Tom Landry is sitting in the first row on the far right; second from the left in that same row is Allie Sherman, who had taken over as offensive coordinator when Vince Lombardi left for Green Bay before the start of the season. Head coach Jim Lee Howell is standing on the left in the second row, and Wellington Mara is the third person from the right. (New York Giants)

scampered for 65 yards and a touchdown on his team's first play from scrimmage, but the Giants defense settled down and allowed only a field goal the rest of the way. The score was tied 10-10 with time running out when the Giants got the ball back near midfield. Three Conerly passes fell incomplete, and to most everyone's surprise, Jim Lee Howell sent in Summerall to try a field goal.

"I couldn't believe he was asking me to do that," Summerall said later on. "The field was in horrible shape, and I had never made a kick that long." No one was exactly sure how long it was because the yard markers were covered with snow. But Summerall drilled it through the uprights—it was recorded as a 49-yarder—and the Giants were still alive.

The two teams met again at Yankee Stadium the next week. Again, it was biting cold, but this time the field was clear of snow. The Giants were ready for Jim Brown, and he gained a career low eight

yards on seven carries before Sam Huff knocked him out of the game. The Giants won 10-0 on a Summerall field goal and a touchdown run by 37-year-old Charlie Conerly, who had taken a lateral from Frank Gifford off a double reverse and scrambled eight yards for the score. "The double reverse didn't surprise me," Paul Brown said after the game. "But the lateral to Conerly? They couldn't have planned it. What the hell was he doing there?"

The championship game was held the following week, and it had all the earmarks of a classic confrontation. The Giants boasted the league's toughest defense, the Colts the NFL's most potent offense, and as could be expected, momentum seesawed throughout the contest. The Colts built a halftime lead of 14-3, but the Giants came back to go ahead 17-14 in the fourth quarter. With little more than two minutes remaining, the Giants faced a third-and-four. The Colts were looking for a pass,

but Conerly crossed them up by pitching to Gifford on a sweep. Gino Marchetti wrestled Gifford to the ground close to the first down marker, and it appeared that the Giants had made it. But Big Daddy Lipscomb fell across Marchetti in the pile-up and broke his leg. Marchetti screamed in pain, and in the ensuing confusion, the officials forgot to mark the ball. Only after the big defensive end had been carried from the field did the referee place the ball down. But when he did it was inches short. "I know I made that first down," Gifford says. "But the referee was so concerned about Marchetti that he forgot where he had picked up the ball."

Rather than risk going for it, the Giants punted. The Colts got the ball back on their own 14-yard line and with Johnny Unitas handing off to Lenny Moore and Alan Ameche and throwing to Raymond Berry, proceeded to march down the

"It was pretty low-budget for everybody. Emlen Tunnell told me that the players all had to buy their own shoes, and most of their uniforms were patched. If they tore any part of their jersey, it got patched up. If their shoes broke, the Giants had someone repair the shoes, a team cobbler, I guess you'd call him."

William N. Wallace,
New York Times.

field. Steve Myhra, who had made only four of ten field goal attempts all season, booted the tying kick with only seven seconds remaining. Never before had a championship game ended in a tie at the end of regulation play.

League rules called for a sudden death overtime period, and Unitas met Giants co-captains Kyle Rote and Bill Svoboda at midfield for the coin toss. The Giants won the right to receive, but their offense sputtered, and they punted after only three plays. The Colts took over at their own 20-yard line, and Unitas began an exhilarating, 13-play drive that ended with Alan Ameche plunging over the goal line from two-yards out for the win, 23-17.

It was a tough defeat for the Giants, but a wonderful day for pro football. The year before, CBS had begun televising NFL games, and for thousands of viewers across the country, the overtime contest had been their first taste of professional

ANDY ROBUSTELLI AND THE REST OF THE GIANTS DEFENSE TAKES A
BREAK IN A 1961 GAME AT YANKEE STADIUM (FRED ROE)

JOHNNY UNITAS THROWS A PASS OVER DICK MODZEWELSKI IN THE
1958 NFL CHAMPIONSHIP GAME. (ROBERT RIGER)
(OPPOSITE) JOE MORRISON PLAYED FOR THE GIANTS FROM 1959-1972.
(NEW YORK GIANTS)

football. Sports Illustrated's Tex Maule described it as "the best game ever played," and it helped lift the NFL to new heights of popularity, not only among fans but also within the New York advertising community, which suddenly began to see the sport as a viable marketing tool.

More losses were to follow the overtime game. Tim Mara passed away six weeks later, and then Vince Lombardi announced he was leaving the Giants to become head coach of the Packers, which had posted a dismal 1-10-1 record the previous year. Jim Lee Howell brought Allie Sherman back to handle the offense, drafted a scrappy halfback named Joe Morrison and traded for cornerback Dick Lynch. Big things were expected from the Giants that year, and they didn't disappoint, winning 10 games and losing only two during the regular season. The defense, in particular, was magnificent, and it led the league in almost every category. "The thing that struck me about our team in those days was its intelligence," Summerall says. "We just outsmarted a lot of people. Especially on defense. Everyone knew so thoroughly what they were supposed to do. I remember that our offense really struggled at

"Rosey Grier was a musician and a singer, and he always came to training camp with a lot of high-tech audio equipment. We'd stick him up in the top floor of one of the Fairfield University dorms so he wouldn't disturb so many people. The first ten days or so all you'd hear from his room was lowdown blues. Sad, sad stuff, you know. But then, Rosey would start to pick it up a bit. And that's when we knew he was getting in shape, because he was feeling better. The coaches used to say, 'We can go to one-a-days now cause Rosey's in shape.' "

Allie Sherman

one point during the 1959 season, and we won some games without even scoring a touchdown, thanks to our defense."

The defense developed something of a glamorous reputation. Linebacker Sam Huff made the cover of *Time* magazine and was the subject of a television special entitled, "The Violent World of Sam Huff," in which he was wired for sound during an exhibition game. A serious rivalry developed between the offensive and defensive units, and it wasn't uncommon to hear a member of the defense mutter to a player on the offense as they ran onto the field during a game, "See if you can hold them."

To New York Giants fans, it didn't matter what side of the ball they played on—they simply loved their football team. "It was an amazing time to be in New York," Webster recalls. "We were something of a people's team. Everybody knew us, everybody was behind us. New York kind of make us into heroes, and it was a great feeling to walk around Manhattan and get all that attention."

The Giants met the Colts again in the 1959 championship game and held a 9-7 lead going into the fourth quarter. But the Colts exploded for 24

(top) SAM HUFF LOOKING TO PLUG A HOLE AGAINST THE GREEN BAY PACKERS. THAT'S FORMER HEISMAN TROPHY WINNER PAUL HORNUNG CARRYING THE BALL. (ROBERT RIGER)

(bottom left) VERSATILE JOE MORRISON PLAYED HALFBACK, FLANKER AND TIGHT END DURING HIS 14 YEARS IN A GIANTS UNIFORM. AND HE PLAYED THEM ALL WELL. (FRED ROE)

(left inset) THE GIANTS HAD A LOGJAM AT QUARTERBACK IN 1961; CHARLEY CONERLY, Y.A. TITTLE AND LEE GROSSCUP LINE UP BEHIND CENTER GREG LARSON. (NEW YORK GIANTS)

(right inset) MIDDLE LINEBACKER SAM HUFF ZEROES IN ON A LONGTIME NEMESIS JIM TAYLOR. (ROBERT RIGER)

(bottom right) ANDY ROBUSTELLI AND DICK MODZEWELSKI WRAP UP CLEVELAND QUARTERBACK FRANK RYAN AS JIM KATCAVAGE COMES IN TO HELP. (ROBERT RIGER)

THE 1962 NFL
CHAMPIONSHIP GAME WAS
PLAYED IN BITTERLY COLD
CONDITIONS AT YANKEE
STADIUM. (ROBERT RIGER)

(inset) ALEX WEBSTER SEEMS
TO BE SCALING THE GOAL
POSTS IN THIS 1959 TOUCH-
DOWN AGAINST THE
BROWNS. (ROBERT RIGER)

(upper left) CHARLIE CONERLY BARKS THE SIGNALS UNDER THE WATCHFUL EYE OF EAGLES MIDDLE LINE-BACKER CHUCK BEDNARIK. (ROBERT RIGER)

(upper right) VINCE LOMBARDI (HERE WITH FRANK GIFFORD) COACHED THE GIANTS OFFENSE FOR FIVE YEARS BEFORE TAKING OVER AS HEAD COACH OF THE GREEN BAY PACKERS IN 1959. (ROBERT RIGER)

(lower left) BALTIMORE'S LENNY MOORE STRETCHES OUT THE GIANTS DEFENSE. (ROBERT RIGER)

(lower right) NO ONE EVER SAID THAT PRO FOOTBALL WAS AN EASY GAME. (ROBERT RIGER)

The Giants had some epic battles with Cleveland and its star running back Jim Brown. (Robert Riger)

(right) Y.A. Tittle was a terrific thrower, but he wasn't much of a scrambler. (Robert Riger)

Frank Gifford rushed for over 3,600 yards during his 12 years with the team. (Robert Riger)

Frank Gifford plunges over for a touchdown against the Eagles. (Robert Riger)

(inset) Alex Webster arrived in New York from the Canadian Football League prior to the 1955 season and went on to lead the Giants running attack for ten seasons. (New York Giants)

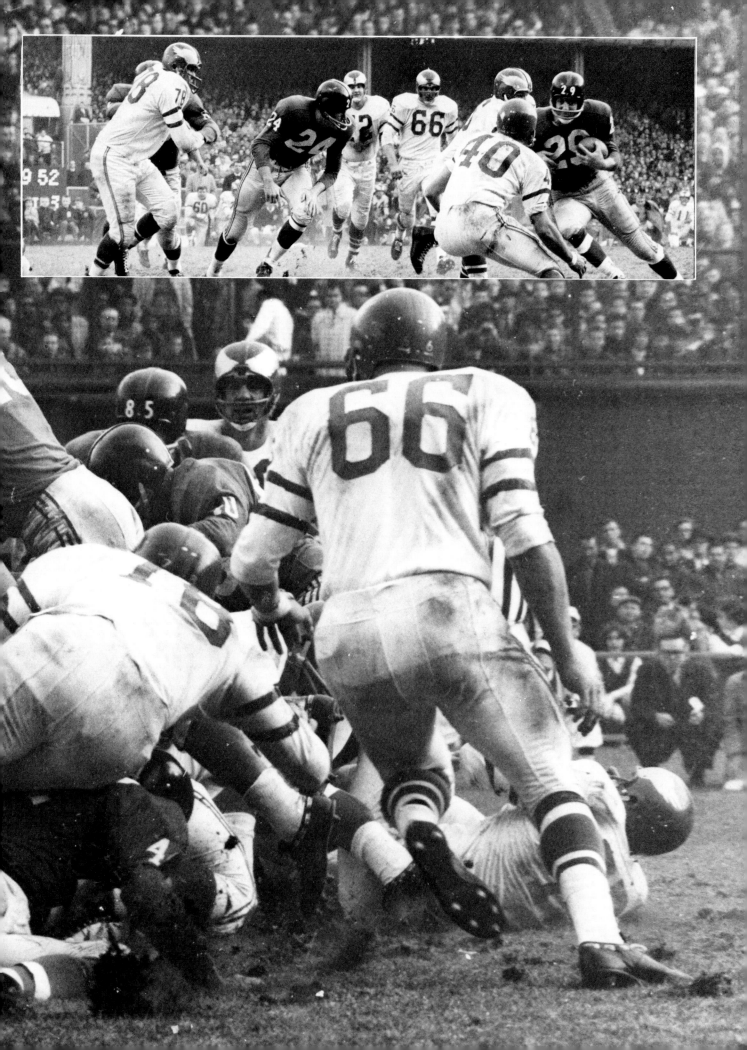

Y.A. Tittle shows
some young fans in
Puerto Rico how
an NFL quarterback
throws a ball
during a 1963
promotional tour.
(New York Giants)

points in the final period and won 31-16.

Bert Bell had died during the 1959 season, and after the championship game, the owners met to pick a new commissioner. They haggled over several candidates, but after four days were still at an impasse. Then Wellington Mara suggested a compromise, Pete Rozelle, the 33-year-old general manager of the Los Angeles Rams, and soon after he was elected for the job. Rozelle inherited a league that was expanding—new franchises were scheduled to start playing in Dallas in 1960 and Minnesota the following year—and facing competition from the upstart American Football League. Wellington Mara was in favor of expansion, but it cost him another top assistant coach when Tom Landry returned home to Texas to coach the new Dallas Cowboys.

"I left the Giants after the 1959 season because I was planning on leaving football altogether," Landry recalls. "The money just wasn't very good, and it was pretty much a part-time job. I was looking to get into some sort of business when the Cowboys got a franchise and asked me to be their head coach. I figured I'd do it for a few years and be on my way. But in 1964 they offered me a ten-year extension, and I decided to stay in it a while longer."

It was Wellington Mara who put the Cowboys onto Landry. "We hated losing Tom, but I understood his desire to get back to Texas," Wellington Mara says. "Not long after he did return home, however, Bud Adams called and asked Tom if he'd be interested in coaching the Houston Oilers of the new American Football League. Now, I didn't want Tom to leave the Giants, but I was even more concerned about the rival league getting him. So I phoned Tex Schramm of the Cowboys and recommended that they keep Tom in the NFL and hire him for their coach."

The 1960 season began well enough for the Giants, and they had a 5-1-1 record when the Philadelphia Eagles came to Yankee Stadium for their first meeting of the year. But the team's fortunes turned when Eagles linebacker Chuck Bednarik put Frank Gifford into the hospital with a savage hit. Gifford suffered a severe concussion and sat out the rest of the year. And as if they were feeling the effects of that tackle themselves, the Giants went on to drop three of their last four games to finish 6-4-2.

Jim Lee Howell retired as head coach in the off-

"I started getting into broadcasting when I was going to school at Southern Cal. I worked on a number of films as an extra or stunt man, and every now and again I'll be watching a late movie and see myself in the background. In the late 1950s I signed a contract with Warner Bors. to do a television series pilot. I didn't realize it at the time, but I would have had to have quit football if the pilot was picked up. But it didn't sell, and I, of course, kept playing. Prior to the 1959 season I began doing a TV show before Giants games with Chris Schenkel. The year I sat out I did some color commentary for CBS radio on Giants games, and the following year, when I was playing again, I began doing the sports report on the local CBS news show. I did that for three years, going to practice from 9 a.m. to 2 p.m., then going over to the station to get ready for my reports. Could you imagine Phil Simms doing local news while he was playing for the Giants?

Frank Gifford

67

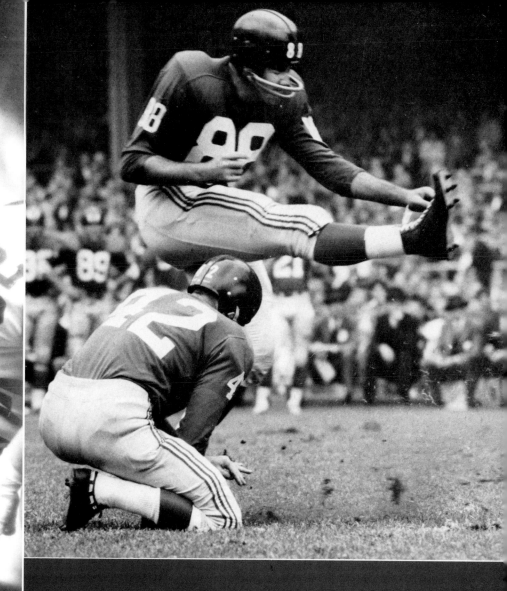

(upper left) Chuckin' Charlie Conerley calls the signals in a 1959 game. (Robert Riger)

(lower left) The Giants practice in Yankee Stadium before the 1959 Championship Game. (Robert Riger)

(upper right) A sure-handed tight end, Pat Summerall also excelled as a place kicker. (New York Giants)

(lower right) Charlie Conerly looks for a receiver in the 1959 NFL Championship game against the Colts. The Giants lost that one, too, 31-16. (Robert Riger)

Giant defenders closing in on
yet another quarterback. (New
York Giants)

SAM HUFF WENT TO FOUR PRO
BOWLS AS A GIANT AND WAS
ELECTED TO THE HALL OF FAME
IN 1982. (ROBERT RIGER)

(opposite) DICK NOLAN (25),
SAM HUFF (70) AND JIMMY
PATTON (20) TRY TO WRESTLE
JIM BROWN TO THE GROUND.
(ROBERT RIGER)

(opposite inset) BART STARR AND
SAM HUFF SEEM TO BE STARING
EACH OTHER DOWN DURING THE
1962 NFL CHAMPIONSHIP GAME AT
YANKEE STADIUM. (ROBERT RIGER)

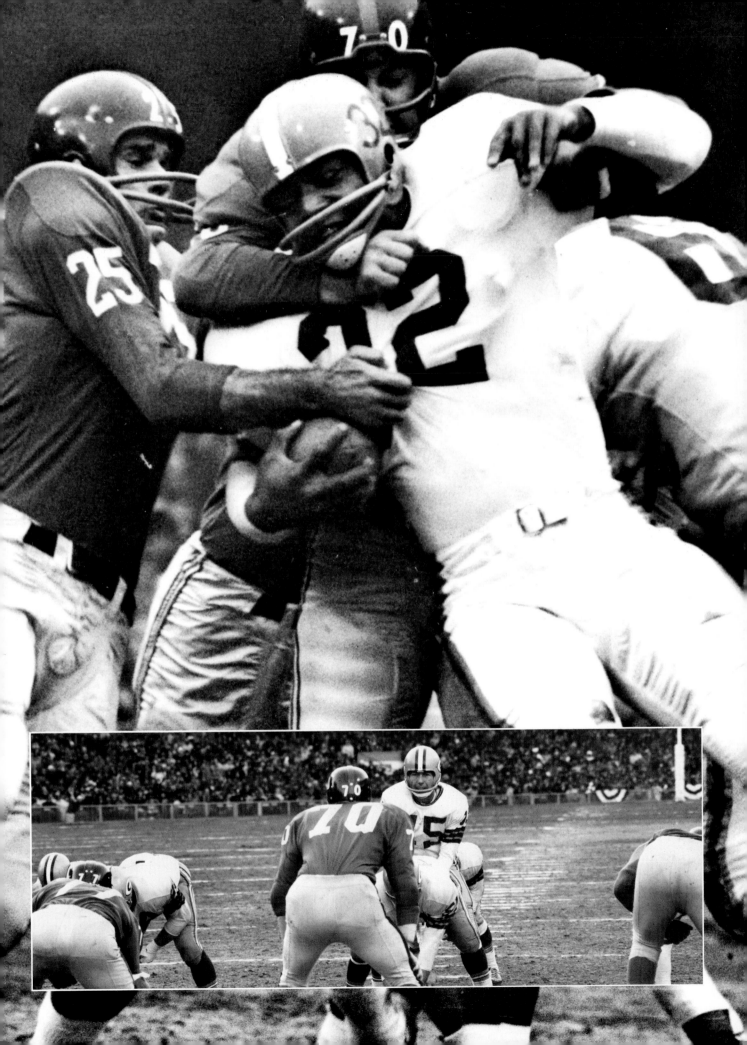

(background) THE GIANTS OFENSE WAS IN CAPABLE HANDS WITH CHARLIE CONERLY AND Y.A. TITTLE AT THE HELM. (ROBERT RIGER)

(lower left inset) CBS STARTED TELEVISING NFL GAMES IN 1957. (ROBERT RIGER)

(lower right inset) IN THE DAYS BEFORE GATORADE, SAM HUFF SIPS FROM THE WATER BUCKET. (ROBERT RIGER)

JOHNNY UNITAS UNCORKS A PASS IN THE SUDDEN DEATH GAME OF 1958. (ROBERT RIGER)

(*inset*) SAM HUFF NAILS A REDSKINS RUNNER; THE HALL OF FAME LINEBACKER WAS TRADED TO WASHINGTON AFTER THE 1963 SEASON. (ROBERT RIGER)

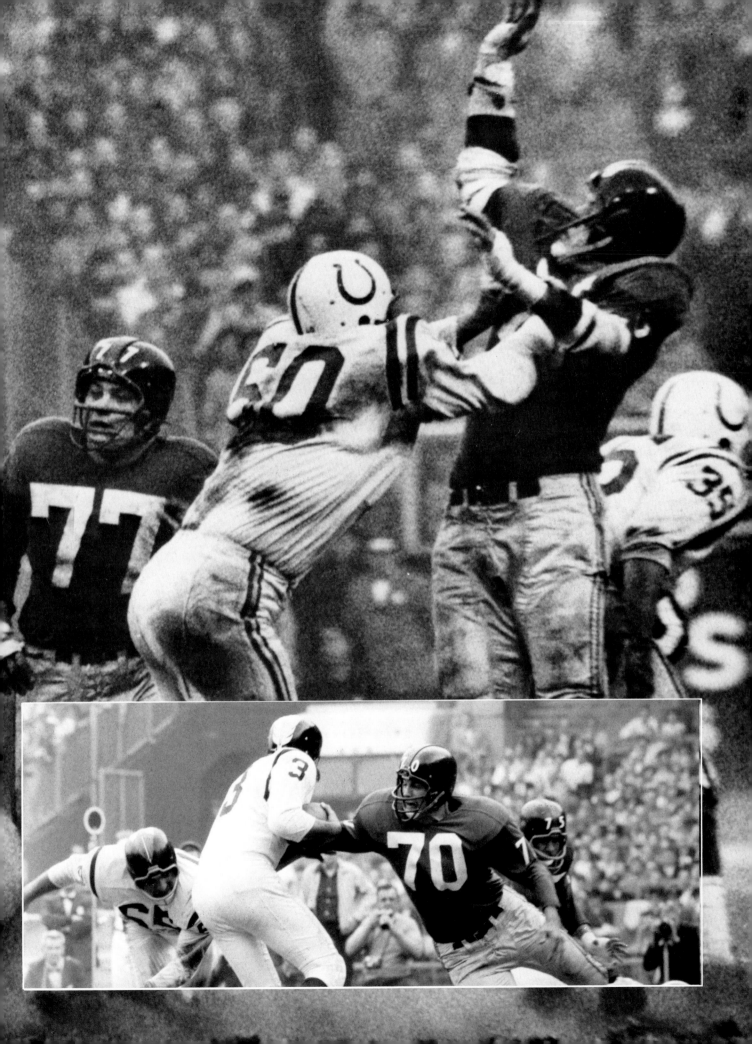

season, and the first call Wellington Mara made was to his old Fordham classmate, Vince Lombardi. "I had told Vince when he left for Green Bay that I would give him first shot the next time a head coaching opened up here," Mara explains. "But he felt a commitment to the Packers and decided to stay put." So the top job went to offensive coach Allie Sherman.

"The first thing Jack and Well Mara asked me to do was evaluate the team," Sherman says. "I told them our defense was getting older, but it was still experienced and could keep a game together. Our offense was getting older, too, but there were some gaps there that we needed to take care off. I wanted us to be more of a passing team and said we needed a pressure guy, a receiver with speed who could stretch out defenses. And with Charlie Conerly being 41, I thought we needed another quarterback. He didn't have to be a Hall-of-Famer, but someone we could use for a couple of games and keep us in the running."

Training camp opened not long after Sherman's meeting with the Mara brothers, and the most noticeable absence was Frank Gifford, who had decided to retire as a result of the concussion he sustained from Bednarik's tackle. But the head coach's concern over that loss was eased considerably when Wellington Mara said he could get a balding, 36-year-old quarterback from the San Francisco 49ers named Y.A. Tittle. "The Niners were employing a shotgun offense," Sherman says, "and they thought Tittle was too slow-footed for that. So we got him for second-year tackle Lou Cordileone." Tittle was thrilled with the deal. "It was great going to a team that expected to win," he says. "I remember Sam Huff asking me not long after I arrived about my Christmas plans for

> *We were playing Philadelphia in the 1961 season, and Allie sent in this formation that had Erich Barnes and Jimmy Patton lined up as receivers. It was a real schoolyard stunt, sort of a 'spread 'em out and go deep' type play that had been diagrammed the week before by our equipment man Pete Privete. Most of our regular offense was in there; Barnes and Patton had just replaced a couple of linemen. The Eagles didn't know what to make of the formation or who to cover, and Tittle was able to complete a pass to Barnes for a touchdown."*
>
> **Pat Summerall**

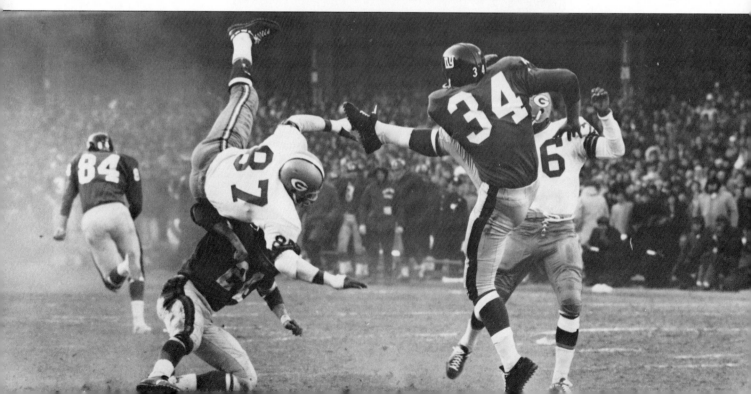

ALEX WEBSTER IS
UPENDED BY AN EAGLE
DEFENDER. (FRED ROE)

(OPPOSITE) DON
CHANDLER BOOMS A
PUNT IN THE 1962
CHAMPIONSHIP GAME AS
PHIL KING TAKES OUT
GREEN BAY'S WILLIE
DAVIS. (ROBERT RIGER)

Y.A. TITTLE WAS A DEADLY ACCURATE PASSER.
(ROBERT RIGER)

the year. 'I'll be home in California, like always,' I said. 'No, you'll be here,' he growled. 'We'll be in the championship game that week.' He said it like it was on the schedule or something. That's how much confidence those guys had."

A few weeks later Mara filled another hole in the Giants offense when he acquired speedy Del Shofner from the Rams. "I said we should do whatever we had to get him," Sherman says. "He was a beautiful receiver with great hands." Mara gave up a number one draft pick for Shofner, and also traded for tight end Joe Walton and cornerback Erich Barnes.

The Giants entered the 1961 season with more firepower than they had had in years, but the team got off to a slow start. They lost their opener to the Cardinals and struggled miserably during the first half of their second game. "Charlie wasn't doing very well, so I sent Y.A. in, and we pulled the game out," Sherman recalls. Conerly started the next week, but Tittle relieved him again with the Giants down two touchdowns and won another game. He became the starter the following Sunday.

Conerly sat on the bench for much of the year season after that, but he did play a major part in a key win late in the season. "We were playing our next-to-last game at Philadelphia, and though our record was 9-3, we really needed a win," Sherman recalls. "But the Eagles were handling us. They kept doubling on the outside, so I told Y.A., 'Let's go with the tight end over the middle, that's open.' We called it the Giants special. But Y.A. liked to throw the out pattern to the wide receivers, and he kept trying to do that, without success. I turned to Charlie at halftime and said, 'See what's happening,' and he

> *"I kind of fell into broadcasting. Charlie Conerly and I were staying in a Manhattan hotel one weekend during the preseason when the phone rang. I was sitting on the bed watching television and Charlie was in the shower, so I answered the phone. This man wanted to speak with Charlie. I said he's unavailable and asked if he wanted to leave a message. 'Just remind him to be at CBS at four this afternoon.' I said I'd tell him and was about to hang up the phone when the man asked me what I was doing. When I said nothing special, he suggested that I come down as well. So I did. There were four of us auditioning—Conerley, Rote, Webster and myself—and I got the job. I started working for CBS in 1960, while I was still playing. And I stayed there for almost 25 years.*
>
> **Pat Summerall**

replied, 'Giants Special.' So I started him for the second half, Joey Walton caught seven or eight passes, including two for touchdowns, and we won the game."

The Giants finished with a 10-3-1 record and went to Green Bay to face Vince Lombardi and the Packers for the championship. The Pack routed Sherman's squad 37-0, and while the loss stung, the team could look back on 1961 with great pride. Sherman was named Coach of the Year in his rookie season, and Tittle was league MVP. The defense, which was now being coached by Andy Robustelli, led the league with 33 interceptions, including one that Erich Barnes ran back 102 yards for a touchdown, and nine Giants—Rosey Brown, Sam Huff, Jimmy Patton, Jim Katcavage, Alex Webster, Robustelli, Tittle, Shofner and Barnes—went to the Pro Bowl.

Conerly retired after the 1961 season, as did Pat Summerall, who wanted to concentrate on a burgeoning career in broadcasting, and Kyle Rote, who stayed on with the team as an assistant coach. But the core of the ball club remained, and while it was a year older, it was still one of the most talented franchises in the NFL. One of the pleasant surprises in training camp was the return of Frank Gifford, who had grown antsy during his year off and wanted to get back into the game. Sherman moved him to Rote's old flanker back position, and while Gifford looked rusty in the early-going, he came on to have a good year.

Most of the Giants had a good year. Tittle threw a league record 33 touchdown passes, including seven in one game against the Washington Redskins, and Sherman was named Coach of the Year again as his team finished atop

NOTHING LIKE A ONE-ON-ONE; JIM BROWN AND JIMMY
PATTON FACE OFF IN A GAME AT YANKEE STADIUM.
(ROBERT RIGER)

(upper right) HERE IS DICK MODZEWELSKI TRYING TO
TACKLE THE BROWN'S GREAT RUNNER. (ROBERT RIGER)

(lower right) ALLIE SHERMAN REPLACED VINCE LOMBARDI
AS OFFENSIVE COORDINATOR IN 1959 AND THEN BECAME
HEAD COACH TWO YEARS LATER WHEN JIM LEE HOWELL
RETIRED. (NEW YORK GIANTS)

the Eastern Conference again with a 12-2 record.

The Giants had never been more popular, and fans regularly filled Yankee Stadium for their games. Those who couldn't get tickets took extreme measures to catch the contests on TV. League rules forced teams to black-out home games from local television coverage, but enterprising fans flocked to area motels that had installed tall antennas capable of pulling down signals from a Hartford station that broadcast the games.

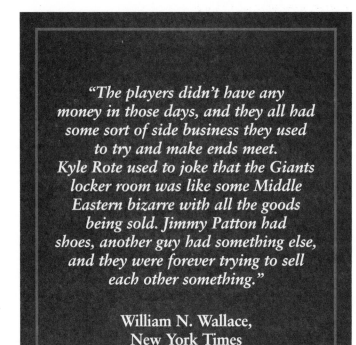

"The players didn't have any money in those days, and they all had some sort of side business they used to try and make ends meet. Kyle Rote used to joke that the Giants locker room was like some Middle Eastern bizarre with all the goods being sold. Jimmy Patton had shoes, another guy had something else, and they were forever trying to sell each other something."

William N. Wallace,
New York Times

The 1962 championship game was held at Yankee Stadium. "I remember waking up the morning of the game, taking a walk up Park Avenue and marveling at what a beautiful day it was," Sherman recalls. "It was cold, but calm." All that changed by game time, however, and the wind was gusting up to 40 knots at kick-off. "I knew we were in trouble when we left the hotel for Yankee Stadium and saw that vans had been blown all over the street," Tittle says.

"It was just freezing cold," Sherman says, "and people told me later it was as cold as it had ever been in New York. Y.A. was throwing passes in our pre-game warm-ups, and he always threw a very tight spiral. But the first ball he tossed died after five yards and went right into the ground. I looked over at Y.A., and his eyes were as big as silver dollars.

One of our coaches, Ken Kavanaugh, saw what had happened and came up to me. 'We might have just lost our passing game.' he said. And he was right."

They had, and that was a bad sign for a team that relied heavily on the pass, especially the long pass. Both Tittle and Bart Starr had tough days throwing—Y.A. completed just 18 of 41 passes, and Starr 10 of 21—and the Giants were only able to muster one touchdown, on a blocked punt recovered in the end zone. But thanks to a Jim Taylor run and three Jerry Kramer field goals, the Pack won 16-7. The Giants were stung by the defeat, and afterwards Kyle Rote said, "I never saw a team that tried so hard and lost."

The Giants were still thinking about that loss when they assembled for training camp the following year. It had been a quiet offseason, with the big news being the opening of the Pro Football Hall of Fame in Canton, Oh. Appropriately, one of the charter members was Tim Mara, the man who had brought pro football to New York.

It was still a confident team that gathered at Fairfield University in Fairfield, Ct. the summer of 1963. Confident but old. Ten of the 36 players who made the final roster were over 30, and many of them were starting to show their age. Sherman made only minor adjustments with the squad, but he did trade Rosey Grier to the Los Angeles Rams. "Rosey had come to me after the previous season to say he was retiring," Sherman recalls. "He said he wanted to go out West and become a singer. I said, 'How about if I trade you to Los Angeles, Rosey, and while you're out there you can still pursue your singing career while you play football. And we could get something for you instead of your just retiring."

Tittle had another marvelous year in 1963, and he broke his own record by throwing 36 touchdown passes. The team started off slowly, going 3-2 for the first five games of the season. But then the Giants won five in a row, averaging 39.5 points per game in the process. They ended the regular season in first place again, this time at 11-3, and went off to Wrigley Field to play the Bears for the championship.

As it had been the case the two previous years, the weather for the championship game was brutal, and the temperature stood at nine degrees at kick-off. The Giants got off to a good start with Tittle hurling a TD pass to Gifford for a 7-0 lead. Later in the first quarter, Y.A. found Shofner in the end zone all alone, but the ball slipped off his frozen fingers and fell harmlessly to the ground. The Bears

picked off a Tittle pass on the next play and ran it all the way down to the five-yard line. Quarterback Bill Wade scored two plays later. The Giants added a Don Chandler field goal before the half ended and went into the locker room leading 10-7.

The Giants would not score another point. Tittle's sprained a knee just before the half, and even a dose of painkillers and a tight tape job could not help. The 37-year-old could barely walk, let alone run, and he was hassled by the Bears defense, which was coached by George Allen, for the rest of the game. In all, Tittle threw five interceptions, including two on screen passes and one on a Hail Mary play the with time expiring that defensive halfback Richie Petibon snatched in the Giants end zone to seal his team's 14-10 victory.

The Giants had lost three championship games in a row, and no one associated with the team found that very easy to take. But it is important to also note that over the eight seasons from 1956 to 1963, the team had captured six Eastern Conference crowns, one NFL championship and compiled a regular season mark of 73-25-3. They truly were Beasts of the East.

THE 1962 GIANTS POSTED A 12-2 REGULAR
SEASON MARK BUT LOST THE TITLE GAME
TO GREEN BAY 16-7 IN A BITTERLY COLD
YANKEE STADIUM.
(NEW YORK GIANTS)

(background) ONE OF THE BEST DEFENSIVE LINES IN NFL HISTORY: (FROM LEFT) ANDY ROBUSTELLI, ROSEY GRIER, DICK MODZEWELSKI AND JIM KATCAVAGE. (ROBERT RIGER)

(bottom insets) PAT SUMMERALL'S KICK WAS GOOD IN THIS 1958 CONTEST AGAINST THE BROWNS, AND THE TWO TEAMS MET AGAIN THE FOLLOWING WEEK TO DETERMINE WHO WOULD FACE THE COLTS IN THE CHAMPIONSHIP GAME. THE GIANTS WON THAT ONE BUT THEN LOST THE TITLE GAME TO THE COLTS IN THE FAMED SUDDEN DEATH GAME. (NEW YORK GIANTS)

(opposite lower right inset) THE GIANTS TAKE THE FIELD IN YANKEE STADIUM FOR THE FIRST TIME AT THE START OF THE 1956 SEASON. (ROBERT RIGER)

(opposite lower left inset) THE GIANTS' CHANCES IN THE 1963 CHAMPIONSHIP GAME TUMBLED AFTER Y.A. TITTLE HURT HIS KNEE ON THIS PLAY AGAINST THE BEARS AT WRIGLEY FIELD. HE THREW FIVE INTERCEPTIONS THAT DAY, AND THE GIANTS LOST 14-10. (ROBERT RIGER)

(background) Y.A. TITTLE GOT THIS PASS AWAY JUST IN TIME. (ROBERT RIGER)

(left) Y.A. TITTLE HAD A TOUGH TIME DURING THE 1963 CHAMPIONSHIP GAME LOSS TO THE CHICAGO BEARS. (NOTICE THE CRACKS IN HIS HELMET.) (NEW YORK GIANTS)

(upper right) DICK LYNCH TRIES TO BRING DOWN JIM BROWN IN A 1963 GAME. (ROBERT RIGER)

(lower right) ASSISTANT COACH VINCE LOMBARDI (IN RED HAT AND SWEATS) WATCHES SOME OF HIS PLAYERS DURING TRAINING CAMP IN 1956. THAT'S FRANK GIFFORD IN THE RED HAT AND JERSEY WALKING BEHIND HIM. (ROBERT RIGER)

(left) FEW TEAMS WERE ABLE TO STOP Y.A. TITTLE DURING HIS YEARS WITH THE GIANTS. (ROBERT RIGER)

BEFORE HE BECAME HEAD COACH OF THE NEW YORK JETS, JOE WALTON CAUGHT A FEW PASSES AS A TIGHT END FOR THE GIANTS. (ROBERT RIGER)

PAT SUMMERALL JOINED THE GIANTS BEFORE THE 1958 SEA-
SON AND HELPED KICK THEM INTO THE CHAMPIONSHIP GAME
THAT YEAR. (FRED ROE)

(inset) ALEX WEBSTER (IN RED HAT) RUNS THROUGH A PLAY
DURING TRAINING CAMP IN 1956. (ROBERT RIGER)

FRANK GIFFORD FOLLOWS DARRELL DESS THROUGH THE LINE IN A 1961 CONTEST. (ROBERT RIGER)

(left inset) ALEX WEBSTER WAS NEVER EASY TO BRING DOWN. (ROBERT RIGER)

(right inset) FRANK GIFFORD BOLTS THROUGH THE CLEVELAND DEFENSE. (ROBERT RIGER)

SAM HUFF BEAR HUGS
CLEVELAND RECEIVER BOBBY
MITCHELL IN A 1959 GAME.
(ROBERT RIGER)

(opposite background)
EVEN THOUGH HE SCORED A
TOUCHDOWN ON THIS PLAY,
JIM BROWN ALWAYS FOUND THE
GIANTS DEFENSE TOUGH TO RUN
ON. (ROBERT RIGER)

(opposite upper inset)
A NATIVE OF KEARNEY, N.J.,
WEBSTER CAME TO NEW YORK
AFTER A BRIEF STINT IN THE
CANADIAN FOOTBALL LEAGUE.
HE SOLD TICKETS FOR THE
GIANTS IN THE OFFSEASON AFTER
HIS FIRST YEAR WITH THE TEAM.
(FRED ROE)

(opposite lower inset)
Y.A. TITTLE AND JACK MARA
LEAVE WRIGLEY FIELD AFTER THE
GIANTS DROPPED THE 1963 TITLE
GAME TO THE CHICAGO BEARS.

(above) Y.A. TITTLE GETS READY TO UNLEASH A PASS. (ROBERT RIGER)

(top left)
CHARLIE CONERLY DROPS BACK DURING A GIANTS PRACTICE UNDER THE WATCHFUL EYE OF ANDY ROBUSTELLI. (ROBERT RIGER)

(bottom left) RAYMOND BERRY GETS READY TO SNARE A PASS FROM JOHNNY UNITAS IN THE 1958 SUDDEN DEATH GAME. (ROBERT RIGER)

GUARD JACK STROUD
WAS A GIANT FOR
12 SEASONS.
(ROBERT RIGER)

(opposite) DEFENSIVE WHIZ
TOM LANDRY OUTLINES A
PLAY FOR THE GIANTS WHILE
ANDY ROBUSTELLI PORES
OVER HIS PLAYBOOK.
(NOTICE THE PHOTOGRAPHS
OF THE NEW YORK YANKEES
IN THE BACKGROUND.)
(ROBERT RIGER)

EMLEN TUNNELL WAS AN ASSISTANT COACH WITH
THE GIANTS FOR 11 SEASONS AFTER HE HAD
RETIRED AS A PLAYER.
(ABOVE: ROBERT RIGER; RIGHT: NEW YORK GIANTS)

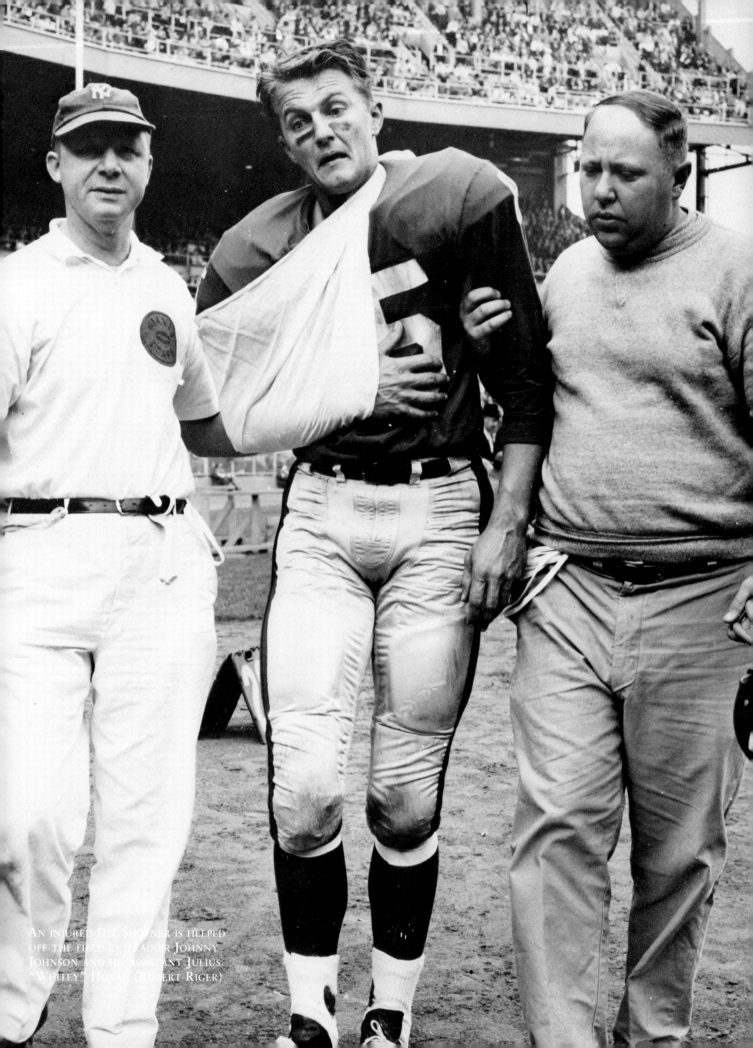

An injured Del Shofner is helped off the field by trainer Johnny Johnson and his assistant Julius "Whitey" Horst (Robert Riger)

(above) FRANK GIFFORD PLAYED IN THE DEFENSIVE
SECONDARY DURING HIS FIRST FEW YEARS WITH THE GIANTS AND
EVEN MADE THE PRO BOWL AS A CORNERBACK. (FRED ROE)

(left) JIMMY PATTON AND AARON THOMAS TAKE A BREAK.
(FRED ROE)

Joe Morrison and Don Chandler wait to go back on the field. (Fred Roe)
(opposite) Buzz Guy, Dick Modzewelski and Dick Lynch prepare before the 1958 NFL Championship game. (Robert Riger)

(left) Y.A. Tittle unleashes a pass as his offensive line holds off a fierce Colts rush. (Robert Riger)

(left bottom) Colts fullback Alan Ameche about to score the winning touchdown in the "greatest game ever played." (Robert Riger)

(right) Training camp was never easy. (Robert Riger)

(right bottom) Frank Gifford is carried off the field after taking a vicious hit from Eagle linebacker Chuck Bednarik in a 1961 game. (Robert Riger)

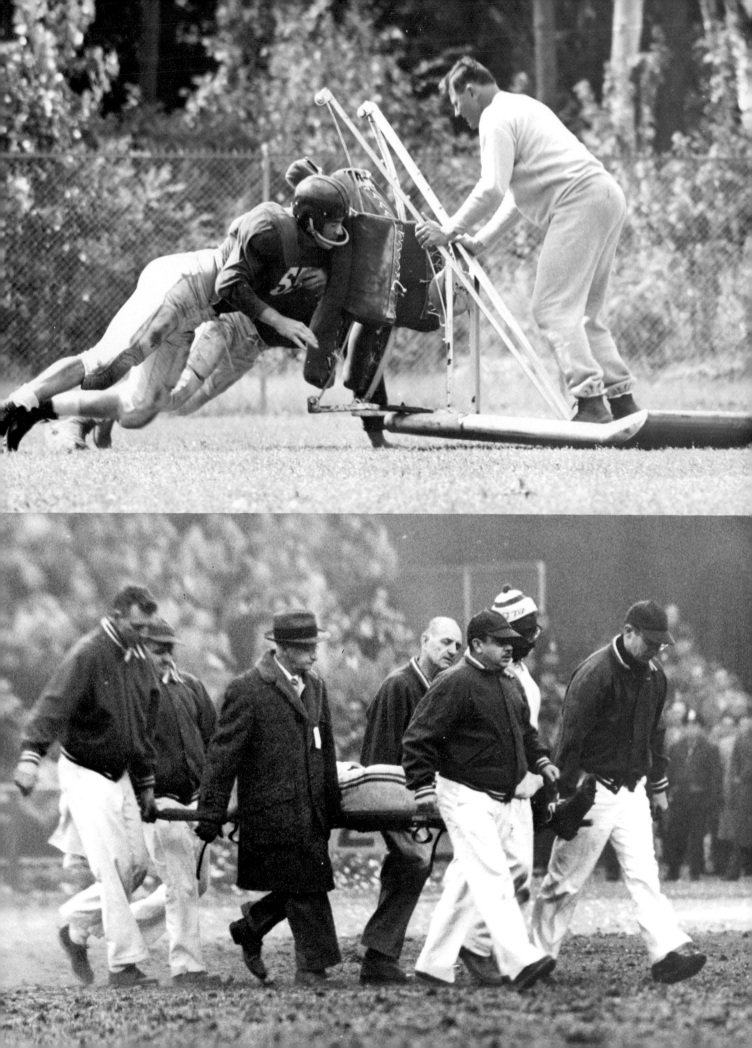

Two defensive stalwarts during
some of the Giants leanest years were
end Jack Gregory (81) and
tackle John Mendenhall (64).
(Joe McKenna)

THE WILDERNESS YEARS

How quickly the Giants' fortunes turned. The formidable beasts who had ruled the Eastern Division for the previous eight years behaved more like pussycats in 1964. Though many of the faces were the same, it was a much different ball club than the one that had battled the Bears for the NFL championship the year before. That was a result, primarily, of two offseason trades that sent Sam Huff to the Washington Redskins and Dick Modzewelski to the Cleveland Browns.

"Allie was not satisfied with coming in second three years in a row," Wellington Mara recalls, "and he felt the defense was starting to show some wear and tear. So he dealt Sam and Mo, with my consent I might add. What neither of us realized at the time was just how integral a part of the defense those two

JOE MORRISON IS ONE OF ONLY SEVEN GIANTS WHO HAVE HAD THEIR NUMBER RETIRED. (BOB SULLIVAN)

were. We didn't understand the attachment that the guys on defense had for one another, that the whole of the unit was greater than the sum of its parts. The defense lost its feeling of togetherness, and things fell apart very quickly after that."

The offense didn't fare much better, and though the Giants still had Tittle, Shofner, Gifford and Webster, they won only one of their first seven games. Y.A. started the season at quarterback, but in the team's second game at Pittsburgh he was hammered by a blitzing John Baker while attempting a screen pass. His ribs severely bruised from the hit, Tittle ripped off his helmet and struggled to his knees to catch his breath. And there he knelt for a moment, with blood trickling down his mostly bald head, his mouth slightly ajar, looking like a tired, old man at the

ONE OF THE FAMED BABY BULLS, HALFBACK ERNIE KOY ALSO PUNTED AND THREW THE OCCASIONAL OPTION PASS FOR THE GIANTS. (FRED ROE)

RON JOHNSON (30) CAME OVER FROM THE CLEVELAND BROWNS IN THE HOMER JONES TRADE IN 1970 AND BECAME THE FIRST GIANTS BACK TO EVER RUSH FOR 1,000 YARDS IN A SEASON. (FRED ROE)

end of his career. Tittle didn't play the next two games, and when he did come back he was ineffective. By mid-season he had lost his job to Cornell rookie Gary Wood.

But Wood couldn't move the team either, and Sherman began to feel the heat. The team finished last in their division at 2-10-2, and no longer did the Giants faithful chant "DEE-FENSE, DEE-FENSE" from their seats in Yankee Stadium. Instead they began deriding the Brooklyn-born head coach by singing "Good-Bye Allie" whenever games started to get out of hand. And plenty of games got out of hand that year.

Not surprisingly, there were a lot of changes

SCRAPPY DOUG KOTAR LED THE GIANTS IN RUSHING HIS FIRST SEASON WITH THE TEAM (1974) AND WAS A FAN FAVORITE DURING HIS SEVEN YEARS IN GIANTS BLUE. SADLY, HE DIED OF BRAIN CANCER SHORTLY AFTER RETIRING. (FRED ROE)

before the 1965 season began. Frank Gifford, Alex Webster, Jack Stroud, Andy Robustelli and Y. A. Tittle all retired. Tittle tried to put a humorous spin on his departure. "I knew it was time to get out," he said, "when Gary Wood asked me if he could date my daughter."

On the basis of their last-place finish, the Giants had the first pick in the 1965 draft. They passed on

LINEBACKER BRAD VAN PELT WAS NAMED TO THE PRO BOWL FIVE YEARS IN A ROW AND WAS ONE OF THE TEAM'S BRIGHTEST STARS DURING SOME OF ITS DARKEST YEARS. (JERRY PINKUS).

DICK LYNCH (22), ROOSEVELT DAVIS (77) AND MIKE BUNDRA (74) WRAP UP A CARDINALS RUNNER IN A 1963 GAME. (FRED ROE)

Gale Sayers, Joe Namath and Dick Butkus in favor of Tucker Frederickson, a running back from Auburn. The team also selected Texas halfback Ernie Koy, Yale fullback Chuck Mercein and cornerback Spider Lockhart from North Texas State.

The Giants were excited about their new players, and the team looked forward to the next season. But a month before training camp was to open, team president Jack Mara died of cancer. He left his 50-percent share of the team to his wife and children, and Wellington took over Jack's former responsibilities for running the business affairs of

EARL MORRALL, ABOUT TO HAND OFF TO ERNIE WHEELWRIGHT, CAME TO THE GIANTS IN A TRADE IN 1965 AND STAYED FOR THREE SEASONS. (FRED ROE)

The Giants held a press conference on Jan. 22, 1965 at Mama Leone's restaurant in Manhattan in which Y. A. Tittle announced his retirement from football.
"This is a moment I have dreaded," he said.
"I don't want to come back and be a mediocre football player again. I was one last fall."
A few hours later, the Jets hosted a press conference of their own at Toots Shor's to introduce a fellow from Alabama named Joe Namath, who had just signed a $400,000 contract to quarterback that franchise.

ing, perhaps, to work the same sort of magic with this veteran signal caller as he had with Y.A. Tittle four years before.

Morall arrived only a few weeks before the season was scheduled to begin, and his first game was

IN HIS FIVE YEARS WITH THE GIANTS, FRAN TARKENTON LED THE GIANTS TO A 33-37 RECORD. (FRED ROE)

the ballclub while retaining his control over football operations.

It was that new arrangement that prompted Wellington to tear up Sherman's contract and ink him to a new, ten-year deal. "I was worried about my ability to spend as much time with the football side of things as I had in the past," Wellington recalls. "I had a lot of respect for Allie's abilities, and I wanted to make sure that he was there to help me out."

In the wake of Tittle's retirement, Gary Wood seemed set as the starting job. But he failed to impress in the preseason, and Sherman traded Erich Barnes and offensive lineman Darrell Dess in a three-way deal for Detroit QB Earl Morrall, hop-

NORM SNEAD, ABOUT TO TAKE THE SNAP FROM SENTER BOB HYLAND, QUARTERBACKED THE GIANTS FOR FOUR SEASONS. (GUS BOYD)

CRAIG MORTON HAD TWO ROUGH SEASONS WITH THE GIANTS IN THE MID-1970S; TWO YEARS AFTER BEING TRADED TO DENVER, HOWEVER, HE LED THE BRONCOS TO THE SUPER BOWL. (GUS BOYD)

a disaster, with the Cowboys thrashing the Giants 31-2. The team settled down the following two weeks, won games against the Steelers and Eagles, and went on to finish 7-7, tied with Dallas for second place in the Eastern Conference. As befitting an Allie Sherman team, they featured a potent, if not somewhat erratic offense. The young backs, in particular, excelled, and sports writers dubbed Frederickson, Koy and Mercein the "Baby Bulls." Frederickson went to the Pro Bowl after his rookie season, justifying in some eyes his being the first

BILL ARNSPARGER HAD A TOUGH STINT AS GIANTS HEAD COACH, POSTING ONLY A 7-28 RECORD NEFORE BEING FIRED MIDWAY THROUGH THE 1976 SEASON. (FRED ROE)

BIG RED STRIKES A CHEERFUL POSE DUR-ING TRAINING CAMP IN THE SUMMER OF 1973. WEBSTER'S MOOD WOULD DARKEN CONSIDERABLY BY THE END OF THE SEA-SON, HOWEVER, AND HE RESIGNED AS HEAD COACH BEFORE THE FINAL REGULAR SEASON GAME. (DAN RUBIN)

ALLIE SHERMAN COACHED THE GIANTS THROUGH THE 1968 REGULAR SEASON; HE WAS FIRED AFTER GOING 0-5 IN THE 1969 PRESEASON. (NEW YORK GIANTS)

JOHN MCVAY HAD ONLY UNEVEN SUCCESS AS A GIANTS HEAD COACH, GOING 14-23 IN TWO-AND-A-HALF YEARS AT THE HELM. HE WAS FIRED AT THE END OF THE 1978 SEASON. (FRED ROE)

ALEX WEBSTER COMPILED A 29-40-1 RECORD DURING HIS FIVE SEASONS AS GIANTS HEAD COACH. (NEW YORK GIANTS)

selection in the previous year's draft. And new arrival Homer Jones, a burner from Texas Southern, caught 26 passes for a remarkable 709 yards. The defense, however, struggled, giving up 31 or more points a game no fewer than six times.

The offseason used to be a fairly quiet time for National Football League teams, but not this year.

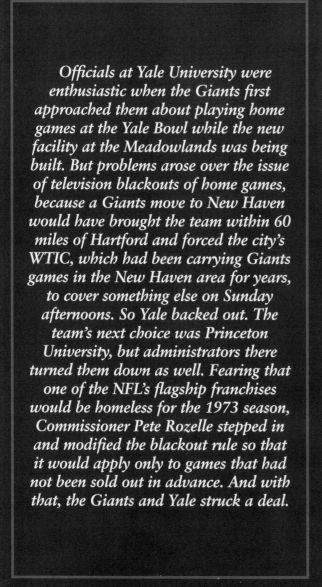

Officials at Yale University were enthusiastic when the Giants first approached them about playing home games at the Yale Bowl while the new facility at the Meadowlands was being built. But problems arose over the issue of television blackouts of home games, because a Giants move to New Haven would have brought the team within 60 miles of Hartford and forced the city's WTIC, which had been carrying Giants games in the New Haven area for years, to cover something else on Sunday afternoons. So Yale backed out. The team's next choice was Princeton University, but administrators there turned them down as well. Fearing that one of the NFL's flagship franchises would be homeless for the 1973 season, Commissioner Pete Rozelle stepped in and modified the blackout rule so that it would apply only to games that had not been sold out in advance. And with that, the Giants and Yale struck a deal.

That spring, Wellington Mara started something of a personnel war with the fledgling American Football League by signing free agent, soccer-style kicker Pete Gogolak, whose contract with the Buffalo Bills had expired the year before. Mara defended his move, correctly pointing out that he had not talked to Gogolak until after his agreement with the Bills had expired. But the AFL was incensed, and commissioner Al Davis began making

plans for his league to raid stars from NFL teams.

Fortunately for football, the battle never really got started. By early June, the two leagues worked out very general terms for a merger. The first Super Bowl was scheduled to be played at the end of the 1966 season, a common draft would be held the following winter and interleague play would begin in 1970.

The Giants' problems in 1966 would not be so easily solved. Tucker Frederickson suffered a knee injury in an exhibition game and was out for the rest of the season. The team fought Pittsburgh to a 34-34 tie on opening day, with Earl Morrall and Homer Jones connecting on a spectacular 98-yard touchdown pass play. But Allie Sherman's squad lost its next four games. In the sixth game they beat the Washington Redskins 13-10 for their first win of the season, but then proceeded to drop their final eight contests. The defense was abysmal, giv-

TIM MARA, SON OF WELLINGTON'S BROTHER JACK, OVERSAW THE BUILDING OF GIANTS STADIUM AND PLAYED A KEY PART IN THE TEAM'S RESURGENCE. (JERRY PINKUS)

ing up a then record 501 points, including 52 to the Cowboys one game, 55 to the Rams and 72 to the 'Skins in a late-season rematch. And the franchise's final 1-12-1 mark was the worst in Giants history.

Distraught over his team's recent performance and worried about the growing popularity of the rival New York Jets, Wellington Mara tried something that had worked so well for his Giants in the 1950s and early 1960s—a blockbuster trade. Once again, he went after a quarterback, this time acquiring Fran Tarkenton from the Minnesota

DEEP THREAT HOMER JONES ONCE SCOREED ON
A 98-YARD PASS PLAY FROM EARL MORRALL.
(NEW YORK GIANTS)

STALWART GEORGE MARTIN PUT IN A LOT OF YEARS
WITH THE GIANTS BEFORE HE HAD A CHANCE TO SMILE.
(JERRY PINKUS)

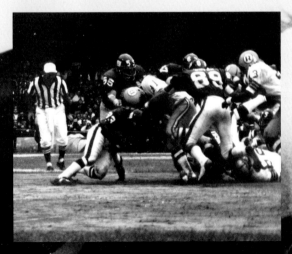

FRED DRYER (89) WAS A STANDOUT DEFENSIVE END
FOR THREE SEASONS BEFORE BEING TRADED TO THE
LOS ANGELES RAMS. (FRED ROE)

DOUG KOTAR DIDN'T HAVE
A LOT OF BLOCKING HELP DURING
HIS TIME WITH THE GIANTS, BUT HE
STILL MANAGED TO GAIN MORE THAN
3,300 YARDS IN HIS SEVEN SEASONS
THERE. (NEW YORK GIANTS)

Vikings. But the price for the scrambling Georgian was high, with the Giants giving up their first and second round picks in the 1967 draft, their first round pick in 1968 and a player to be named later.

Still, Giants fans were thrilled with the addition, and they looked forward to a much-improved season. The prospects of a good year brightened even more when Pope Paul VI, who had met Allie Sherman the year before, bestowed a papal blessing on the franchise and its head coach.

Both the trade and the blessing seemed to work. Tarkenton threw for more than 3,000 yards and tossed 29 touchdown passes in guiding the Giants to a 7-7 record. Homer Jones had another good year, leading the league in TD receptions with 13 and joining Tarkenton and running back Ernie Koy in the Pro Bowl. The only downer was that Tucker Frederickson injured his knee again and sat out much of the season.

The Giants went 7-7 in 1968 and competed for their division title into the last weeks of the season before finishing second. But the big story in New York that year was the New York Jets, who captured the AFL Championship and then stunned the Baltimore Colts 16-7 in Super Bowl III.

There were no offerings from the Vatican prior to the 1969 season, but after the team lost all five of its exhibition games—including a 34-14 shellacking by

> "I was doing a lot of league work on the labor committee, and we had a conference call one day to pick a new chairman for the committee.
> I was still signing players back then, and part way through the meeting I had to get off the phone to finalize a contract. I got back on about an hour later and asked everybody how we were doing. 'Fine,' one of the owners said. 'You're the new chairman.' "
>
> Wellington Mara

THE PRESS—AND THE QUESTIONS—GOT TOUGHER FOR ALLIE SHERMAN AS HIS TEAM STRUGGLED THROUGH THE MID-1960S.
(NEW YORK GIANTS)

the New York Jets at the Yale Bowl—it seemed that nothing less than divine intervention would save the Giants that year. Mara wasn't about to put a call into the Pope, but he did decide that the best way to salvage the season was to change head coaches. He fired Allie Sherman just before the opening game and brought in Alex Webster as his replacement.

Webster, the former running back from Kearny, N.J., had been working as an assistant coach for Sherman the previous two years and was a popular choice among fans and players alike. But Big Red, who still held most of the Giants' rushing records,

PUNTER DAVE JENNINGS WAS A PERENNIAL ALL-PRO.
(JERRY PINKUS)

JOE DANELO MADE A NUMBER OF BIG KICKS DURING HIS YEARS
WITH THE GIANTS. (NEW YORK GIANTS)

wasn't sure how good a head coaching job he would do. "I didn't think I was prepared to run a team at that time," he recalls. "I hadn't been coaching for very long, and the squad I took over really wasn't very good. I knew I'd need a lot of starch in my collar."

Webster won his first game, a 24-23 heartstopper against the Minnesota Vikings, and thanks to the play of quarterback Fran Tarkenton and a promising first round pick from San Diego State, defensive end Fred Dryer, the Giants beat three out of the first four teams they faced. But Homer Jones never got untracked, and the team lost seven games in a row on the way to a 6-8 record.

There was another major development for the Giants in 1969: New Jersey State Senator Frank Guarini began speaking with Giants general manager Ray Walsh and Tim Mara, son of the team's late president Jack, about the possibility of building a new stadium for the Giants in the Hackensack Meadowlands. Walsh and Mara were intrigued, and later that year joined Guarini for a tour of the area.

The months before the 1970 season began were busy. The American and National Football Leagues officially merged, and ABC announced plans to begin televising games on Monday nights the upcoming year. Mara engineered another deal to shore up his team, sending a suddenly unproductive Homer Jones to the Cleveland Browns for defensive lineman Jim Kanicki and running back Ron Johnson. In addition, he signed free agent Bob Tucker, a tight end who had played his college ball at Bloomsburg State in Pennsylvania.

The personnel moves worked beautifully. After struggling to an 0-3 mark, the Giants took off. With Johnson and Frederickson running hard and Tarkenton clicking nicely with the rookie Tucker, the team won six games in a row. Their streak was broken by a 23-20 loss to the Eagles in week ten, but the Giants went on to beat their next three opponents. It was the team's best season since 1963, and all that stood between them and a division crown was the Los Angeles Rams. A victory, and the Giants would go to the playoffs.

But it was not to happen. The final game of the season took place at Yankee Stadium, and the Rams romped 31-3. It was small consolation that Johnson had rushed for 1,027 yards, the first time a Giant had ever run for over 1,000 yards in a sin-

PETE GOGOLAK, WHO WAS SIGNED AS A FREE AGENT BY WELLINGTON MARA, WAS THE NFL'S FIRST SOCCER-STYLE KICKER. (NEW YORK GIANTS)

gle season, and that he and Tarkenton were invited to the Pro Bowl.

The 1971 season began badly. Tarkenton and the Giants became embroiled in a contract dispute during training camp, and it got so heated that prior to a preseason game in Houston, Tarkenton decided to leave the team and go home to Atlanta. Back-up quarterback Dick Shiner started the game against the Oilers, and the Giants lost 35-6. Four days later, Tarkenton returned to the team and settled his contract problems. But his relationship with the Giants would never be the same.

The Giants had another falling out that summer, this one with the City of New York after the team signed a 30-year lease to play at a new stadium that would be built in the Hackensack Meadowlands. Wellington Mara was delighted with the deal. "I felt the move would give us a chance to provide better seats and more of them for our fans," he says. "And for the first time we would be the number one tenant in a facility instead of number two. I wasn't crazy about leaving Yankee Stadium; after all I had grown up watching games there. But we felt it was the best things for our fans." In response to criticism that by moving the Giants were harming New York fans who had supported the team for so many years, Mara also pointed out that the new stadium would be only 6.9 miles from Times Square while Yankee Stadium was 6.6 miles. "And the same fans will have tickets," he added.

It may have made perfect sense to the Mara family, but New York Mayor John Lindsay was irate. He characterized the team's decision as "selfish, callous and ungrateful," and suggested that the city might prohibit the Giants from playing in Yankee Stadium while their new facility was being built.

Giants fans probably wished their team was moving to Alaska with the way it played that season. Tarkenton threw only 11 touchdown passes and after he was benched toward the latter part of the season asked Wellington Mara to trade him. Ron Johnson sat out much of the year with a thigh injury, and Tucker Frederickson hurt his knee again. The running duties were left to rookie halfback Rocky Thompson, a speedster from West Texas State the Giants had selected with their first pick in the 1971 draft. But he proved less than adequate. The team finished 4-10, and for the first time in history, no Giants were selected to play in the Pro Bowl.

The 1971 season had been over for only a few weeks old when Wellington Mara granted Tarkenton his

PLAYERS HAVE DIFFERENT WAYS OF GETTING UP FOR A GAME.
(FRED ROE)

also brought the retirement of Tucker Frederickson and his aching knees. A talented runner full of heart, he never was able to achieve the promise he had shown in his rookie season.

The Giants prepared for their eventual move to the Garden State by holding their 1972 training camp at Monmouth College in West Long Branch, N.J. The team lost its first two games of the regular season, then won their next four and went on to finish with an 8-6 mark. Snead proved a fine acquisition, and he led the NFL in completion percentage. Ron Johnson recovered from his thigh injury and rushed for over 1,000 yards again. And before the last game of the season, New Jersey Governor William Cahill officially broke ground

> *"I remember the fumble against the Eagles only too well. Andy Robustelli and I were sitting in a booth next to the coaches that game, and as time was running out we heard one of the coaches screaming over the telephone insisting that they run a play rather than falling on the ball. He kept calling for the play. It was an indication to me that the guy in a position we depended on had just lost it. He made a terrible error, and the next thing we knew the Eagles had scored the winning touchdown."*
>
> *Wellington Mara*

request and traded the veteran QB back to Minnesota for quarterback Norm Snead, receiver Bob Grimm, running back Vince Clements and two draft choices. Some weeks later, Mara orchestrated another deal, this one for Cleveland Browns defensive end Jack Gregory. The team missed badly with its first draft pick that year—Eldridge Small, a defensive back from Texas A&I who lasted only three seasons—but picked up a solid defensive tackle in the third round with stocky John Mendenhall from Grambling. Sadly, the offseason

for the Giants new stadium. In an interesting twist, the man in charge of the Meadowlands project was none other than Sonny Werblin, the former Jets owner and a longtime football rival of the Maras.

The 1973 season was not an easy one for the Giants, mainly because they didn't have one place they could call home. The previous year, New York City had announced plans to renovate Yankee Stadium, and in what many observers thought was a fit of pique, told the Giants they would have to move out once the 1973 baseball season ended.

The new facility in the Meadowlands was three years from completion, and the team wasn't sure where it would go. The Maras asked Yale and Princeton Universities if the Giants could play a couple of seasons in their football stadiums, but both schools turned them down, and when the NFL released its official schedule for the upcoming year, they didn't list a home site for the Giants games. A month later, however, Yale changed its mind and said the university would welcome the team. The Giants still needed a practice facility, however, and a few weeks later signed a two-year contract with Jersey City officials that allowed the team to practice at rundown Roosevelt Stadium.

SPIDER LOCKHART (43) LED THE GIANTS DEFENSE FOR 11 SEASONS; BUT HE NEVER GOT TO PLAY IN A PLAYOFF GAME. HERE HE IS ABOUT TO TACKLE MIAMI'S LARRY CSONKA. (FRED ROE)

Some fans suggested the team should change its name to the New York Nomads, but at least the Giants had found places to play and practice. The football season got off to a good start, and led by Snead, Johnson and second round draft pick Brad Van Pelt, the team went undefeated in the preseason. The Giants won their opening game against Houston 34-14, and tied Philadelphia the next week, 23-23, in their final game at Yankee Stadium. But then the wheels fell off. Perhaps its was homesickness, maybe it was all the travelling between New York, New Jersey and Connecticut. Whatever the reasons, the Giants lost 11 of their last 12 games. The defeats became too much for Webster, and Big Red resigned before the season finale—a 31-7 thrashing by Fran Tarkenton and the Minnesota Vikings at the Yale Bowl.

There was a lot of soul searching within the Giants organization after the 1973 season, and with good reason. The team had gone ten years without making the playoffs and had posted some of the worst won-lost records in franchise history. The Giants had drafted poorly, few of their trades had proved successful, and they seemed no closer to winning on a consistent basis than they had a decade earlier.

No one agonized more over the franchise's decline than Timothy Mara II, Wellington's nephew and the son of the late Jack Mara. Tim controlled the half of the team his father once owned, and shortly after Webster resigned, he went to speak to Wellington about how they could turn it around. "Tim was very dissatisfied with a lot of the football decisions I had made," Wellington recalls, "and in retrospect, they weren't very good ones. He said I was trying to do too much and suggested we get a football man to run that end of things."

LARRY CSONKA SLIDES THROUGH THE SNOW IN A WINTRY 1977 GAME AGAINST THE CHICAGO BEARS. (ROBERT RIGER)

Wellington liked the idea. "I started running the football and business sides of the team when my brother Jack died, to the detriment of both," Mara says. "Part of the problem was that I had been very involved in league matters and was away a lot of the time. Tim suggested we hire Andy Robustelli as our head of football operations. I told him it sounded like a good idea to me."

Robustelli had been heading up a successful travel agency in Stamford, Ct. since he retired as a player, and he met Tim and Wellington at Wellington's suburban Harrison, N.Y. home to discuss the job. "Andy had been away from football for a while, but he was excited about working for the team again," Wellington recalls. "We knew it would be tough for him to get his teeth back in the business, but we figured he would do well just the same."

Robustelli accepted the post shortly after the interview. "I had thought about getting into foot-

ball management when I retired as a player," he says. "But I wanted to stay home in Connecticut so I didn't really pursue it. But when Well and Tim offered me the job, I said I'd give it a try. This was my old team calling, and I felt there were things I could do to help."

The Maras gave Robustelli complete charge of football operations, and the first thing the Hall-of-Fame defensive end did was hire Miami Dolphins defensive coordinator Bill Arnsparger as head coach. But even though there had been changes aplenty in the offseason, the Giants played with painfully familiar ineptitude when the games started. At midway point they stood at 1-6, and the offense was sputtering so badly that Robustelli traded a first and second round pick to the Dallas Cowboys for quarterback Craig Morton. Morton, who had lost the starting job in Dallas to Roger Staubach, was a skilled, veteran player, but not even he could turn things around for the Giants,

128

and they finished with a dismal 2-12 record.

The team had hoped to play the 1975 season at their new stadium in the Meadowlands, but construction delays forced them to push the facility's opening back a year. However, New York City Mayor Abe Beame graciously offered the Giants use of Shea Stadium for their 1975 home games, and the nomads had another new place to hang their helmets.

Having given up their first-round pick to Dallas as part of the Craig Morton trade, the Giants didn't have a choice until the second round. That was too bad, because there were several top players available had they hung on to that selection,

BOB TUCKER WAS ONE OF THE BEST TIGHT ENDS IN GIANT HISTORY. (NEW YORK GIANTS)

including Randy White, Walter Payton and Russ Francis. Instead, the Giants had to settle for Al Simpson, a tackle from Colorado State, in the second round. He lasted only two seasons. In fact, most of the team's choices that year were busts, but the Giants did find a gem in the 11th round with Oregon defensive end George Martin.

Bad drafts had sadly become a part of the Giants legacy during the past decade, and Robustelli was among those who thought it was largely a result of the team letting time pass it by. While other organizations were hiring specialists and employing

computers, they argued, the Giants were still run like a family store, with Wellington Mara taking on much of the responsibility for rebuilding the franchise. "One of the team's problems was that they did things an early way, and they were successful, so they didn't change," Robustelli explained to Michael Katz of the Daily News in 1986. "It was a

Prior to the beginning of the 1978 season, members of the 1958 New York Giants and Baltimore Colts met for a touch football game in New York's Central Park to commemorate their classic sudden death title game that had taken place 20 years before. Playing for the Colts were John Unitas, Lenny Moore, Raymond Berry, Alan Ameche, Gino Marchetti, Art Donovan and Steve Myhra. The Giants had Charlie Conerly, Frank Gifford, Alex Webster, Rosey Brown and Dick Modzewelski. Sonny Jurgensen was the referee. The temperature was in the 90s, and Myhra brought a six-pack of beer for pre-game refreshments. The teams played six to a side, and the Colts opened the scoring with a Unitas-to-Moore TD pass. Conerly's first pass was intercepted, and Unitas went on to throw two more TDs in the first half to Raymond Berry. Gifford threw for two touchdowns in the second half, and it looked as if the '58 Giants might get their revenge. But Unitas intercepted another Gifford toss with less than a minute to go and ran it back for a touchdown. Once again, the Colts prevailed.

mamma and poppa league 30 years ago, but now you can't call up an owner you're friendly with and say, 'I need a flanker. Is there anybody you might be cutting soon that I could use?' and the guy would be pretty good."

"Like Del Shofner?" Katz asked.

"Exactly," Robustelli said.

People also accused Wellington Mara of being loyal to a fault, of sticking with players, coaches and scouts far too long simply because they were part of the Giants family. Some pointed to the hiring of Giants heroes such as Alex Webster and Andy Robustelli when more experienced people might have been available as another example of Mara's blind devotion.

Robustelli admitted that he had a lot of catching up to do after being out of the game for ten years, but he went at his job with a vengeance. The results of his hard work, however, would not be felt for a few years. The 1975 Giants posted a disappointing 5-9 mark, with Craig Morton throwing only 13 touchdown passes and 11 interceptions.

The 1976 draft yielded the best bunch of new players in years. The Giants selected Colorado defensive end Troy Archer with their first pick, and he went on to have an outstanding rookie year. South Carolina State's Harry Carson came in the fourth round, and backer Dan Lloyd of Washington was selected in the sixth. In addition, the Giants added some glamour and power to their offense when they signed free agent running back Larry Csonka.

The Giants played its first four games on the road that year as workers put the finishing touches on their impressive new stadium in the Meadowlands. The team had a new look on their helmets, with the word GIANTS replacing the NY logo, but it didn't help their play much, and they dropped all four contests. Some 76,000 fans showed up for the opening of Giants Stadium, and while most marveled at the wonderful facility that would be the team's home into the next century, they were disappointed to see their club drop their fifth in a row to the Dallas Cowboys. It was the first time a

Giants team had ever started a season 0-5.

Unfortunately, the losing didn't stop. The Giants came up short in their next two games, and Robustelli fired Bill Arnsparger, replacing him with John McVay. McVay, who had been one of Arnsparger's assistants, lost his first two games to put the team at 0-9. But he managed to guide the Giants to victories in three of their remaining five contests. Robustelli liked what he saw, and at season's end, signed McVay to a two-year contract.

While Robustelli may have been pleased with McVay's work, he was certainly not happy with his quarterback situation. He traded Craig Morton to Denver for quarterback Steve Ramsey and then signed a Canadian Football League refugee named Joe Piscarik, a 6'4", 220-pound signal caller from New Mexico State. And with their first choice in the draft, the Giants selected defensive tackle and pass rush specialist Gary Jeter

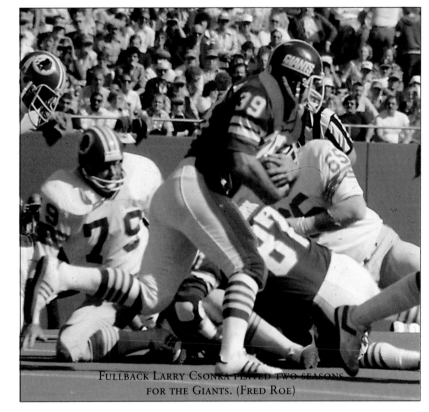

FULLBACK LARRY CSONKA PLAYED TWO SEASONS FOR THE GIANTS. (FRED ROE)

from USC.

The year started off reasonably well, and the Giants stood 3-3 after their first six games, with two of the wins coming against George Allen's Washington Redskins. But they would win only twice more that season and finish at 5-9.

Again, the 1978 campaign began well. The Giants prevailed in three of their first four contests and were 5-3 at midseason. But then they lost three away games in a row—to New Orleans, St. Louis and Washington—and their year seemed to be slipping away. Their twelfth game was at home against the Philadelphia Eagles, and the crowd was rightfully anxious. Desperate for a winner, they had revelled during the team's early season's successes. But the three losses had tempered much of their enthusiasm, and many of them had a sense of foreboding as their team faced off against the Eagles that day.

And with good reason. With just 31 seconds remaining in the game, the Giants were leading 17-

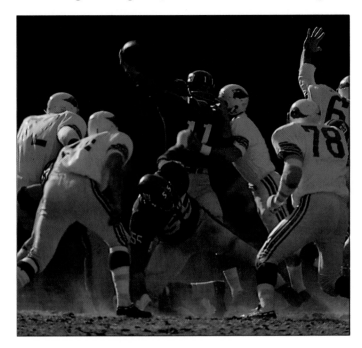

12 and had the ball. The Eagles had used up their time-outs, and all the Giants had to do to win the game was have quarterback Joe Piscarik take the snap and fall on the ball. But for some reason, Bob Gibson, McVay's offensive coordinator, sent in a running play. Piscarik and Csonka fumbled the hand-off, and Eagles defensive back Herm Edwards scooped up the ball and sprinted in with it for the winning touchdown.

The Giants Stadium crowd sat in stunned silence when that happened, but by the time their team faced off against the Los Angeles Rams two weeks later, they had become a very vocal, very angry bunch. A group of fans organized a ticket burning outside the stadium before the game. The following week it got even uglier when a group calling itself the "Committee Against Mara Insensitivity to Giants Fans" hired a small plane to fly over the stadium during a game with the St. Louis Cardinals with a banner that read "15 Years of Lousy Football…We've Had Enough."

The Giants went on to drop their final contest of the season to the Eagles in Philadelphia's Veterans Stadium 20-3, and the next day the John McVay

was fired. Robustelli, who had told the Giants back in 1974 that he would only stay a few years, resigned to return to his travel agency in Connecticut. "I hated to see Andy go," Wellington Mara says. "He had started from scratch and was just getting to know the league again when he left."

The end of the 1978 season was among the darkest times in Giants history. Though the team had a decent core of players, including Harry Carson, George Martin, Brad Van Pelt and punter Dave Jennings, they couldn't seem to shed the losing image that had become so much a part of this once-proud franchise. The team didn't have a director of football operations, it had lost its head coach and its loyal fans, who had helped the Maras sell out every game for more than 20 years, were near revolt. And though the public was not aware of it at the time, a feud over the direction and operation of the team had developed between Wellington Mara and his nephew Tim, and since each side of the family owned 50 percent of the franchise, there was no simple tie-breaker when it came time to vote on decisions.

It had been 15 years since the last playoff game,

"Of course, there is a less serious side to my addiction to the Giants. One Monday morning after an especially grueling loss to the Redskins under Coach George Allen, I checked into the hospital for minor surgery. When it was time to leave, the young resident who discharged me announced, 'Mrs. Concannon, if I knew you better I'd tell you what you said about George Allen while you were under anesthia.' "

Maura Mara Concannon, daughter of Jack Mara and granddaughter of team founder Tim.

15 years of looking for a permanent home, looking for a winning quarterback, looking to improve upon a shaky draft and trade record. The Giants had been lost in a sort of football wilderness, and at the end of the 1978 season, few people gave the franchise much hope of turning it around any time soon.

EVEN TWO-A-
DAYS CAN'T KEEP
SIMMS FROM
SMILING DURING
TRAINING CAMP.
(JERRY PINKUS)

CHAPTER 5

GEORGE AND BILL, LAWRENCE AND PHIL

The biggest obstacle to reversing the Giants' slide was the discord that had poisoned the Mara family. The primary issue was control. Wellington had run the football operations for more than three decades, and since his brother Jack's death in 1965 had been more or less in charge of the team's business affairs as well. Now in his early 60s and one of the senior owners in the league, he wanted to continue playing the lead role. That, however, did not sit well with his nephew Tim. Tim, who was listed as vice president and treasurer of the team, had become displeased with the results of Wellington's work and wanted a greater say in the operation of the ball club. It was a problem that had begun brewing in the early 1970s, and it came to a boil after the 1978 season when the Giants started to look for a new director of football operations and a new head coach.

The Giants had hoped to find a replacement for Andy Robustelli first, but rumors began surfacing after the beginning of the new year that Wellington and Tim Mara could not agree on a choice. Commissioner Pete Rozelle got wind of the conflict and tried to intervene. "Pete was

father confessor to every team in the league, and he knew what was going on with us," Wellington recalls. "We talked about it several times, and during the course of one conversation he gave me a list of five or six people he thought would be good for the job. One of the names was George Young, who was working for Don Shula in Miami."

"I had known of George through work he had done in NFL scouting meetings," Mara says. "I had seen him in action, I had read his reports, and I thought he was very good. But I told Pete that I didn't think Tim would go for him, especially if it was someone I recommended or liked."

Weeks passed, and still the Giants had not come up with a man to fill Robustelli's position. At one point, the commissioner asked Wellington and Tim to each submit a list of acceptable candidates, and he was delighted to find a common name—that of Jan Van Duser, an executive who worked in the league offices—on both lists. But Van Duser wanted nothing to do with a pair of quarreling Irishmen and turned down the job.

"I started to get anxious about the whole

(opposite) WILLIAM
ROBERTS JOINED
THE GIANTS IN
1984 AND HAS
BEEN AN INTREGAL
PART OF THE
TEAM'S OFFENSIVE
LINE. (FRED ROE)

CORNERBACK
MARK HAYNES
CAME TO THE
GIANTS IN THE
1980 DRAFT AND
QUICKLY BOLSTERED
THE TEAM'S DEFEN-
SIVE BACKFIELD.
(FRED ROE)

thing," Mara says. "I felt we were losing our shot at hiring a good coach—Bill Walsh and John Robinson were among those available—and so I held a press conference and announced that I was going to hire a coach first. Tim walked into the room shortly after I had spoke and basically said, 'No, you're not.' Pete was at a tennis tournament with Pat Summerall down in Florida when news of the press conference broke, and he called me immediately. And I told him it was time he recommended George Young to us."

Rozelle did just that, and on Feb. 14, 1979 Young flew to New York for a meeting with the Maras. A bespectacled, rumpled hulk of a man, he had taught history and political science and coached football at two Baltimore high schools before joining Don Shula's Colts as a scout in 1968. He coached the team's offensive line in 1970, when Baltimore captured the Super Bowl, and followed Shula to Miami four years later to work in the Dolphins' front office.

"I only brought the suit I was wearing when I came up," Young recalls. "I didn't even have a toothbrush, and I had a nine o'clock ticket back to Miami. The Maras had booked a room for me at the Drake Hotel, and I was registered under a fictitious name, Wayne Rosen, who I later found out was Pete

> *"I grew up a Giants fan and I recall being as young as 10 and watching the Giants Quarterback Huddle on television with Marty Glickman. I started going to games when they were still playing at the Polo Grounds. I remember one against the Steelers, and Pittsburgh's quarterbacks were Jim Finks and Ted Marchibroda. I was at the Cleveland game in 1958 when Pat Summerall kicked that field goal for the win, sitting in the right field bleachers at Yankee Stadium. And I'll never forget the overtime loss to the Colts a couple of weeks later. I had gone ice skating with a bunch of friends of mine. They were all on the ice, and I was sitting in the car listening to the radio."*
>
> Bill Parcells

Rozelle's driver. I spent about two hours at the commissioner's office with Tim and Wellington, then went out to lunch and walked back to my room. Around 2:45 p.m. the Maras called and asked me to come back. First, I spoke with Pete, then the Maras came in and offered me the job."

It didn't take Young long to make up his mind. "About half a second," he says. "This was a flagship franchise, a very special job and a terrific opportunity for me. I was very aware of the Giants, I knew the tradition of the team, and I was excited about working there."

Was there any trepidation about stepping into the middle of a family feud? "I had worked for Carroll Rosenbloom, Joe Thomas, Bob Irsay and Joe Robbie, so I knew a little bit about being in sensitive situations," Young says. "Compared to those guys, the Maras were choirboys."

Tim and Wellington wanted to announce Young's appointment right away. "I asked if I could go back and talk to my wife about it, or at least talk to her on the phone," Young says. "They said I should

talk to her because, after all, it was Valentine's Day. So I called her, then spoke to Joe Robbie on the phone, and we went over to Gallagher's for the press conference." It was there Young got his first taste of the New York press. "One guy said I looked like Khrushchev, but I'm 6'3", and he was 5'5", he says. "Another guy said I looked like a tourist who had wandered up to the press conference to see what all the commotion was about. But I wasn't upset by that. My father had taken the New York papers for years, and I knew a little bit about the city's press. I told the Maras that as long as I had a fence around my office and a gate that locked, I'd be all right."

As was the case with Robustelli, Young would be in charge of all football operations. "I wanted George to inform me of any major player or coaching moves," Wellington explains. "And I wanted to feel free to give my opinion. I still went to practice and kept in touch with what was going on personnel-wise. But George was the one making the decisions."

Young had an important decision to make right away: who would be the head coach? "I went to the West Coast and interviewed a few people," he says. "And it came down

PHIL SIMMS AND THE GIANTS CAME UP SHORT IN THE MUCH-ANTICIPATED MONDAY NIGHT MEETING WITH THE SAN FRANCISCO 49ERS IN THE 1990 SEASON; AFTER THE GAME'S FINAL PLAY, SIMMS AND RONNIE LOTT (42) GOT INTO A HEATED SHOUTING MATCH ON THE FIELD. (ROBERT RIGER)

to Ray Perkins and Dan Reeves. I felt they would both be good coaches, but I knew Ray better because he and I had been in Baltimore the same time, and I thought the adjustment there would be quicker. He had coached for a northern team (the New England Patriots), and I liked the idea that he had been in rebuilding programs before. Dan had only been in Dallas, and I worried about the frustration he would feel coming from a successful franchise to one that needed to dig itself out of a hole. Ray had done that before, so I made him my choice."

His next move involved the 1979 draft. "We did a lot of scouting, and in the end had to choose between Phil Simms and Ottis Anderson," Young recalls. "It was a tough call. Phil had had a good junior year, but his school switched to a veer offense when he became a senior and didn't throw the ball very much. Ray worked him out, however, and liked him a lot. And so did a number of other people I talked to along the way. I thought we needed to build the team around a quarterback, and Ray had had good success with San Diego and the great offenses they had out there."

The reaction from the crowd that had gathered in New York for the draft that year was expectedly adverse. "People were booing and shouting 'Rocky Thompson' from the balcony in the hotel there," Young recalls. "It looked like one of those street scenes from 'A Tale of Two Cities' during the French Revolution. But the next day we brought the press out to meet Phil, and they all

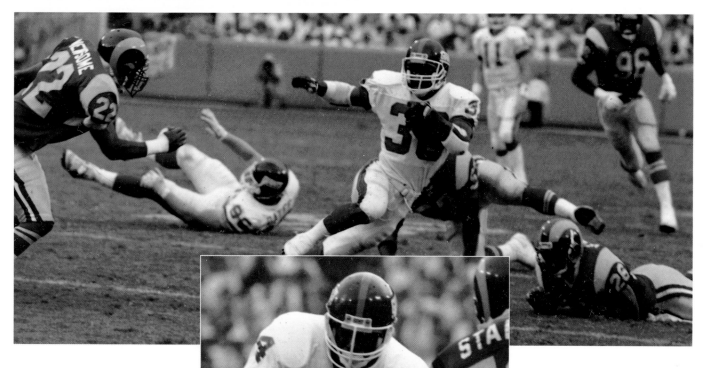

dropped their pens when they discovered that 17 teams had worked him out and that Bill Walsh had said he would have drafted Simms in the first round."

Simms was the number-two quarterback coming out of training camp, and he sat on the bench during the team's first four games, all of which were losses. Perkins had hoped to bring him along slowly, but with the Giants about to drop their fifth in a row, he scuttled those plans and sent in the rookie to finish the game. Simms performed well enough to earn a start the following Sunday, and with the blonde Kentucky native at the helm, the Giants won four straight games and six out of the next eight before dropping the final three con-

(opposite) George Martin sacks John Elway for a safety in Super Bowl XXI. (Robert Riger)

(top) Dave Meggett was a favorite target of Phil Simms' on third down plays. (Robert Riger)

(center) Fullback Maurice Carthon, a punishing blocker, also ran well with the ball. (Robert Riger)

tests to finish 6-10. Ottis Anderson was named rookie of the year, but Simms finished second in the balloting and was selected to the NFL's All-Rookie team.

Young continued the rebuilding process in the offseason. He shored up the defense by taking Mark Haynes, a cornerback from Colorado, with the Giants' first pick in the draft. And after Jim Lee Howell resigned as director of player personnel, a position he had held since he stepped down as Giants head coach after the 1960 season, Young hired Tom Boisture from the Patriots to replace him.

The football season started out in fine fashion, with Simms throwing five touchdown passes—four of them to Earnest Gray, the Memphis State receiver who had been drafted in the second round the year before—in the opener to lead the Giants to a 41-35 victory over the St. Louis Cardinals. But then the team lost its next eight games. Harry Carson, the talented inside linebacker, was so discouraged that he talked about quitting. The mood among the

139

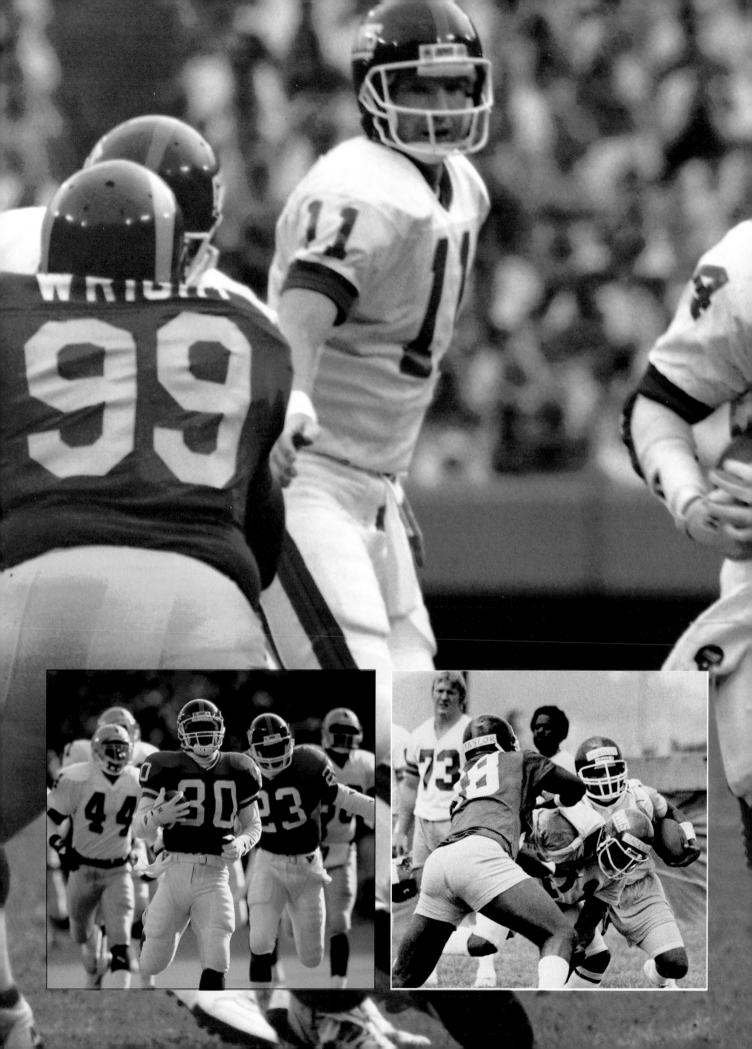

(background) PHIL SIMMS, ARGUABLY THE BEST QUARTERBACK IN GIANTS HISTORY. (ROBERT RIGER)

(extreme left) DAVE MEGGETT DAZZLED GIANTS FANS WITH HIS PUNT AND KICK-OFF RETURNS DURING HIS ROOKIE SEASON. HERE HE RETURNS A PUNT FOR A TOUCHDOWN AGAINST THE LOS ANGELES RAIDERS. (JERRY PINKUS)

(left center) LAWRENCE TAYLOR, WEARING NUMBER 58, WAS IMPRESSIVE IN HIS FIRST TRAINING CAMP. (FRED ROE)

(bottom) SIMMS, ENROUTE TO A RECORD-SETTING PERFORMANCE, GETS SET TO LEAD THE GIANTS TO ANOTHER SCORE IN SUPER BOWL XXI. (JERRY PINKUS)

(background) JOE MORRIS ALWAYS SEEMED TO HAVE A BIG GAME AGAINST THE REDSKINS. (JERRY PINKUS)

(left) SIMMS THREADS THE NEEDLE IN A GAME AGAINST THE RIVAL 49ERS. (ROBERT RIGER)

(opposite) LEONARD MARSHALL CELEBRATES HIS CRUSHING HIT IN THE 1990 NFC CHAMPIONSHIP GAME THAT SENT JOE MONTANA TO THE SIDELINES AND OPENED THE WAY FOR THE GIANTS' COMEBACK VICTORY. (ROBERT RIGER)

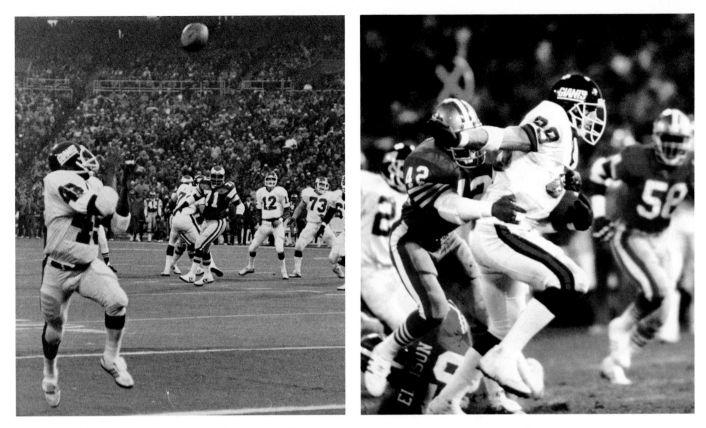

(top left) SCOTT BRUNNER (12) WATCHES LEON BRIGHT GET READY TO TAKE IN HIS PASS FOR THE OPENING TOUCHDOWN IN THE 1981 PLAYOFF VICTORY AGAINST THE PHILADELPHIA EAGLES. IT WAS THE GIANTS' FIRST PLAYOFF APPEARANCE SINCE 1963 AND THEIR FIRST POSTSEASON VICTORY SINCE 1958. (FRED ROE)

(top right) MARK BAVARO DRAGGED HALF A DOZEN 49ER DEFENDERS (INCLUDING FUTURE HALL-OF-FAMER RONNIE LOTT) FOR 20 YARDS IN HIS AWE-INSPIRING PLAY FROM THE CLASSIC 1986 REGULAR SEASON MATCH-UP AT CANDLESTICK PARK. (JERRY PINKUS)

(opposite) IN ONE OF THE GREATEST PLAYOFF PERFORMANCES IN NFL HISTORY, SUPER BOWL MVP PHIL SIMMS COMPLETED 22 OF 25 PASSES AGAINST THE DENVER BRONCOS. (JERRY PINKUS)

players darkened even further when Simms dislocated his shoulder near the end of the season and missed the last three games. The Giants finished the year 4-12, and fans were beginning to wonder if their ballclub would ever post another winning season.

No one realized it at the time, but the dismal 1980 campaign turned out to be a blessing in disguise because it gave the Giants the second choice overall in the 1981 draft, and they used it to select North Carolina defensive end Lawrence Taylor. Taylor impressed from his very first scrimmage in training camp and opened the season as the starting weakside linebacker.

Young brought in a number of good players that year. In addition to Taylor, he drafted nose tackle Bill Neill, guard Billy Ard and SMU linebacker Byron Hunt. And he signed free agent nose tackle Jim Burt.

The season started slowly, and the Giants stood at 2-3 after five games. LT was a terror on defense, and the team gave up only 14 points in its first two wins. But the offense was still sputtering. Young took care of that problem, however, by trading for Houston Oilers running back Rob Carpenter. Carpenter arrived in time for the Cardinals game in week six, and though he only played the second half, he rushed for 103 yards in 14 carries and led the Giants to a 34-14 victory.

The Giants won their next two games and were 5-3 at the halfway point. But they lost their next three games, including a devastating overtime defeat to the Washington Redskins that also saw Simms go down with another separated shoulder, and it looked like the wheels were about to come off again. "The next week we went down to Philadelphia to play the Eagles," says Young. "They had played in the Super Bowl the year before and were riding high at 9-2. It was the perfect chance for our team to fold, but it didn't. We

beat the hell out of the Eagles physically and won 20-10. It was a real turnaround for the franchise, and after that game, the players began to understand that no matter how bad things got, they could still win."

With Scott Brunner, a sixth round pick from Delaware in the 1980 draft, taking over for Simms, the Giants won two of their final three games and then met the Dallas Cowboys the last game of the season.

The Superbowl began as a tight contest, as the Broncos held a 10-9 lead at halftime. But Phil Simms came out smoking in the second half, and the Giants romped to a 39-20 victory and their first NFL Championship since 1956.

win.

The Jets won their game, and so the following week, the Giants traveled to Philadelphia for their first playoff game since 1963. Their offense stalled on the opening possession, and they punted. But the Eagles fumbled the return, and Beasley Reece recovered the ball at the Philadelphia 25. Six plays later, the Giants scored, and they went on to build a 27-7 halftime lead. The Eagles mounted a comeback, but the

To get into the playoffs, the Giants had to beat Dallas and hope the Jets defeated the Green Bay Packers the next day. Dallas owned a 10-7 lead with just over two minutes to play. But George Martin recovered a Tony Dorsett fumble, and with 30 seconds remaining in regulation, Joe Danelo tied the game with a 40-yard field goal into the wind. Danelo came through again in the overtime period after Byron Hunt had intercepted a Danny White pass and booted a 35-yarder for a 13-10

Giants held on to win 27-21, with Rob Carpenter gaining 161 yards on the ground.

Next up were the San Francisco 49ers and Joe Montana. The Giants kept the game close for three quarters, but the Niners pulled away in the fourth to win 38-24. It was a discouraging defeat, but still the team and their fans celebrated their first winning season since 1972 and their first playoff appearance since 1963. Taylor was named Rookie of the Year and Defensive Player of the Year and

LAWRENCE TAYLOR IS
JUST MAKING SURE THE
SAINTS QUARTERBACK
KNOWS EXACTLY WHO
IT WAS THAT SACKED
HIM. (JERRY PINKUS)

(opposite) HARRY CARSON PROUD-
LY CARRIED ON THE TRADITION OF
GREAT GIANTS LINEBACKERS. HERE
HE LISTENS TO DEFENSIVE COORDI-
NATOR BILL BELICHICK OUTLINE
STRATEGY. (JERRY PINKUS)

BILL PARCELLS WAS A TOUGH
TASKMASTER, BUT HE HAD A
LIGHTER SIDE. (JERRY PINKUS)

went to the first of his ten Pro Bowls. Says Mara: "We had concrete evidence that we were turning things around."

The Maras were so confident of the team's resurgence that they gave Ray Perkins a three-year contract extension before the beginning of the 1982 season. Hopes for another good year began to wane, however, when Phil Simms went down with a knee injury during a preseason game against the Jets. And it almost disappeared completely after the Giants lost their first two games of the season and then went out on strike with the rest of the NFL teams.

The strike lasted eight weeks. The Giants lost their first game back and then went on to win their next three. They were preparing to visit the Redskins at RFK Stadium in mid-December and had only to win their final three games to get into the playoffs. But a few days

George Young had also been to plenty of Giants games before he started working for the team. "I saw my first one in 1942," Young recalls. "I was also at the 1956 Championship Game that they won against the Bears. I remember when we beat Green Bay badly in the last game of the 1986 season, they announced that the last time the Giants had scored more than 50 points in a game was against the Colts in 1950. I was there, too."

Whatever the reasons, it was a devastating development, especially coming at such a critical point in the season. Young tried to minimize the damage by quickly naming defensive coordinator Bill Parcells as Perkins' successor. A New Jersey native who had played college ball at Wichita State, Parcells had bounced around as an assistant college coach for more than a decade before taking the head job at the Air Force Academy. In 1980 he became linebackers coach for the New England Patriots and arrived at the Giants the next year to help build what was rapidly becoming one of the toughest defenses in the league.

Given the way they played early on in the Redskins game, the Giants seemed completely unaffected by the moves of the previous week, and they built a 14-3 lead. But with four

before the Washington game, Ray Perkins announced that he was leaving at the end of the year to take over for Bear Bryant as head coach of his alma mater, the University of Alabama. It was a move motivated partly by the opportunity to succeed the legendary Bryant and partly by the disillusionment Perkins felt with the pro game after enduring the fractious strike.

seconds remaining, Mark Moseley kicked his NFL-record 21st straight field goal from 42 yards out to give the 'Skins a 15-14 win. Out of the playoffs, the Giants split their remaining two games.

To many people in and out of the Giants organization, 1982 was an aberration, what with the strike and Ray Perkins' sudden departure, and they fully expected the team to make a strong run for

(top right) LEONARD MARSHALL (70) CELEBRATES AFTER GEORGE MARTIN SACKS JOHN ELWAY FOR A SAFETY IN SUPER BOWL XXI. (JERRY PINKUS)

(left inset) DOUG RIESENBERG HAS BEEN A STALWART AT RIGHT TACKLE SINCE BEING DRAFTED FROM CALIFORNIA IN 1987. (FRED ROE)

(top) LT AND MARK COLLINS PRESSURE JOHN ELWAY IN SUPER BOWL XXI. (JERRY PINKUS)

(middle right inset) STEPHEN BAKER MAKES A BIG TOUCHDOWN CATCH AGAINST THE BILLS IN SUPER BOWL XXV. (JERRY PINKUS)

(right) LT PLAYED THIS 1988 GAME AGAINST THE SAINTS WITH A TORN LIGAMENT AND A DETACHED MUSCLE IN HIS RIGHT SHOULDER, LITERALLY WITH ONE ARM. STILL, HE RECORDED SEVEN TACKLES, THREE SACKS AND TWO FORCED FUMBLES. BILL PARCELLS CALLS IT "LAWRENCE'S MOST SPECTACULAR GAME, HIS FINEST HOUR FROM A COURAGE STANDPOINT." (JERRY PINKUS)

(bottom left) LT OFTEN SAID HE WAS HELL ON QUARTERBACKS; CLEARLY WASHINGTON QB JAY SCHROEDER WOULDN'T ARGUE WITH THAT. (JERRY PINKUS)

(background) STACY
ROBINSON MADE SOME
BIG PLAYS FOR THE
GIANTS DURING HIS SIX
YEARS WITH THE TEAM.
(JERRY PINKUS)

(inset) THE APTLY
NAMED JUMBO ELLIOTT
ANCHORS THE LEFT SIDE
OF THE GIANTS OFFEN-
SIVE LINE. (JERRY
PINKUS)

(top right) ONE OF THE CHANGES BILL PARCELLS MADE IN HIS SEC-
OND YEAR AS HEAD COACH WAS THE CONSTRUCTION OF A WEIGHT
ROOM AND THE HIRING OF STRENGTH AND CONDITIONING COACH
JOHNNY PARKER. THE BENEFITS WERE FELT ALMOST IMMEDIATELY;
INJURIES WENT DOWN, AND THE GIANTS MADE THE PLAYOFFS THE
NEXT THREE YEARS IN A ROW. (JERRY PINKUS)

(top left) TWO DEFENSIVE WAR HORSES—HARRY CARSON AND JIM
BURT—CONGRATULATE EACH OTHER ON A FUMBLE RECOVERY IN A
1985 GAME AGAINST THE CLEVELAND BROWNS. (JERRY PINKUS)

(bottom center) RIGHT TACKLE KARL NELSON PLAYED A BIG ROLE
IN GETTING THE GIANTS THEIR SUPER BOWL TROPHY IN 1986; A
YEAR LATER, HOWEVER, HE WAS STRICKEN WITH CANCER. (JERRY
PINKUS)

(bottom left) WHILE THE GIANTS WERE BEATING THE REDSKINS IN
A MONDAY NIGHT GAME DURING THE 1986 SEASON, THE METS
WERE CLINCHING THE WORLD SERIES WITH A VICTORY OVER THE
BOSTON RED SOX AT SHEA STADIUM. LIKE MANY OTHERS IN THE
MEADOWLANDS THAT NIGHT, THIS GIANTS FAN KEPT CLOSE TABS
ON THE METS' CHAMPIONSHIP WIN. (JERRY PINKUS)

(background) PHIL MCCONKEY CELEBRATES AFTER THE GIANTS' FIRST SUPER
BOWL WIN. (FRED ROE)

(inset) A FOURTH-ROUND DRAFT PICK FROM NORTHWEST LOUISIANA STATE,
GARY REASONS WAS ANOTHER IN A LONG LINE OF TALENTED GIANTS
LINEBAKCERS. (JERRY PINKUS)

THE GATORADE BATHS, ADMINISTERED BY HARRY CARSON, BECAME A GIANTS TRADITION IN THE 1986 SUPER BOWL SEASON. (JERRY PINKUS)

PEPPER JOHNSON JOINED THE
GIANTS IN 1986 AND QUICKLY
BECAME A KEY PART OF THE
TEAM'S VAUNTED DEFENSE.
(JERRY PINKUS)

the playoffs in '83. The year got off to a good start on draft day when the Giants grabbed Terry Kinard in the first round and Leonard Marshall, Karl Nelson, Perry Williams, Andy Headen and kicker Ali Haji-Sheik later on.

Training camp began, as usual, in mid-July, and the main attraction was the battle between Phil Simms, Scott Brunner, Jeff Rutledge for the starting quarterback job. The three played it about even in preseason, but Parcells elected to go with Brunner. Simms was furious with the decision, and after the Giants lost their fifth game of the season to San Diego to fall to 2-3, the former first round draft choice asked to be traded.

Brunner struggled in game six, and part way through the contest Parcells pulled him in favor of Simms. The offense suddenly came to life, but after only a few plays Simms dislocated his right thumb. He was out the rest of the year.

Simms was not the only Giant to go down that season. Twenty-five players, including Harry Carson and Rob Carpenter, spent time on the injured reserve list, and the season quickly unraveled. The Giants ended up 3-12-1 and led the league in turnovers with 58 (31 interceptions, 27 lost fumbles). It got so bad in that one late-season contest against the Cardinals there were a NFL record 51,589 no-shows. "It's only football," Harry Carson remarked to a New York Times sportswriter when the season was over. "But to be a Giant is to always feel sad underneath, always a little bit unsteady. Is that O.K.? Is it O.K. to feel sad about not winning, about seeing your teammates come and go, about seeing other teams that were as bad as you rise out of the ashes? It's only football, but I think it's O.K. to feel sad because it's my life, and I am a football player."

Giants fans were more than just sad when they learned in December that year that Donald Trump, owner of the USFL New Jersey Generals, had signed Lawrence Taylor to a contract obligating the All-World linebacker to join Trump's team after the 1988 season. But the Maras were not about to lose their franchise player, and they eventually negotiated a buy-out of the Generals pact and then inked LT to a six-year extension.

There was plenty of speculation that Parcells would not be back after his disastrous rookie year. But the coach did return, and he made sure that things in 1984 would be different. His first order of business was revamping his roster of players, some

Bill Parcells was a man of many superstitions during the 1986 Super Bowl campaign. He had a collection of toy elephants in his Giants Stadium office, all facing the door, all with their trunks pointing up. Once a cat crossed his path as he was driving his car down a busy expressway; Parcells backed up and drove over its path again to "erase" it. He wouldn't touch a penny sitting tails up. One lay on the floor of the coaches' locker room and another in his locker for most of the season that way because Parcells would not pick them up. And he instructed maintenance workers to clean around them. Jerome Sally had to be the first player to attend team meetings, and Byron Hunt the last. In practice, the Giants always did the same drills from the same yard line. For the national anthem, Parcells always stood at the 50-yard line with Harry Carson on his immediate left. Before every coin flip that year, Carson and Parcells had the exact same conversation. Carson: What do you want me to call, heads or tails?" Parcells: "You decide." And after his players began pouring Gatorade on him after victories, he made sure it became a ritual, no matter how frigid the weather.

163

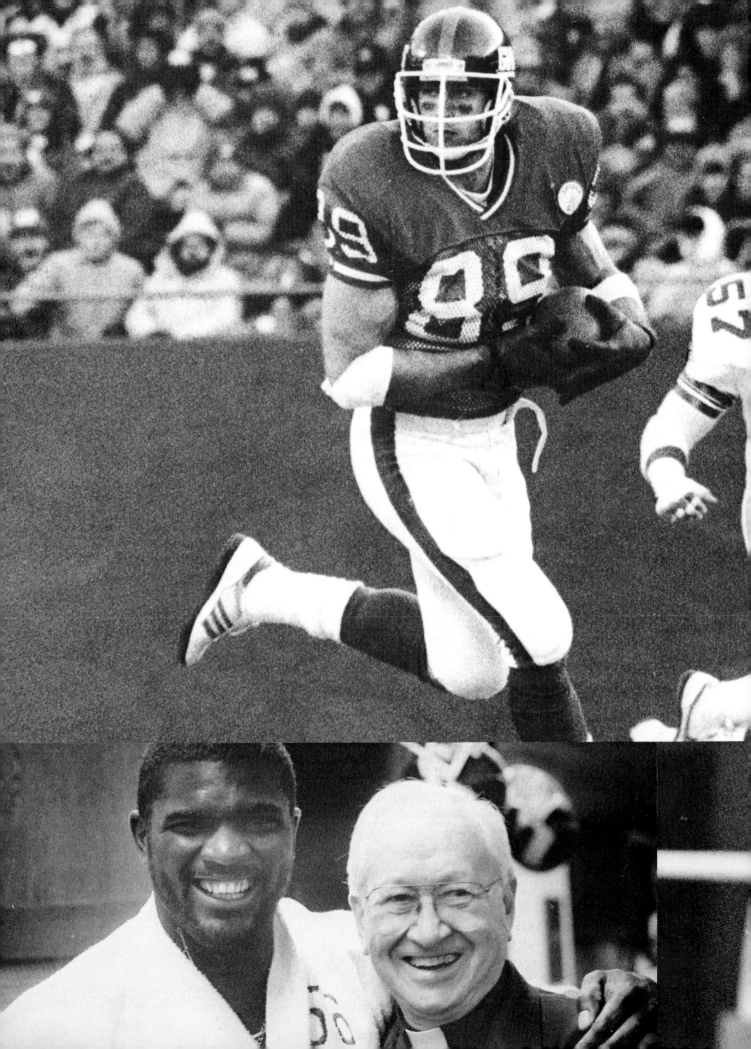

(lower left) LAWRENCE TAYLOR WITH FATHER KENNETH MOORE, A CLOSE FRIEND OF THE MARA'S AND UNOFFICIAL CHAPLAIN OF THE GIANTS. MOORE'S BROTHER TIM WAS THE PRINCIPAL OF A CATHOLIC HIGH SCHOOL IN NEW JERSEY AND GAVE VINCE LOMBARDI HIS FIRST COACHING JOB. LOMBARDI COACHED THREE SPORTS, TAUGHT TWO CLASSES AND OFTEN SAID, "TIM MOORE TOOK A VOW OF POVERTY AND SAW THAT I LIVED UP TO IT." (JERRY PINKUS)

(lower right) LITTLE JOE MORRIS SHATTERED MOST OF THE GIANTS RUSHING RECORDS DURING HIS EIGHT SEASONS WITH THE TEAM. (JERRY PINKUS)

(upper right) MORRIS PICKED UP 181 YARDS IN THIS 1986 CONTEST AGAINST THE WASHINGTON REDSKINS. (JERRY PINKUS)

(upper top) IN HIS SIX SEASONS WITH THE GIANTS, MARK BAVARO WAS ONE OF THE BEST TIGHT ENDS IN FOOTBALL. (JERRY PINKUS)

THE STRONG AND SILENT TYPE, MARK
BAVARO WAS NICKNAMED RAMBO BY
GIANTS FANS, AND HE WREAKED AS
MUCH HAVOC WITH OPPOSING DEFENSES
AS SYLVESTER STALLONE'S MOVIE CHAR-
ACTER JOHN RAMBO DID WITH POLICE
DEPARTMENTS AND COMMUNIST ARMIES.
(FRED ROE)

LT WENT TO A RECORD TEN CONSECUTIVE PRO BOWLS AND WAS ONLY THE SECOND DEFENSIVE PLAYER EVER TO BE NAMED THE NFL'S MOST VALUABLE PLAYER. (JERRY PINKUS)

(*opposite*) LAWRENCE TAYLOR HOLDS COURT ON PRESS DAY BEFORE THE 1986 SUPER BOWL. (JERRY PINKUS)

(*opposite inset*) MANY TIMES WITH LT, A PRESSURE WAS AS GOOD AS A SACK. (JERRY PINKUS)

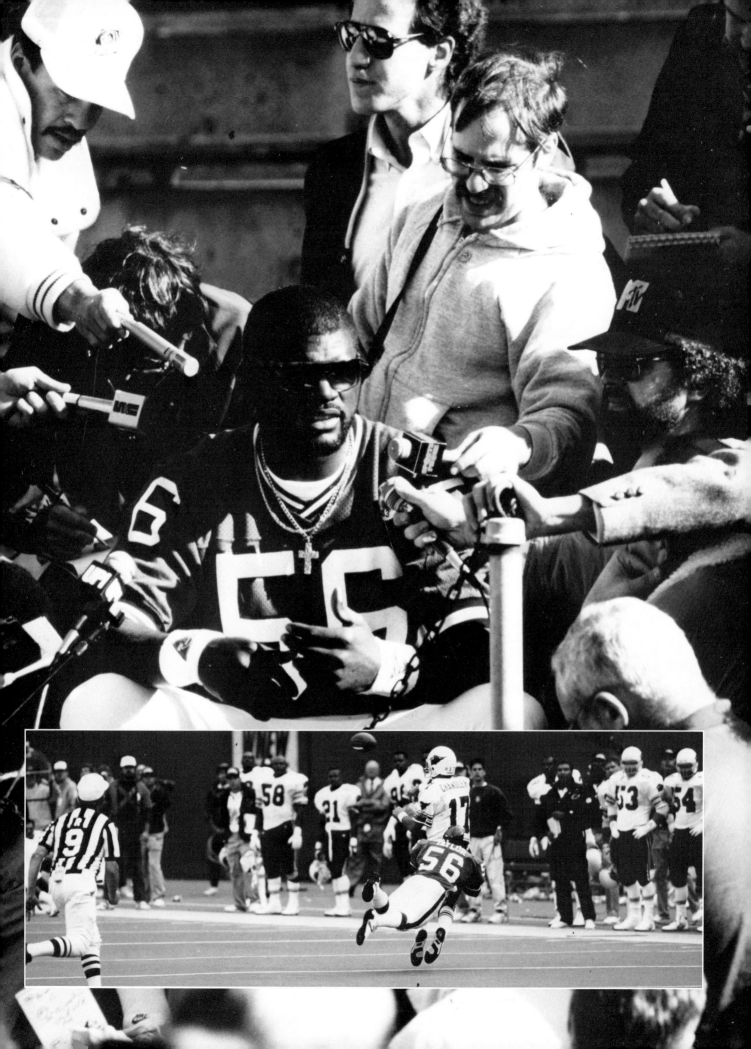

(lower left) BE IT EVER SO HUMBLE, THE ROSE BOWL WASN'T HOME. BUT THE GIANTS FELT VERY COMFORTABLE PLAYING THERE. (JERRY PINKUS)

(left) THE GIANTS PASSED ON O.J. ANDERSON IN 1979 COLLEGE DRAFT, BUT SEVEN YEARS LATER THEY ACQUIRED HIM IN A TRADE WITH THE ST. LOUIS CARDINALS. (JERRY PINKUS)

(lower right) HARRY CARSON LEAVING BALMY NEW JERSEY FOR PASADENA AND SUPER BOWL XXI IN 1986. (JERRY PINKUS)

(opposite) TWO OF THE BEST LINEBACKERS IN GIANTS HISTORY, HARRY CARSON AND LT WENT TO 19 PRO BOWLS BETWEEN THEM. (JERRY PINKUS)

JIM BURT, ANDY HEADEN AND PEPPER
JOHNSON LEAVE THE FIELD AFTER
THE GIANTS THUMPED THE 49ERS IN
THEIR 1986 PLAYOFF MEETING
49-3. (JERRY PINKUS)

(inset) A FIERCE TACKLER,
HARRY CARSON WAITS TO PUT THE
HURTS ON A CHARGER RUNNING BACK.
(JERRY PINKUS)

of whom had bad attitudes, others of whom he suspected were using drugs. "I had become less and less tolerant of people who for whatever reason had problems that were going to continually inhibit the team from performing at the level I wanted," he says. "It was important that we replaced them with a more performance-oriented group of players. I didn't want gangsters or people with no ambition, intelligence or direction. That would all be counterproductive to the type of ballclub I wanted to put on the field."

In essence, Parcells had decided to clean house, and by the time the 1984 season opened he had 27 new players on his squad, including draft choices Carl Banks, Gary Reasons, William Roberts, Jeff Hostetler and Lionel Manuel. Young also traded for Tony Galbreath and Kenny Hill and signed Phil McConkey and Bobby Johnson as free agents.

Parcells' given names are Dwayne Charles, but he didn't keep them for very long. "In the fourth grade the teacher would say, 'Dwayne Parcells, is she here?" the former Giants coach told Dave Anderson of the New York Times in 1982. "The name Bill came when I moved to Oradell, and people confused me with a guy named Bill." Later, Parcells was nicknamed Tuna by his players. "The Patriots gave it to me when I coached there in 1980," he says. "One time they pulled a practical joke on me, and I said, 'Do you think I'm Charlie the Tuna, like a sucker?' After that, they called me Tuna and set up a Tuna award each week. It took me about eight weeks to find out what it was for. It was for the player I had praised the most that week. He got a Charlie the Tuna sticker to wear on his helmet."

Parcells and Young had a different approach to building a football team than those who had been with the Giants in the past. Young, for one, preferred assembling players through the draft and free agent signings rather than trades. And he and Parcells wanted a cold-weather club based on a tough defense and strong running game that could handle the brutal weather conditions that often prevailed in the Northeast late in the season. Passing teams may score a lot of points, but as Giants fans remembered from the championship games their team lost in 1961, 1962 and 1963, they often struggle in December's cold and wind.

Another change Parcells orchestrated was the construction of a weight room for the players and the hiring of Johnny Parker as strength and conditioning coach. "We needed to do something about preventing the sorts of

MARK COLLINS CAME TO NEW YORK IN THE BOUNTIFUL 1986
COLLEGE DRAFT AND QUICKLY BECAME KNOWN AS ONE OF THE
BEST COVER MEN IN THE LEAGUE. (JERRY PINKUS)

(below left) THE 1986 SUPER BOWL CHAMPION GIANTS.
(JERRY PINKUS)

(below) KARL NELSON CAME BACK
AFTER HIS INITIAL BOUT WITH
CANCER, BUT HE HAD TO RETIRE IN
1988 WHEN THE DISEASE
RETURNED. HE NOW BROADCASTS
GIANTS GAMES ON RADIO.
(JERRY PINKUS)

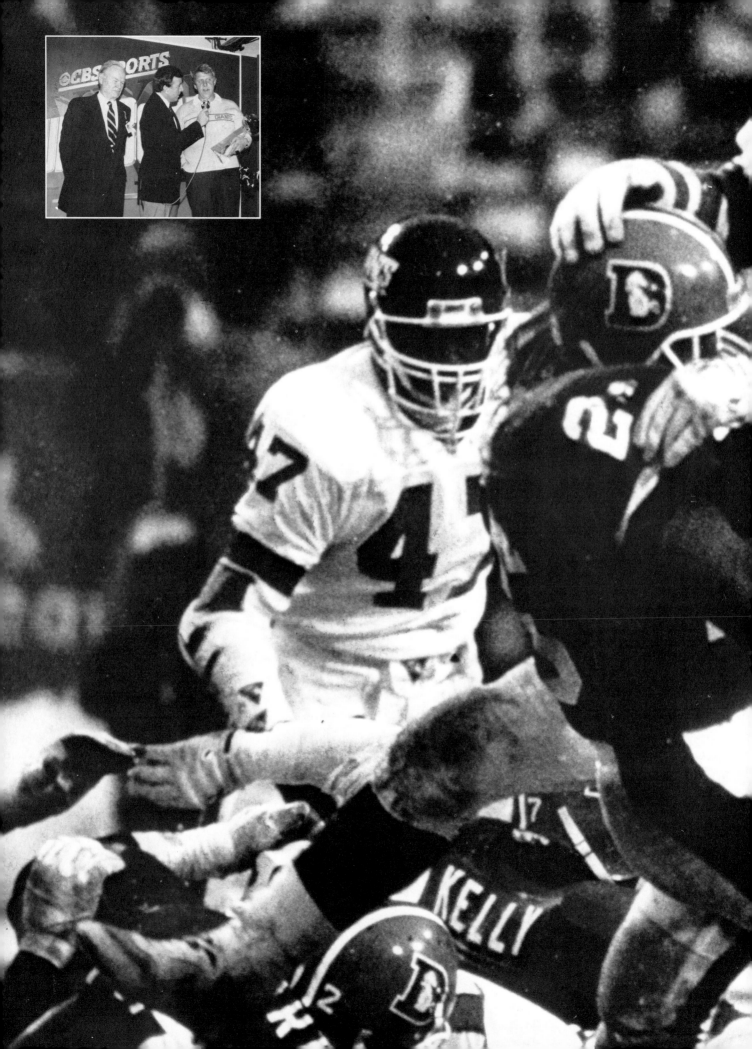

(upper inset) CBS SPORTS' BRENT MUSBERGER INTERVIEWS BILL PARCELLS AFTER THE GIANTS' FIRST SUPER BOWL WIN WHILE WELLINGTON MARA TAKES IT ALL IN. (JERRY PINKUS)

(lower inset) GEORGE MARTIN RUMBLES FOR A TOUCHDOWN WITH THE PASS HE HAS JUST INTERCEPTED FROM DENVER'S JOHN ELWAY IN WEEK 12 OF THE 1986 SEASON. BILL PARCELLS CALLED IT THE GREATEST PLAY HE EVER SAW. (FRED ROE)

GARY REASONS PUTS A CRUSHING HIT ON A BRONCO RUNNING BACK AT THE GOAL LINE, PREVENTING A TOUCHDOWN IN A 1989 GAME. (JERRY PINKUS)

injuries we had in 1983," he says. "And I wanted the players to have a place they could go and be together, a place where the team could get stronger and get closer to each other."

The Giants won three of their first four games and were 4-4 at the midway point of the season. The defense was strong, and Simms was throwing well. But the running game was still sputtering, so Parcells benched Butch Woolfolk, who had been the team's top draft pick in 1982, and replaced him with diminutive Joe Morris. The former Syracuse University halfback gave his coach the spark he was looking for, and the Giants won five of its last eight games to finish with a 9-7 mark and a berth in the playoffs.

Their first postseason game was against the Rams in Los Angeles. The Rams had hammered the Giants 33-12 in the regular season, but this time Parcells' team contained Eric Dickerson and won 16-13. Then it was on to San Francisco for another battle with the Niners. Harry Carson returned an interception for a touchdown, but that was the only TD the Giants could muster, and they fell 21-10 to the eventual Super Bowl champs.

Even with the playoff loss, 1984 had to be considered a very good year. Parcells had put together a solid group of veteran and young players and did a terrific job of coaching. George Young was named NFL Executive of the Year. And Simms, who stayed healthy for the first time in his career, had his best year as a Giant, setting club marks for attempts (533), completions (286) and yards

JIM BURT TOSSES A SOUVENIR TO THE FANS AFTER THE
TEAM'S SUPER BOWL WIN IN PASADENA. (FRED ROE)

AFTER PLAYING IN EARL CAMPBELL'S
SHADOW IN HOUSTON, ROB CARPENTER
SHINED IN NEW YORK.
(JERRY PINKUS)

gained (4,044) and earning an invitation to the Pro Bowl.

The Giants were even better in 1985. They had another solid draft that spring, picking up receiver Stacy Robinson in the second round, tight end Mark Bavaro in the fourth, running back Lee Rouson in the seventh and safety Herb Welch in the 12th. And Young signed punter Sean Landeta, center Bart Oates, fullback Maurice Carthon and guard Chris Godfrey from the defunct USFL. The team went 5-0 in preseason and then won seven of their first ten regular season games. They split their remaining contests to wind up 10-6 and in the play-offs again.

It was a banner year for a squad that had 25 players with three years or less experience in the NFL. Joe Morris became only the second Giant to ever rush for more than 1,000 yards, and his 21 touchdowns led the league. Five players, including Morris, were named to the Pro Bowl, and 12 team and 16 individual club records were set. And for the first time since 1962-63 the team posted back-to-back winning seasons.

The opening round of the playoffs that year pitted the Giants against the Super Bowl Champion San Francisco 49ers. But this time, the Giants were the home team, and in the first playoff game ever held at the Meadowlands, they shut down Bill Walsh's squad for a 17-3 win.

The Giants had to travel to Chicago, however, for their next game. Their opponent was the Chicago

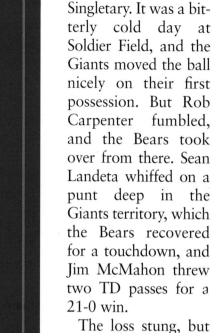

"The booing was pretty bad the day we drafted Phil Simms. And the television people made it even worse when they missed Pete Rozelle's first trip to the podium and asked him to announce our selection again for the cameras. Pete had a slight smile on his face as he got ready to repeat Phil's name because he knew how the crowd in the balcony would react. And sure enough, the booing started up again as soon as Pete began to speak."

Wellington Mara

Bears, which featured a fierce defense anchored by middle linebacker Mike Singletary. It was a bitterly cold day at Soldier Field, and the Giants moved the ball nicely on their first possession. But Rob Carpenter fumbled, and the Bears took over from there. Sean Landeta whiffed on a punt deep in the Giants territory, which the Bears recovered for a touchdown, and Jim McMahon threw two TD passes for a 21-0 win.

The loss stung, but the Giants were in no way demoralized. In fact, the defeat actually gave them something to build on for 1986. "I remember Bill talking to Harry Carson and George Martin after the game," says Wellington Mara. "He promised them that he'd win them a championship before they retired. The entire locker room seemed upbeat. Players and coaches kept saying they had grown a little bit with this game, and that they would be ready next year."

Next year began on a shaky note when it was reported that Lawrence Taylor had sought treatment for a drug problem in the offseason. But he was with the team when the season started with a Monday night loss to the Dallas Cowboys. The Giants rebounded to win their next five games. And after a loss to the Seahawks in Seattle, they came back to capture all their remaining contests to finish 14-2.

The team, which had added Eric Dorsey, Mark Collins, Erik Howard and Pepper Johnson through the draft, played well all year, especially through a dramatic three-game stretch that saw them beat Minnesota, Denver and San Francisco.

Perhaps the entire season hinged on the Minnesota win. Down 20-19 with time running out, the Giants faced a 4th-and-17 from midfield. But Simms found Bobby Johnson open on the right sideline and completed a 22-yard pass for the first down. Raul Allegre came in five plays later to boot the winning field goal with 12 seconds remaining.

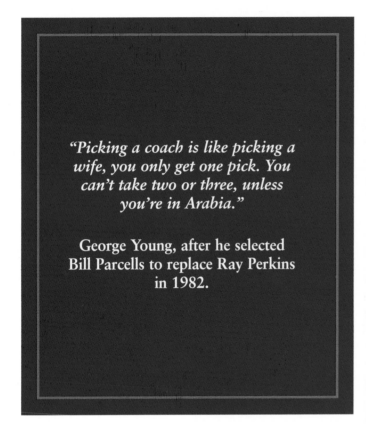

"Picking a coach is like picking a wife, you only get one pick. You can't take two or three, unless you're in Arabia."

George Young, after he selected Bill Parcells to replace Ray Perkins in 1982.

Denver visited New York the following week. The Broncos had driven deep into Giants territory shortly before the half when George Martin picked off a John Elway pass and rumbled 78 yards for a touchdown. "It was the greatest play I ever saw," Parcells says. "People forget that Denver had gone the length of the field. The defense was exhausted, and for a lineman who has been chasing Elway for seven or eight plays in a row to run the ball all the way back like that was something else." Martin wasn't the only hero in that contest, however. The game was tied with less than two minutes to go when Simms completed a 24-yard pass to Johnson on 3-and-21 from the Giants 18 yard line and then followed that with a 46-yard pass to Phil McConkey to set up the winning field goal.

Then there was San Francisco. The Giants came

CENTER BRIAN WILLIAMS, A NUMBER ONE DRAFT PICK FROM MINNESOTA, TOOK OVER FOR BART OATES IN 1994.
(JERRY PINKUS)

184

out flat and were down 17-0 at the half. But in the third quarter Simms completed eight of nine passes for 167 yards and two touchdowns. No completion was more important than one he made to Bavaro, who seemed to inspire the entire team when he dragged half a dozen 49er defenders for an additional 20 yards after catching the ball. The offense tacked on another score that period, thanks to a one-yard plunge by newly-acquired running back Ottis Anderson, and the Giants won 21-17.

The Giants dominated their opponents for the rest of the season and earned homefield advantage throughout the playoffs. Their first postseason match-up brought the 49ers to the Meadowlands, but this game was no contest. Jim Burt knocked Montana out of the game with a savage hit, and the Giants rolled to a 49-3 win.

The next week the Giants faced the Redskins for the NFC Championship. It was a frigid day with the wind gusting up to 40 knots, and when the Giants won the coin toss they elected to kick off. The move paid instant dividends because the

After taking the hand-off from Phil Simms,
O.J. Anderson is about to cut inside a block by
Eric Moore (60) in a 1990 game against the Dolphins.
(Jerry Pinkus)

'Skins couldn't move the ball and managed only a 23-yard punt into the wind on fourth down. The Giants drove for a field goal on their first possession and went on to score two more touchdowns for a 17-0 victory and a trip to Pasadena and the Super Bowl two weeks later. Many of the Giants players distinguished themselves in that victory, but none more than punt returner Phil McConkey. "The Washington punt returner let all his balls roll that day," Parcells says. "The wind was just that bad. But Phil caught every one of his, and when I added it up after the game there was 106 yards difference in field position as a result. Al Davis called me up a few days later and told me McConkey was great that day. He certainly was."

The Super Bowl began as a tight contest, and the Broncos held a 10-9 lead at halftime. But Phil Simms came out smoking in the second half, and the Giants romped to a 39-20 victory and their first NFL Championship since 1956. In one of the strongest performances an NFL quarterback has ever had in a title game, Simms completed 22 of 25 passes and was named the MVP. Parcells was selected the NFL's Coach of the Year, and Lawrence Taylor received the league's Most Valuable Player award. Joe Morris shattered his old team record by gaining more than 1,500 yards in the regular season and joined seven other Giants in the Pro Bowl.

Hopes were high for another Super Bowl win as the Giants readied themselves for 1987. But it turned out to be a miserable year. Doctors found a lump in tackle Karl Nelson's shoulder in the off-season and determined that he had cancer and would be out indefinitely. The Giants lost its first two regular season contests, including a 34-19 thrashing by the Chicago Bears in the opening Monday night game, and then went out on strike with the rest of the league. The NFL canceled game three but resumed play the next three weeks with ragtag squads of "replacement" players. The Giants had one of the weakest replacement teams and lost all three of those games. The strike ended after week six, and the regulars rebounded to win six of its final ten contests. But it was too little too late, and the Giants finished the 1987 campaign last in their division at 6-9.

The next year went a little better as the Giants posted a 10-6 record. One of their best wins that season was a 13-12 triumph over the New Orleans Saints, in which Lawrence Taylor added *(background)* JIM BURT'S FEROCIOUS HIT ON JOE MONTANA PUT THE FUTURE HALL-OF-FAME QUARTERBACK OUT OF THE 1986 PLAYOFF CONTEST THAT THE GIANTS WON 49-3. (FRED ROE)

(below left) A REFLECTIVE PHIL SIMMS ANSWERS REPORTERS' QUESTIONS AFTER SUPER BOWL XXI. (JERRY PINKUS)

(below ...) WHO SAYS ADVERTISING ... SIMMS LOST ALL HIS HAIR (... TEMPORARILY) FOR A TELEVISION COMMERCIAL. (JERRY PINKUS)

(opposite) LINEMAN JOHN ... WASHINGTON STUFFED THE CHICAGO BEARS ON THIS 4TH-AND-GOAL PLAY FROM THE ONE-YARD LINE IN THE OPENING PLAYOFF GAME OF THE 1990 SUPER BOWL SEASON WITH HELP FROM PEPPER JOHNSON, WHO LOSES HELMET IN THE PROCESS. (JERRY PINKUS)

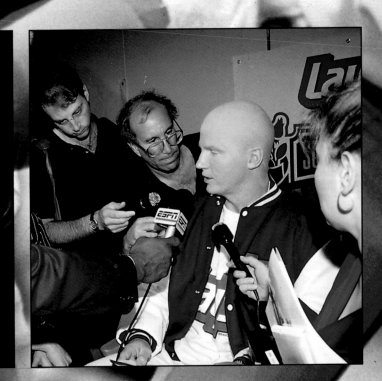

to his remarkable legacy by recording seven tackles, three sacks and two forced fumbles even though he had a torn ligament and detached muscle in his right shoulder. "Lawrence played that game literally with one arm," says Bill Parcells, "I told him afterwards he was great that night. I thought it was his most spectacular game, his finest hour from a courage standpoint."

But the Giants, as a team, were not great the final game of the season, in which they met the Jets. A win, and they were in the playoffs. But the Jets prevailed 27-21, and the Giants went home for the holidays. The season was not a total loss, however. The Giants had still won ten games, and their five-year record stood at 54-32, a winning percentage of .628 and the most victories over a five-year period a Giants team had ever compiled. Joe Morris rushed for 1,000 yards for a third time and surpassed Alex Webster as the team's all-time leading runner.

Sadly, 1988 would be Joe Morris' last season with the Giants. The following summer he hurt his knee in an exhibition game and spent the year on the injured reserve list. Little-used Ottis Anderson took over, and the ageless wonder rushed for over 1,000 yards as the Giants won 12 games and captured the Eastern Division crown. Another bright spot that season was rookie Dave Meggett, who Young had selected in the fifth round of the 1989 draft. The 5'7", 180 lbs. running back and return specialist played his way into the Pro Bowl by compiling over 1,800 all-purpose yards.

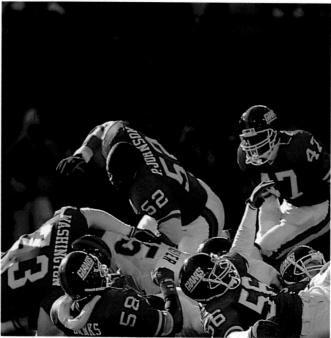

(background) O.J. ANDERSON BUSTING LOOSE AGAINST THE 49ERS. (JERRY PINKUS)

(bottom left) SEAN LANDETA AND HIS BOOMING PUNTS CAME TO THE GIANTS WHEN THE USFL FOLDED. (JERRY PINKUS)

(top right) ANOTHER GEM FROM THE 1986 DRAFT, NOSE TACKLE ERIK HOWARD HAS BEEN AN IMMOVABLE FORCE IN THE MIDDLE. (JERRY PINKUS)

(bottom right) BUTCH WOOLFOLK HAD AN ERRATIC CAREER WITH THE GIANTS; AFTER STARTING FOR A WHILE, HE LOST HIS JOB TO JOE MORRIS AND WAS EVENTUALLY TRADED TO HOUSTON. (JERRY PINKUS)

The Giants met the Rams at the Meadowlands for their opening playoff game that year. It was a tight contest that stood at 13-13 at the end of regulation. But Jim Everett threw a touchdown pass to Flipper Anderson in overtime for a 19-13 victory.

To say the Giants bounced back nicely from that overtime loss would be an understatement, for 1990 would go down as one of the greatest seasons in franchise history. Young drafted Rodney Hampton and Mike Fox with his first two picks that year, but the team went to training camp minus Lawrence Taylor, who was looking to negotiate a new contract. Parcells cut Joe Morris in camp and acquired veteran defensive backs Everson Walls and Dave Duerson. LT returned only a few days before the season opener against the Philadelphia Eagles and showed how little preseason meant to him by sacking Randall Cunningham three times and leading the team to a 27-20 victory.

The Giants won their first ten games that year. After back-to-back losses to the Eagles and 49ers, they beat Minnesota and then faced the Buffalo Bills and their potent "offense of the '80s." The game was played in a cold, steady drizzle at the Meadowlands, and the Giants fell 17-13. But their biggest loss that day was Phil Simms, who went down with a season-ending foot injury.

Jeff Hostetler, who had been so desperate for playing time in previous years that he had talked his way into some special teams play, took over at quarterback and engineered victories in the last two games of the regular season. No one was sure, however, how he would do in the playoffs. No one, that is, except Bill Parcells. "I remember asking Bill before the playoffs how he thought we would do with Hoss in charge," Young recalls. "And he said, 'If we lose, it won't be because of him.' "

Parcells' confidence in his quarterback proved to be well-founded. Hoss played brilliantly in a 31-3 rout of the Bears in their first playoff game, and the Giants went out to San Francisco to face the Niners. "You have to remember, these were the three-peat 49ers," Parcells says, "and people were about to anoint them as the greatest football team in history if they went on to the Super Bowl that year." The Giants didn't score a touchdown that day, but they held Joe Montana and his explosive offense to 13 points and won 15-13 when Matt Bahr kicked a field goal with time running out. "It

(left) PHIL SIMMS SPORTED THE PRINCE VALIANT LOOK WHEN
HE FIRST ARRIVED AT THE GIANTS. (NEW YORK GIANTS)

A FREE AGENT MANY THOUGHT WAS TOO SMALL TO PLAY
IN THE NFL, BURT WAS A BIG REASON FOR THE TEAM'S
RESURGENCE IN THE 1980s. (JERRY PINKUS)

may have been the greatest game I ever witnessed," Parcells says. "There were six or seven future Hall-of-Famers on the field that day, and the intensity was unbelievable."

Perhaps even more unbelievable was the Giants second trip to the Super Bowl in four years. Few of the pundits had given them much hope of getting to Tampa for the game, let alone winning it. But thanks to a hard-hitting defense and an efficient, ball-control offense, the Giants captured their second NFL Championship 20-19. "I don't want to say the 1990 team was the best I ever coached," Parcells explains. "But it was certainly the most underestimated. People didn't give us much of a chance to win it all, especially after we lost Simms. But we allowed the fewest points of any team in the league that year and had the fewest turnovers in the history of the NFL. And then we beat the 49ers and the Bills with our back-up quarterback."

Wellington Mara was just as impressed. "The 1990 team got more out of its abilities than any other team I've ever been associate with," he says. "And Bill did a great job coaching them."

DEFENSIVE COORDINATOR BILL BELICHICK (WITH HIS DEFENSIVE BACKS) WAS A HOT COACHING COMMODITY AFTER HIS DEFENSE SHUT DOWN THE POWERFUL BILLS DEFENSE IN SUPER BOWL XXV. HE WENT ON TO BECOME HEAD COACH OF THE BROWNS THE NEXT YEAR. (JERRY PINKUS)

(right) EARNEST GRAY WAS DRAFTED AFTER PHIL SIMMS IN 1979 AND SOON BECAME ONE OF THE QUARTERBACK'S FAVORITE RECEIVERS. (FRED ROE)

A THIRD ROUND PICK FROM WEST VIRGINIA IN 1984,
HOSTETLER SAT ON THE BENCH FOR MOST OF HIS FIRST SEVERAL YEARS
WITH THE GIANTS; HE WAS SO DESPERATE FOR ACTION THAT HE EVEN TALKED THE
COACHES INTO LETTING HIM PLAY ON SOME OF THE SPECIAL TEAMS. (JERRY PINKUS)

(opposite background)
JEFF HOSTETLER WAS AS DANGEROUS RUNNING
WITH THE BALL AS HE WAS THROWING IT. (JERRY PINKUS)

(opposite top inset)
005-78   HOSTETLER FILLED IN ADMIRABLY FOR SIMMS IN 1990. (JERRY PINKUS)

(opposite bottom inset)
PHIL MCCONKEY FLIES THROUGH THE AIR IN AN ATTEMPT TO
SCORE A TOUCHDOWN AGAINST THE BRONCOS IN SUPER BOWL XXI;
HE CAME UP ONE YARD SHORT. (JERRY PINKUS)

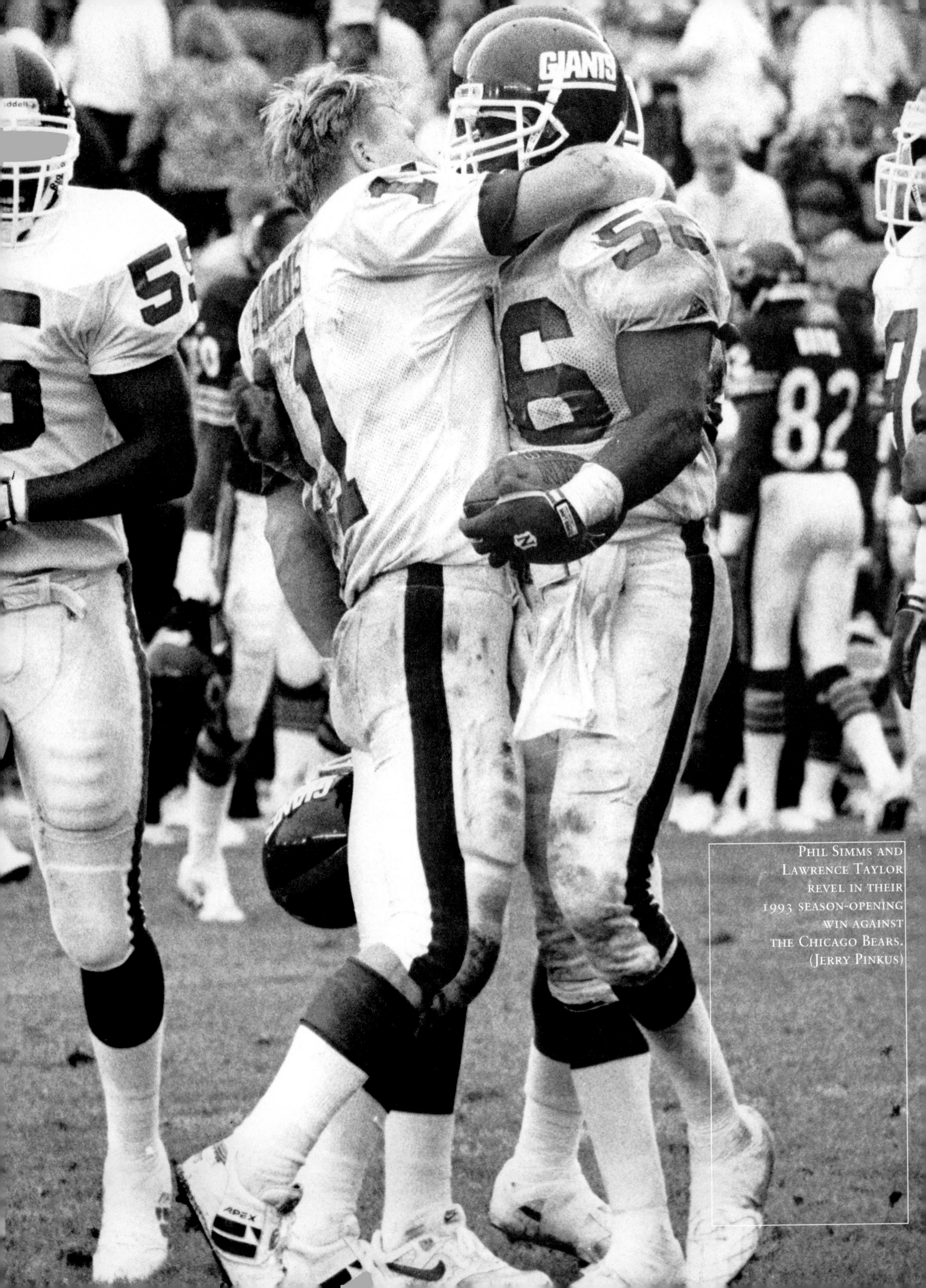

Phil Simms and Lawrence Taylor revel in their 1993 season-opening win against the Chicago Bears. (Jerry Pinkus)

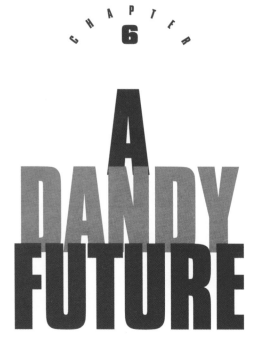

A DANDY FUTURE

Super Bowl winners rarely have quiet offseasons, but the changes that rocked the Giants in the months following their victory in Tampa Bay were unusual even for an NFL champion. The first tremor came in late February when Tim Mara announced that he was selling his family's 50 percent share of the ballclub to Robert Preston Tisch for a reported $75 million. The president and co-chief executive officer of the Loews Corp.—a conglomerate with interests in hotels, broadcasting, watches, tobacco and insurance—Tisch was a successful businessman who had served as Postmaster General during the Reagan Administration. More importantly to Giants fans, he was a longtime season ticket holder who liked professional football so much that he had attended all 25 Super Bowls.

Tisch had long expressed interest in owning an NFL franchise. Several years before he had talked to the Sullivan family of Boston about acquiring the New England Patriots and had also looked into the possibility of backing an expansion franchise in Baltimore. "Art Modell (owner of the Cleveland Browns) knew that Bob wanted to get into football, and he had some inkling that Tim wanted to sell his share of the Giants," Wellington Mara recalls. "So he arranged a lunch with Bob and myself. We talked about the Giants,

and Art told Bob that half of our team was better than 100 percent of any other NFL franchise."

That reasoning apparently made sense to Tisch, and he worked out a deal that gave him 50 percent of the franchise and made him the first person out-

LT SEEMS IN A PENSIVE MOOD BEFORE HIS FINAL GAME AS A GIANT, THE 1993 PLAYOFF LOSS TO THE 49ERS. (JERRY PINKUS)

READY FOR WAR, LAWRENCE TAYLOR WAITS TO GO ON THE FIELD
FOR THE 1993 WILDCARD GAME AGAINST THE VIKINGS.
IT WAS HIS LAST GAME AT GIANTS STADIUM. (JERRY PINKUS)

time to get a new head coach, and much as he had done when Ray Perkins resigned unexpectedly in 1982, he turned to an assistant already with the organization. His choice this time was Ray Handley, who Parcells had promoted to offensive coordinator several weeks before.

Handley had come to the Giants in 1984 from Stanford University, where he had been associate head coach, and was lauded by Bill Walsh as "an excellent alternative to Bill Parcells." But even Walsh admitted that Handley had a tough act to follow. Parcells had compiled an 85-51-1 mark in his eight years with the team, including two Super Bowl championships, and had won more games than any other Giants coach except Steve Owen, who was with the ballclub for 23 years.

Handley faced a tough decision right from the start, and that was who would be his starting quarterback. It was made even more difficult by the fact

side of the Mara family to own a piece of the storied NFL team. Tisch assumed the title of co-chief executive officer and said he would work on financial matters while Wellington Mara oversaw the football operations.

Next to feel the winds of change was the coaching staff. Defensive coordinator Bill Belichick resigned to take the head job with the Cleveland Browns. And shortly before mini-camp opened in May, Bill Parcells announced that he was stepping down as well. The main reason for his departure, he says, was health. "My instincts are generally very good," Parcells says, "and I thought something was wrong with me physically because I just wasn't feeling very well. I didn't know what it was, but I knew I didn't feel right. And I knew it was time for me to take care of myself."

For George Young, it was

LT AND COACH DAN REEVES SHARE A LAUGH THE DAY BEFORE THE 1993 PLAYOFF GAME
AGAINST THE 49ERS. (JERRY PINKUS)

202

that he was the first NFL head coach to ever have two QBs on the same team—Phil Simms and Jeff Hostetler—who had won Super Bowls. Most Giants fans felt Simms would get the nod, mainly because he had been the starter before going down with an injury the year before. But at the end of preseason, Handley picked Hostetler.

Hoss led the Giants to an opening game victory over the 49ers, and the team built a 7-5 record over 12 contests. But the Giants lost three of their last four games to finish out of the playoffs at 8-8. Rodney Hampton rushed for over 1,000 yards, and Simms, who had filled in when Hostetler went down with an injury late in the year, set his 15th all-time club record when he broke Charlie Conerly's mark for touchdown passes in a career.

To be sure, more had been expected of the Giants the year after their second Super Bowl victory. But to many in the organization, the fans and media had been unnecessarily hard on the team. "I didn't think our year was that horrendous," George Young remarks. "Teams struggle after Super Bowls, and we had a late change of head coaches. But the way some people talked about it, you would have thought we went 0-16."

In an effort to improve on his first

THE DAY BEFORE HIS LAST GAME, LT WAS PREPARING FOR LIFE AFTER FOOTBALL; HERE HE IS TALKING WITH HIS AGENT ABOUT A POSSIBLE ACTING ROLE IN A MOVIE. (JERRY PINKUS)

year at the helm, Handley reshuffled his coaching staff in the offseason. One of his hires was Rod Rust, a longtime NFL assistant who planned to implement a new "read and react" defense with the Giants. George Young was also busy, picking up Derek Brown, Phillipi Sparks, Aaron Pierce, Keith Hamilton, Stacy Dillard and Kent Graham in the regular college draft and adding quarterback Dave Brown from Duke in the supplemental draft three months later.

Jeff Hostetler entered training camp in the summer of 1992 as the number one QB, but he went down with an injury, and when the season opened Phil Simms was running the offense. Simms played well, and early in the year became only the 14th quarterback in NFL history to pass for over 30,000 yards. But he hurt his elbow in the fourth game and was out for the rest of the season. Hoss took over again, but soon after he suffered a severe concussion, and the quarterbacking duties were left to rookies Kent Graham and Dave Brown. In addition, Lawrence Taylor ruptured his Achilles tendon during a week nine win over Green Bay and did not play another game that year.

Not surprisingly, the Giants struggled as a result, and after starting off 5-4, dropped six of their last seven games to finish 6-10. It was a tough year for

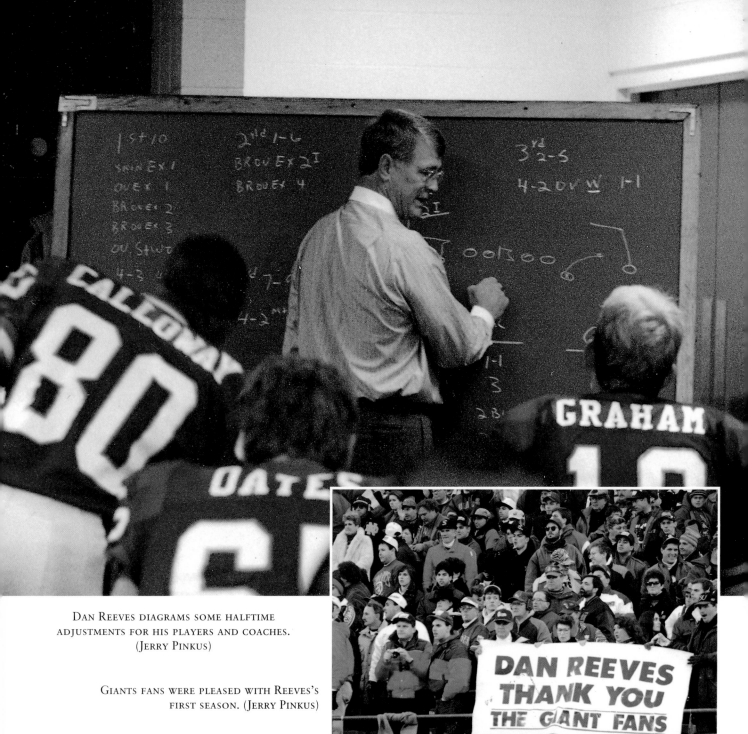

DAN REEVES DIAGRAMS SOME HALFTIME
ADJUSTMENTS FOR HIS PLAYERS AND COACHES.
(JERRY PINKUS)

GIANTS FANS WERE PLEASED WITH REEVES'S
FIRST SEASON. (JERRY PINKUS)

"Don't ever tell Dan Reeves he can't do something in or out of football. When he learned the parlor trick of blowing a dime off a table up into a paper cup inches away, he was challenged by a sportswriter to do it with a nickel. When he did it with a nickel, he was challenged to do it with a quarter. But he couldn't. The quarter was too heavy."
"Hours later, Reeves beckoned the sportswriter.
'Watch this,' he said, then blew a quarter into the cup.

Dave Anderson, from a column in the *New York Times*.

Handley. He had come under criticism for selecting Hostetler over Simms the season before, and later that year alienated several members of the media when he stalked out of a news conference. His relations with the press only got worse in 1992, and many observers felt he lost control of his players, some of whom openly revolted over Rod Rust's new defense and challenged the way Handley ran the team. George Young had stuck by Handley during his first year as head coach, but three days after the 1992 season ended, he let him go.

Once again, Young had to find a new head coach. He spoke first with Tom Coughlin, who had worked as an assistant coach on Bill Parcells' staff for three years before becoming head coach at Boston College. And then he met with Dallas Cowboys defensive coordinator Dave Wannstedt, who was also being wooed by the Chicago Bears. A third candidate surfaced unexpectedly when Dan Reeves, who had been fired by the Denver Broncos at the end of the 1992 season, put in a call to the Giants general manager and said he'd like to be considered as well.

"I had read that the Giants were interviewing different people, and there were some comments in the papers suggesting they weren't interested in

PHIL SIMMS WAS ONE OF ONLY A HANDFUL OF NFL QUARTERBACKS WHO STARTED EVERY ONE OF HIS TEAM'S GAMES IN 1993. (JERRY PINKUS)

205

and the New England Patriots, courted Simms, but he decided to stay with the Giants and signed a two-year, $5 million contract. Shortly afterwards, Hoss hooked up with the Los Angeles Raiders and inked a multi-year deal with them.

Hoss was not the only Giants player to seek greener pastures that offseason. Carl Banks moved to the Redskins, and receiver Mark Ingram joined the Miami Dolphins. But Young and Reeves were able to fill those gaps, and then some, by adding receivers Mike Sherrard and

DEFENSIVE END KEITH HAMILTON, SACKING DALLAS COWBOYS QB TROY AIKMAN, IS AN UP-AND-COMING STAR. (JERRY PINKUS)

FREE AGENT RECEIVER CHRIS CALLOWAY BECAME A FAVORITE TARGET OF PHIL SIMMS. (JERRY PINKUS)

me because I'd want the same sort of control over personnel decisions that I had had in Denver," Reeves says. "Some New York area reporters called me and asked if that was true, and I said no. Then Frank Gifford phoned and suggested that I give George a call and tell him that myself."

Reeves followed Gifford's advice and spoke to Young on the telephone. George must have liked what he heard, for two weeks later he flew out to Denver and offered Reeves the job.

The Giants' new head coach took charge right away. His first move was to decide on a quarterback because he did not want the controversy over who would start to continue. After mulling it over for a couple of weeks, he told Phil Simms that the job was his and suggested that Jeff Hostetler seek employment elsewhere.

Reeves had come on board at the beginning of a brave new world for pro football as players were able to become true free agents for the first time. Several teams, including the Washington Redskins

Mark Jackson and linebackers Michael Brooks and Carlton Bailey. They also signed Lawrence Taylor, who had come back strong from his Achilles injury, to a two-year deal similar to the one Simms had negotiated and picked up promising rookies Michael Strahan, Marcus Buckley and Jesse Armstead in the college draft.

It didn't take long for the players to discover that Reeves wouldn't put up with the sort of dissent and controversy that had been so much a part of the Handley years. The first sign of that came during the three-day May mini-camp. As had been his practice for most of his time with the Giants, Lawrence Taylor did not attend the camp, opting instead to play golf in a Kansas City charity event. Reeves was not pleased. "I thought Lawrence would be here," the coach said at the time. "I've heard what his feelings have been in the past, but

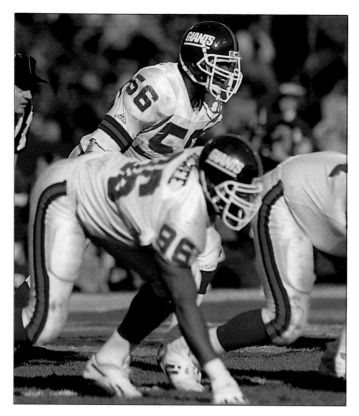

At 6'3, 243 lbs., Lawrence Taylor was a defensive end when he came out of the University of North Carolina in 1981; the Giants switched him to linebacker in his first training camp. (Jerry Pinkus)

this is the future now. So if he wants to be a part of it, I want to sit down and talk to him. To help us from a team standpoint, he certainly needs to be here and to be physically ready to go. I don't know if anybody has ever rehabbed an Achilles on the golf course."

LT got the message and arrived on the last day of camp to meet with Reeves. "There's no problem,"

Dan Reeves talks to LT after the perennial All-Pro played his last game. (Jerry Pinkus)

Taylor said. "It's just one of those classic cases of miscommunication. Nobody ever asked me to come. Reeves assumed that when he said mini-camp, he meant everybody. I assumed that when you say mini-camp, you ain't talking to me."

"Reeves said some things that kind of got me upset," the linebacker continued. "The old LT would have said, 'To hell with it.' But I thought it was important to defuse everything around here. That's why I came over. Now we're on the same page."

Reeves made sure the Giants stayed on the same page as training camp opened and they began

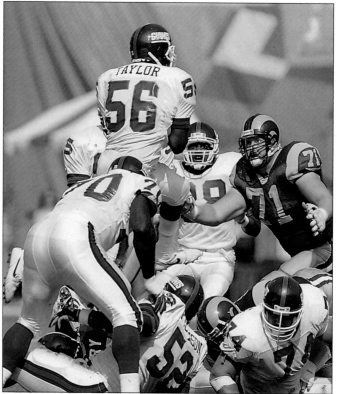

LT intercepts a pass against the Rams in 1992. (Jerry Pinkus)

preparing for the regular season. When nose tackle Erik Howard complained about a lack of playing time in an exhibition game, Reeves lashed back. "I won't have anybody...on the football team if they are more concerned with their own individual selves," he said. "I wasn't here in the past. If they want to make the team, it's on what I've seen since I've been here. The guys have to do it in practice and the game."

One player who apparently didn't do it anywhere for Reeves was linebacker Pepper Johnson, who was a surprise cut at the end of preseason. Johnson had been an integral part of the Giants'

PART-OWNER
BOB TISCH
AND LT GET
TOGETHER
BEFORE A
1993 GAME.
(JERRY PINKUS)

"I remember when Bob Tisch bought his share of the team, he told me that he was looking for ten years of fun. I said he'd have to stay in the game for 30 years if he wanted ten years of fun. And so far, that's proved true, because Bob's had fun one out of his first three years here."

Wellington Mara

A BEMUSED LT GETS READY FOR A GAME.
PERHAPS HE WAS THINKING OF A
QUARTERBACK SACK. (JERRY PINKUS)

JOHN MADDEN MAKES A POINT DURING PRACTICE BEFORE
THE 49ERS PLAYOFF GAME WHILE WELLINGTON MARA AND
PAT SUMMERALL LOOK ON. (JERRY PINKUS)

MANY THOUGHT THAT LAWRENCE TAYLOR'S CAREER WAS OVER WHEN HE TORE HIS ACHILLES TENDON IN THE MIDDLE OF THE 1992 SEASON; BUT THE SUPERSTAR LINEBACKER CAME BACK TO ENJOY ONE MORE SEASON IN THE SUN. (JERRY PINKUS)

defense the past few seasons, but he was also openly critical about some of the changes Reeves was implementing and had derisively referred to the Giants, which had added several former coaches and players from Reeves' former team in Denver, as the "New Jersey Broncos." Says Reeves: "I was making a conscious effort to put together the best possible team, and attitude is an essential part of that. No one is bigger than the team, no one is more important, and there were some around here who felt they were. I wanted guys with the right physical make-up and the right attitude."

It seems Reeves found what he was looking for. The Giants jumped out to a 3-0 start and went on to compile an 11-5 record. They were in the running for the Eastern Division title up until the last game of the season, but fell to Dallas 16-13 in a thrilling contest at the Meadowlands. They beat the Vikings at Giants Stadium 17-13 in one of the

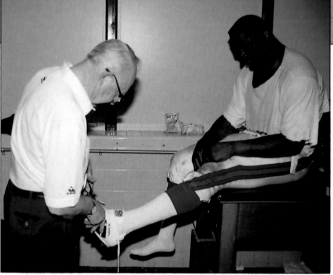

TRAINER JOHNNY JOHNSON, WHO HAS BEEN WITH THE TEAM SINCE THE MID-1950S, TAPES LT FOR THE LAST TIME IN SAN FRANCISCO, 1993. (JERRY PINKUS)

wildcard games the following week, but then got thumped by the 49ers in San Francisco 44-3.

It was a tough way to end what had otherwise been a terrific season. Rodney Hampton had gained over 1,000 yards for the third year in a row. Simms stayed healthy the entire season and completed 61.8 percent of his passes to earn a spot on the Pro Bowl team. Dan Reeves was named Coach

of the Year and George Young was honored as NFL Executive of the Year for the fourth time. The only downer was that Lawrence Taylor, who had returned from his Achilles injury to play a solid season, decided to retire after 13 brilliant years.

The Giants front office didn't have much time to savor Reeves' first year as head coach because the new rules governing free agency—and the introduction of a salary cap—threatened to break the team apart. They had 15 unrestricted free agents, 11 restricted free agents and very little financial room to work with under the salary cap.

The team began negotiating with several of those players as soon as the 1993 season had ended. But much as they feared, the Giants could not compete with the clubs that had more room under the cap, and they began to lose key

AGELESS O.J. ANDERSON RUSHED FOR OVER 1,000 YARDS IN 1989 AND WAS NAMED SUPER BOWL MVP THE FOLLOWING YEAR. HERE HE TAKES A HANDOFF FROM PHIL SIMMS IN A GAME AGAINST THE REDSKINS. (JERRY PINKUS)

BILL PARCELLS CALLED HIS 1990 SQUAD THE MOST UNDERESTIMATED EVER. (JERRY PINKUS)

211

the GIANTS are
AMERICA'S [FLAG] TEAM
the RED, WHITE & BLUE

WHO'S AMERICA'S TEAM?
(JERRY PINKUS)

GIANTS FANS HAVE BEEN COMING FOR YEARS.
(JERRY PINKUS)

NO QUARTERBACK HUNG IN THE POCKET BETTER THAN PHIL SIMMS. (JERRY PINKUS)

SIMMS TALKING TO ANOTHER PRETTY GOOD QUARTERBACK, DAN MARINO OF THE MIAMI DOLPHINS. (JERRY PINKUS)

MARK COLLINS STRETCHING BEFORE A GAME. (JERRY PINKUS)

Reeves explains. "We needed some money to sign players, and if we didn't have the $2.5 million that was earmarked for Phil, I don't know where we would have come up with it." But money was only one of the reasons for turning loose the greatest quarterback the franchise ever had. "We were also looking at Phil's age and the shoulder surgery he's coming off of," Reeves adds. "It would have been a gamble whether he would have been able to come back from that. I didn't like having to make the decision, I would have loved it if we could have gone some other way. But that was what we had to do."

No one in the Giants organization took Simms' release harder than Wellington Mara. The day the decision was announced, the longtime Giants owner appeared shaken and near tears when he spoke to members of the news media who had gathered for a press conference at the

RODNEY HAMPTON IS THE ONLY GIANTS BACK
TO RUSH FOR MORE THAN 1,000 YARDS
THREE CONSECUTIVE YEARS. (JERRY PINKUS)

people. Bob Kratch and safety Myron Guyton went to the New England Patriots. Cornerback Mark Collins signed with the Kansas City Chiefs. Running back Lewis Tillman moved to the Chicago Bears. Guard Eric Moore cut a deal with the Cincinnati Bengals. And safety Greg Jackson joined the Philadelphia Eagles.

But the biggest loss of all came in June when the Giants released Phil Simms. "That never would have happened under the old system," Dan

Meadowlands. In an unusual move for him, Mara read from a prepared statement. "I apologize for having something written out," he said. "I don't usually do that. There are some questions that need to be answered, and I want to answer them before they are asked. I am not sure I can control my emotions so I have things written out."

"It goes without saying that this is a day of

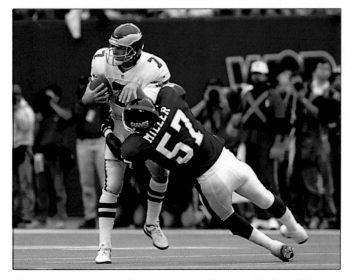

LINEBACKER COREY MILLER, SACKING EAGLES QB KEN O'BRIEN
IN A 1993 CONTEST, IS A RISING STAR. (JERRY PINKUS)

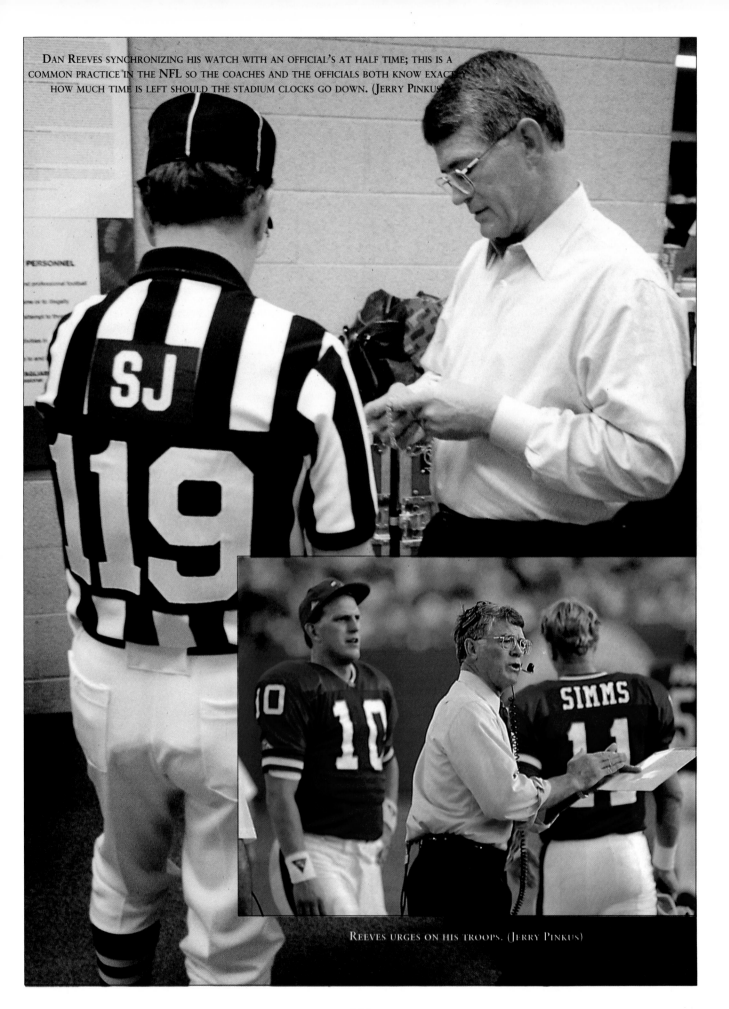

DAN REEVES SYNCHRONIZING HIS WATCH WITH AN OFFICIAL'S AT HALF TIME; THIS IS A COMMON PRACTICE IN THE NFL SO THE COACHES AND THE OFFICIALS BOTH KNOW EXACTLY HOW MUCH TIME IS LEFT SHOULD THE STADIUM CLOCKS GO DOWN. (JERRY PINKUS)

REEVES URGES ON HIS TROOPS. (JERRY PINKUS)

215

DAVE BROWN GOT THE NOD TO SUC-
CEED PHIL SIMMS AS THE GIANTS'
STARTING QUARTERBACK IN 1994.
(JERRY PINKUS)

(INSET) KENT GRAHAM IS BACKING
HIM UP. (JERRY PINKUS)

RAY HANDLEY
WAS THINKING
ABOUT GOING
TO LAW SCHOOL
WHEN GEORGE
YOUNG TAPPED
HIM TO SUCCEED
BILL PARCELLS.
(JERRY PINKUS)

SECOND TIME'S THE CHARM;
PASSED OVER BY THE GIANTS IN
1979, REEVES REPLACED
RAY HANDLEY AFTER
THE 1992 SEASON.
(JERRY PINKUS)

RODNEY HAMPTON STRETCHES FOR A TOUCHDOWN AGAINST THE COLTS. (JERRY PINKUS)

BILL PARCELLS ANNOUNCES HIS RESIGNATION FROM THE
GIANTS. HE WON 85 GAMES AND TWO NFL TITLES IN HIS
EIGHT YEARS WITH THE TEAM. (JERRY PINKUS)

RAY HANDLEY NEVER HAD AN EASY TIME DEALING WITH
THE NEW YORK AREA PRESS. (JERRY PINKUS)

ANOTHER PRODUCTIVE FREE AGENT SIGNEE, MICHAEL BROOKS, PLAYED IN DENVER WITH DAN REEVES BEFORE COMING TO THE GIANTS IN 1993. (JERRY PINKUS)

tions about how the team will perform with a green quarterback directing the offense. And no one is really sure how the franchise will react to the loss of so many good players to free agency. But Wellington Mara isn't bothered by all the uncertainty. In fact, he's excited about the future.

"The NFL is as stable as it has been in a long time," he says. "We have labor peace until the year 2000, we have a new television contract, and we've been getting glowing reports about the prospects of satellite TV and overseas growth. Sure, the changes in free agency and the salary cap are making it tough on teams like ours. But our ownership remains strong, we have a good mix of young and veteran players, and with George Young and Dan Reeves taking care of the football operations, I believe this club will thrive for many seasons to come."

Get ready for another 70 years of championship Giants football.

almost overwhelming sadness for me and my family," Mara continued. "I think you need to understand the relationship that I have with George Young and that I had with Andy Robustelli. Except for one or two exceptions, George has the ultimate decision-making authority on personnel on football matters and on our team. Whenever I have an opinion, and I have lots of opinions, I convey them to George. He accords it the weight that he think it merits, and he makes his decision. That decision becomes the decision of the Giants, and there is no further discussion on the matter. In this particular case, I told George that I disagreed with him. He considered my position, and he made his decision. He made it for what he sees as for the best interest of the Giants. I might say that on the few occasions in the past where George and I have differed, his track record is a lot better than mine. So that is the Giants' decision. I accept it. I support it. It is a fact of life. We will go on from here."

The Giants opened the 1994 season with young Dave Brown in Simms' old job and lots of ques-

FREE AGENT ACQUISITION CARLTON BAILEY PLAYED BRILLIANTLY IN 1993, HIS FIRST SEASON WITH THE GIANTS. (JERRY PINKUS)

RETIRED GIANTS NUMBERS

1	Ray Flaherty	End-Assistant Coach (1928-1935)
7	Mel Hein	Center-Linebacker (1931 -1945)
14	Y.A. Tittle	Quarterback (1961 -1964)
32	Al Blozis	Tackle (1942-1944)
40	Joe Morrison	End-Halfback (1959-1972)
42	Charlie Conerly	Quarterback (1948-1961)
50	Ken Strong	Fullback-Kicker (1933-1935,1939-1947)
56	Lawrence Taylor	Linebacker (1981-1993)

MEMBERS OF THE GIANTS IN THE PRO FOOTBALL HALL OF FAME

TIM MARA
FOUNDER, PRESIDENT (1925-1959)
ELECTED IN 1963

MEL HEIN
CENTER (1931-1945)
ELECTED IN 1963

PETE HENRY
TACKLE (1927)
ELECTED IN 1963

CAL HUBBARD
TACKLE (1927-1928, 1936)
ELECTED IN 1963

JIM THORPE
HALFBACK (1925)
ELECTED IN 1963

JOE GUYON
HALFBACK (1927)
ELECTED IN 1966

ARNIE HERBER
QUARTERBACK (1944-1945)
ELECTED IN 1966

STEVE OWEN
HEAD COACH (1931-1953)
ELECTED IN 1966

KEN STRONG
HALFBACK (1933-1935, 1939-1947)
ELECTED IN 1967

EMLEN TUNNELL
DEFENSIVE BACK (1948-1958)
ELECTED IN 1967

HUGH McELHENNY
HALFBACK (1963)
ELECTED IN 1970

VINCE LOMBARDI
ASSISTANT COACH (1954-1958)
ELECTED IN 1971

ANDY ROBUSTELLI
DEFENSIVE END (1956-1964)
ELECTED IN 1971

Y.A. TITTLE
QUARTERBACK (1961-1964)
ELECTED IN 1971

ROOSEVELT BROWN
TACKLE (1953-1965)
ELECTED IN 1975

RAY FLAHERTY
END (1928-1935)
ELECTED IN 1976

FRANK GIFFORD
BACK-END (1952-1960, 1962-1964)
ELECTED IN 1977

TUFFY LEEMANS
RUNNING BACK (1936-1943)
ELECTED IN 1978

RED BADGRO
END (1927-1935)
ELECTED IN 1981

SAM HUFF
LINEBACKER (1956-1963)
ELECTED IN 1982

ARNIE WEINMEISTER
TACKLE (1950-1953)
ELECTED IN 1984

FRAN TARKENTON
QUARTERBACK (1967-1971)
ELECTED IN 1986

LARRY CSONKA
RUNNING BACK (1976-1978)
ELECTED IN 1987

DON MAYNARD
END (1958)
ELECTED IN 1987

TOM LANDRY
DEFENSIVE BACK (1950-1955)
ELECTED IN 1990

vs NFC EAST

Year	PHI	WAS	DAL	CARD	Home	Away	Overall
1970	1-1	2-0	1-1	2-0	4-0	2-2	6-2
1971	0-2	0-2	0-2	1-1	1-3	0-4	1-7
1972	2-0	0-2	1-1	2-0	2-2	3-1	5-3
1973	0-1-1	0-2	0-2	1-1	1-2-1	0-4	1-6-1
1974	0-2	0-2	1-1	0-2	0-4	1-3	1-7
1975	1-1	0-2	0-2	0-2	0-4	1-3	1-7
1976	0-2	1-1	0-2	0-2	1-3	0-4	1-7
1977	0-2	2-0	0-2	1-1	2-2	1-3	3-5
1978	0-2	1-1	0-2	1-1	2-2	0-4	2-6
1979	0-2	1-1	0-2	0-2	1-3	0-4	1-7
1980	0-2	0-2	1-1	1-1	1-3	1-3	2-6
1981	1-1	1-1	1-1	2-0	2-2	3-1	5-3
1982	2-0	0-2	0-0	0-1	1-1	1-2	2-3
1983	1-1	0-2	0-2	0-1-1	0-4	1-2-1	1-6-1
1984	1-1	1-1	2-0	1-1	4-0	1-3	5-3
1985	2-0	1-1	0-2	2-0	3-1	2-2	5-3
1986	2-0	2-0	1-1	2-0	4-0	3-1	7-1
1987	2-0	0-2	0-2	1-1	2-2	1-3	3-5
1988	0-2	2-0	2-0	1-1	3-1	2-2	5-3
1989	0-2	2-0	2-0	2-0	3-1	3-1	6-2
1990	1-1	2-0	2-0	2-0	4-0	3-1	7-1
1991	0-2	0-2	1-1	2-0	2-2	1-3	3-5
1992	0-2	1-1	0-2	1-1	1-3	1-3	2-6
1993	2-0	2-0	0-2	1-1	3-1	2-2	5-3
Totals	18-29-1	21-27	15-31	26-20-1	47-46-1	33-61-1	80-107-2

GIANTS TEAM RECORDS
GAME

OFFENSE

SCORING

MOST POINTS
62 vs. Philadelphia, Nov. 26, 1972
56 vs. Philadelphia, Oct. 15, 1933
55 at Baltimore, Nov. 19, 1950

MOST TOUCHDOWNS
8 vs. Philadelphia, Nov. 26, 1972
8 at Baltimore, Nov. 19, 1950
8 vs. Philadelphia, Oct. 15, 1933
7 vs. Green Bay, Dec. 20, 1986
7 vs. St. Louis, Dec. 7, 1969
7 vs. Washington, Oct. 28, 1962
7 vs. Washington, Nov. 5, 1961

MOST POINTS AFTER TOUCHDOWN
8 vs. Philadelphia, Nov. 26, 1972
8 vs. Philadelphia, Oct. 15, 1933
7 vs. Green Bay, Dec. 20, 1986
7 vs. St. Louis, Dec. 7, 1969
7 vs. Washington, Oct. 28, 1962
7 vs. Washington, Nov. 5, 1961
7 at Baltimore, Nov. 19, 1950
7 at Green Bay, Nov. 21, 1948
7 vs. Cleveland Rams, Nov. 16, 1941

MOST FIELD GOALS ATTEMPTED
6 at Minnesota, Nov. 16, 1986
6 at Washington, Dec. 17, 1983
6 at Seattle, Oct. 18, 1981
6 at Philadelphia, Nov. 25, 1973
6 vs. Philadelphia, Nov. 14, 1954
5 vs. Tampa Bay, Nov. 3, 1985
5 vs. Seattle, Dec. 11, 1983
5 at Philadelphia, Jan. 2, 1983
5 at Detroit, Nov. 17, 1974
5 vs. Chicago, Sept. 19, 1970
5 at Cleveland, Dec. 9, 1966
5 at St. Louis, Oct. 9, 1966
5 at Cleveland, Oct. 27, 1963
5 vs. Philadelphia, Nov. 18, 1962
5 vs. Dallas, Oct. 29, 1961

MOST FIELD GOALS
6 at Seattle, Oct. 18, 1981
5 at Minnesota, Nov. 16, 1986
5 vs. Tampa Bay, Nov. 3, 1985
5 vs. Washington, Dec. 17, 1983
4 13 times; Last time: at Chicago, Sept. 5, 1993

MOST SAFETIES
2 vs. Washington, Nov. 5, 1961
2 at Pittsburgh, Sept. 17, 1950

FIRST DOWNS

MOST FIRST DOWNS
34 at Cincinnati, Oct. 13, 1985
33 vs. St. Louis, Dec. 7, 1969
31 at Pittsburgh, Dec. 5, 1948

FEWEST FIRST DOWNS
0 at Washington, Sept. 27, 1942
0 at Green Bay, Oct. 1, 1933

MOST FIRST DOWNS RUSHING
19 at Baltimore, Nov. 19, 1950
18 at Philadelphia, Dec. 15, 1956

MOST FIRST DOWNS PASSING
29 at Cincinnati, Oct. 13, 1985
22 vs. St. Louis, Dec. 7, 1969
22 at Washington, Oct. 1, 1961
22 at Pittsburgh, Dec. 5, 1948

MOST FIRST DOWNS BY PENALTY
9 vs. Pittsburgh, Oct. 12, 1969
6 at Washington, Nov. 27, 1966
6 at Philadelphia, Oct. 5, 1957
5 at Dallas, Nov. 7, 1993
5 at Dallas, Nov. 26, 1992
5 vs. Philadelphia, Nov. 22, 1992
5 at Washington, Dec. 12, 1965

NET YARDS

MOST YARDS GAINED
625 vs. N.Y. Yankees, Dec. 3, 1950

RUSHING
602 vs. Washington, Oct. 28, 1962

MOST RUSHING ATTEMPTS
61 at Philadelphia, Oct. 3, 1937
59 vs. Philadelphia, Nov. 10, 1946

MOST YARDS RUSHING
423 at Baltimore, Nov. 19, 1950
377 vs. N.Y. Yankees, Dec. 3, 1950

MOST TOUCHDOWNS RUSHING
6 at Baltimore, Nov. 19, 1950
5 at Chicago Cardinals, Sept. 28, 1958
5 vs. Philadelphia, Oct. 15, 1933

PASSING

MOST PASSES ATTEMPTED
62 at Cincinnati, Oct. 13, 1985
53 at Pittsburgh, Dec. 5, 1948
52 vs. Seattle, Dec. 11, 1983
51 vs. San Diego, Oct. 2, 1983
51 at St. Louis, Dec. 26, 1982

MOST PASSES COMPLETED
40 at Cincinnati, Oct. 13, 1985
36 at Pittsburgh, Dec. 5, 1948
31 vs. San Diego, Oct. 2, 1983
30 at St. Louis, Dec. 13, 1987
30 vs. Philadelphia, Dec. 19, 1971
29 vs. Rams, Sept. 25, 1988
29 vs. Seattle, Dec. 11, 1983
29 at St. Louis, Dec. 26, 1982
28 at Dallas, Sept. 29, 1991
28 vs. New Orleans, Sept. 20, 1981
28 vs. New England, Sept. 22, 1974
28 at St. Louis, Oct. 28, 1973

MOST YARDS GAINED (NET) PASSING
505 vs. Washington, Oct. 28, 1962
443 at Cincinnati, Oct. 13, 1985
409 vs. Philadelphia, Sept. 2, 1984
395 vs. San Diego, Oct. 2, 1984
384 at San Francisco, Dec. 1, 1986
372 vs. Philadelphia, Dec. 19, 1971

MOST TOUCHDOWNS PASSING
7 vs. Washington, Oct. 28, 1962
6 vs. Dallas, Dec. 16, 1962

MOST PASSES HAD INTERCEPTED
7 at Pittsburgh, Nov. 30, 1952
5 at New Orleans, Nov. 22, 1987
5 at Washington, Dec. 5, 1971
5 at Washington, Nov. 27, 1966
5 vs. St. Louis, Oct. 30, 1960

PUNTING

MOST PUNTS
14 at Detroit, Nov. 7, 1943
11 at Atlanta, Oct. 25, 1981
11 at Washington, Sept. 13, 1981
11 at St. Louis, Oct. 8, 1961
11 vs. Cleveland, Nov. 18, 1951
11 vs. Philadelphia, Nov. 26, 1950

MOST YARDS PUNTING
583 at Detroit, Nov. 7, 1943
511 at Washington, Sept. 13, 1981

PUNT RETURNS

MOST PUNT RETURNS
9 at Philadelphia, Nov. 20, 1983
9 vs. Philadelphia, Dec. 11, 1982
9 at Philadelphia, Dec. 15, 1956
9 vs. N.Y. Yankees, Dec. 3, 1950
8 at Dallas, Nov. 4, 1984
8 at Washington, Sept. 13, 1981
8 vs. Green Bay, Nov. 1, 1959

MOST FAIR CATCHES
6 vs. Minnesota, Oct. 31, 1971
5 vs. Philadelphia, Nov. 20, 1988
4 at Pittsburgh, Oct. 14, 1991
4 at Philadelphia, Sept. 29, 1985
4 at Detroit, Sept. 28, 1969
4 at Minnesota, Oct. 9, 1965
4 at Cleveland, Oct. 27, 1963
4 at Pittsburgh, Sept. 22, 1963
4 vs. Washington, Oct. 28, 1962

MOST YARDS GAINED
149 vs. Chicago Cardinals, Oct. 14, 1951
143 vs. Philadelphia, Dec. 11, 1982
114 vs. Raiders, Dec. 24, 1989

KICKOFF RETURNS

MOST KICKOFF RETURNS
12 at Washington, Nov. 27, 1966
10 vs. Chicago Cardinals, Oct. 17, 1948

MOST YARDS GAINED
274 at Washington, Nov. 27, 1966
236 at Cleveland, Dec. 4, 1966

FUMBLES

MOST FUMBLES
8 vs. San Francisco, Dec. 1, 1957
7 vs. Philadelphia, Oct. 18, 1964
7 vs. Washington, Nov. 5, 1950

MOST FUMBLES RECOVERED
5 vs. Philadelphia, Oct. 18, 1964
5 vs. Washington, Nov. 5, 1950
5 at Philadelphia, Nov. 3, 1946
5 vs. Pittsburgh, Oct. 21, 1945

MOST OPPONENTS' FUMBLES RECOVERED
6 at Pittsburgh, Sept. 17, 1950
5 at Dallas, Oct. 11, 1971
4 vs. Pittsburgh, Nov. 22, 1964
4 at Chicago Cardinals, Nov. 22, 1959
4 at Chicago Cardinals, Sept. 28, 1958
4 vs. Chicago Cardinals, Oct. 7, 1956
4 at Chicago Cardinals, Nov. 2, 1952

PENALTIES

MOST PENALTIES
17 at Washington, Oct. 9, 1949
17 vs. Boston, Nov. 28, 1948
15 at Buffalo, Oct. 18, 1987
12 at Rams, Nov. 24, 1968
12 vs. Chicago Cardinals, Nov. 10, 1957

MOST YARDS PENALIZED
177 at Washington, Oct. 9, 1949
145 at Buffalo, Oct. 18, 1987
127 vs. Washington, Oct. 28, 1962

DEFENSE

SCORING

FEWEST POINTS ALLOWED
0, Many Games; Last: vs. Detroit, Nov. 18, 1990 (20-0)

MOST POINTS ALLOWED
72 at Washington, Nov. 27, 1966
63 at Pittsburgh, Nov. 30, 1952
63 vs. Chicago Cardinals, Oct. 17, 1948

MOST TOUCHDOWNS ALLOWED
10 at Washington, Nov. 27, 1966
9 at Pittsburgh, Nov. 30, 1952
9 vs. Chicago Cardinals, Oct. 17, 1948

MOST POINTS AFTER TOUCHDOWN, OPPONENT
9 vs. Washington, Nov. 27, 1966
9 vs. Pittsburgh, Nov. 30, 1952
9 vs. Chicago Cardinals, Oct. 17, 1948

MOST FIELD GOALS, OPPONENT
4 vs. Philadelphia, Dec. 8, 1991
4 vs. Rams, Sept. 8, 1991
4 vs. Phoenix, Oct. 21, 1990
4 vs. Kansas City, Dec. 11, 1988
4 at New Orleans, Nov. 27, 1988
4 at Dallas, Nov. 2, 1987
4 vs. Rams, Nov. 10, 1985
4 at Green Bay, Nov. 8, 1981
4 vs. Jets, Nov. 1, 1981
4 at Cleveland, Sept. 30, 1973
4 vs. Washington, Nov. 15, 1970
4 vs. New Orleans, Nov. 16, 1969

FIRST DOWNS

FEWEST FIRST DOWNS ALLOWED
1 at Pittsburgh, Sept. 20, 1933
2 at Philadelphia, Oct. 3, 1937
2 vs. Brooklyn, Oct. 14, 1934

MOST FIRST DOWNS ALLOWED
38 at Rams, Nov. 13, 1966
29 vs. St. Louis, Nov. 4, 1962

MOST FIRST DOWNS ALLOWED, RUSHING
19 at Buffalo, Nov. 26, 1978
19 vs. Green Bay, Oct. 22, 1967
16 at Rams, Nov. 13, 1966
16 vs. Cleveland, Oct. 2, 1966
16 at Green Bay, Dec. 3, 1961
16 vs. Brooklyn, Dec. 7, 1941

MOST FIRST DOWNS ALLOWED, PASSING
20 at Rams, Nov. 13, 1966
20 at San Francisco, Sept. 30, 1956
17 at Dallas, Nov. 10, 1968
17 at Philadelphia, Sept. 23, 1962

NET YARDS ALLOWED

FEWEST YARDS ALLOWED
48 at Brooklyn, Oct. 17, 1943
62 at Pittsburgh, Sept. 20, 1933

MOST YARDS ALLOWED
682 vs. Chicago Cardinals, Nov. 14, 1943
579 vs. Chicago Cardinals, Oct. 17, 1948

RUSHING

FEWEST ATTEMPTS, OPPONENT
7 at Houston, Dec. 8, 1985
9 at Philadelphia, Nov. 20, 1983
11 vs. Miami, Sept. 23, 1990
11 at Dallas, Sept. 16, 1990
12 at New Orleans, Dec. 12, 1993
12 at Washington, Oct. 10, 1993
13 vs. San Diego, Sept. 14, 1986
13 vs. Philadelphia, Nov. 26, 1967
13 at Philadelphia, Sept. 23, 1962
14 vs. Philadelphia, Dec. 11, 1982
14 at Seattle, Oct. 18, 1981
14 at Cleveland, Oct. 27, 1963

MOST ATTEMPTS, OPPONENT
60 at Washington, Dec. 9, 1945
58 at Washington, Nov. 18, 1956
58 at Philadelphia, Oct. 5, 1947

FEWEST YARDS ALLOWED
-24 at Brooklyn, Oct. 17, 1943
-1 vs. Chicago Cardinals, Oct. 18, 1953

MOST YARDS ALLOWED
396 at Boston (Redskins), Oct. 8, 1933
366 vs. Buffalo, Nov. 26, 1978

MOST RUSHING TOUCHDOWNS ALLOWED
5 at Buffalo, Nov. 26, 1978
5 vs. Green Bay, Oct. 22, 1967

PASSING

FEWEST ATTEMPTS, OPPONENT
3 at Detroit, Sept. 23, 1934
4 vs. Brooklyn, Dec. 7, 1941

MOST ATTEMPTS, OPPONENT
59 vs. Chicago Bears, Oct. 23, 1949
57 at Philadelphia, Sept. 23, 1962

FEWEST COMPLETIONS ALLOWED
0 at Washington, Dec. 11, 1960
1, many games; Last: vs. Brooklyn, Dec. 6, 1942

MOST COMPLETIONS ALLOWED
34 vs. Chicago Bears, Oct. 23, 1949
33 at Philadelphia, Sept. 23, 1962

FEWEST YARDS ALLOWED (NET)
0 at Chicago Cardinals, Nov. 22, 1959
6 at Washington, Dec. 11, 1960

MOST YARDS ALLOWED (NET)
488 vs. Chicago Bears, Nov. 14, 1943
460 at Philadelphia, Nov. 8, 1953

MOST TOUCHDOWNS ALLOWED
7 vs. Chicago Bears, Nov. 14, 1943
6 vs. Cleveland, Dec. 12, 1964

INTERCEPTIONS

MOST INTERCEPTIONS BY GIANTS
8 at N.Y. Yankees, Dec. 16, 1951
8 at Green Bay, Nov. 21, 1948
7 vs. Washington, Dec. 8, 1963

MOST YARDS, RETURNS
144 at Philadelphia, Sept. 13, 1941
138 at Dallas, Oct. 15, 1961

MOST RETURNS FOR TOUCHDOWN
2 vs. Washington, Dec. 8, 1963

GIANTS ALL-TIME LEADERS

(**BOLD** indicates active Giants)

TOP TEN RUSHERS
based on rushing yardage

Player	Years	Attempts	Yards	Avg	Lg	TDs
1. Joe Morris	1982-89	1,318	5,296	4.0	65t	48
2. Alex Webster	1955-64	1,196	4.638	3.9	71	39
3. Ron Johnson	1970-75	1,066	3,836	3.6	68	33
4. RODNEY HAMPTON	**1990-93**	**914**	**3,732**	**4.1**	**63t**	**31**
5. Frank Gifford	1952-60, 62-64	840	3,609	4.3	79	34
6. Doug Kotar	1974-81	900	3,378	3.8	53	20
7. Eddie Price	1950-55	846	3,292	3.9	74	23
8. Tuffy Leemans	1936-43	919	3,142	3.4	NA	20
9. Joe Morrison	1959-72	677	2,472	3.7	70	18
10.Rob Carpenter	1981-84	677	2,371	3.5	37	17

TOP TEN PASSERS
(Based on Passing Yardage)

Player	Years	Att.	Comp.	Yards	Pct.	TDs	Ints
1. Phil Simms	1979-93	4,647	2,576	33,462	55.4	199	157
2. Charlie Conerly	1948-61	2,833	1,418	19,488	50.0	173	167
3. Fran Tarkenton	1967-71	1,898	1,051	13,905	55.4	103	72
4. Y.A. Tittle	1961-64	1,308	731	10,439	55.9	96	68
5. Scott Brunner	1980-83	986	482	6,121	48.9	28	48
6. Craig Morton	1974-76	884	461	5,734	52.1	29	49
7. Jeff Hostetler	1984-92	632	365	4,409	57.8	20	12
8. Norm Snead	1972-74,76	602	349	4,029	57.9	24	38
9. Joe Pisarcik	1977-79	650	289	3,979	44.5	18	43
10.Ed Danowski	1934-41	581	282	3,408	48.5	33	38

TOP TEN RECEIVERS
Based on Number of Receptions

Player	Years	No.	Yards	Avg	Lg	TD
1. Joe Morrison	1959-72	395	4,993	12.6	70	47
2. Frank Gifford	1952-60, 62-64	367	5,434	14.8	77	43
3. Bob Tucker	1970-77	327	4,376	13.4	63	22
4. Kyle Rote	1951-61	300	4,795	15.9	75	48
5. Mark Bavaro	1985-90	266	3,722	13.9	61	28
6. Aaron Thomas	1962-70	247	4,253	17.2	71	35
7. Earnest Gray	1979-84	243	3,768	15.5	62	27
8. Alex Webster	1955-64	240	2,679	11.2	59	17
9. Del Shofner	1961-67	239	4,315	18.1	70	35
10. Lionel Manuel	1984-90	232	3,941	16.9	53	23

TOP TEN SCORERS
Based on Total Points

Player	Years	Touchdowns Tot	Rush	Rec	Ret	Kicking FGs	PATs	Total Points
1. Pete Gogolak	1966-74	0	0	0	0	126	268	646
2. Frank Gifford	1952-60, 62-64	78	34	43	1	2	10	484
3. Joe Danelo	1976-82	0	0	0	0	104	170	482
4. Joe Morrison	1959-72	65	18	47	0	0	0	390
5. Raul Allegre	1986-91	0	0	0	0	77	109	340
6. Alex Webster	1955-64	56	39	17	0	0	0	336
7. Ken Strong	1933-35, 39, 44-47	13	12	1	0	35	141	324
8. Pat Summerall	1958-61	0	0	0	0	59	136	313
9. Kyle Rote	1951-61	52	4	48	0	0	0	312
10.Ward Cuff	1937-45	19	7	12	0	31	98	305

GIANTS HEAD COACHES RECORDS

Regular Season

Coach	Seasons	Years	W	L	T	Pct
Robert Folwell	1925	1	8	4	0	.667
Joseph Alexander	1926	1	8	4	1	.667
Earl Potteiger	1927-28	2	15	8	3	.635
LeRoy Andrews*	1929-30	2	24	5	1	.817
Benny Friedman	1930	1	2	0	0	1.000
Steve Owen	1930-53	23	153	100	17	.598
Jim Lee Howell	1954-60	7	53	27	4	.655
Allie Sherman	1961-68	8	57	51	4	.527
Alex Webster	1969-73	5	29	40	1	.421
Bill Arnsparger**	1974-76	3	7	28	0	.200
John McVay	1976-78	3	14	23	0	.378
Ray Perkins	1979-82	4	23	34	0	.404
Bill Parcells	1983-90	8	77	49	1	.610
Ray Handley	1991-92	2	14	18	0	.438
DAN REEVES	**1993**	**1**	**11**	**5**	**0**	**.688**

*Andrews was replaced by Friedman and Owen after 15 games in 1930.

**Arnsparger was replaced by McVay after first seven games in 1976.

Postseason

Coach	Games	Seasons	W	L	T	Pct
Steve Owen	10	1931-53	2	8	0	.200
Jim Lee Howell	4	1954-60	2	2	0	.500
Allie Sherman	3	1961-68	0	3	0	.000
Ray Perkins	2	1979-82	1	1	0	.500
Bill Parcells	11	1983-90	8	3	0	.727
DAN REEVES	**2**	**1993**	**1**	**1**	**0**	**.500**

Preseason

Coach	Games	Seasons	W	L	T	Pct
Jim Lee Howell	5	1954-60	1	3	1	.300
Allie Sherman	37	1961-68	14	22	1	.392
Alex Webster	29	1969-73	11	16	2	.414
Bill Arnsparger	18	1974-76	10	8	0	.555
John McVay	10	1976-78	3	7	0	.300
Ray Perkins	16	1979-82	5	11	0	.313
Bill Parcells	33	1983-90	27	6	0	.818
Ray Handley	8	1991-92	4	4	0	.500
DAN REEVES	**4**	**1993**	**2**	**2**	**0**	**.500**

Opening Day Games

Coach	Games	Seasons	W	L	T	Pct
Robert Folwell	1	1925	0	1	0	.000
Joseph Alexander	1	1926	1	0	0	1.000
Earl Potteiger	2	1927-28	2	0	0	1.000
LeRoy Andrews	2	1929-30	1	0	1	.750
Steve Owen	23	1931-53	13	7	3	.630
Jim Lee Howell	7	1954-60	5	2	0	.714
Allie Sherman	8	1961-68	3	4	1	.438
Alex Webster	5	1969-73	3	2	0	.600
Bill Arnsparger	3	1974-76	1	2	0	.333
John McVay	2	1976-78	2	0	0	1.000
Ray Perkins	4	1979-82	1	3	0	.250
Bill Parcells	8	1983-90	5	3	0	.625
Ray Handley	2	1991-92	1	1	0	.500
DAN REEVES	**1**	**1993**	**1**	**0**	**0**	**1.000**

TOP TEN INTERCEPTORS
Based on Number of Interceptions

Player	Years	No	Ret. Yds	Avg	TD
1. Emlen Tunnell	1949-58	74	1240	16.7	4
2. Jim Patton	1955-66	52	712	13.7	2
3. Carl Lockhart	1965-75	41	475	11.6	3
4. Dick Lynch	1959-66	35	568	16.2	4
Willie Williams	1965, 67-73	35	462	13.2	0
6. Tom Landry	1950-55	31	360	11.6	3
7. Terry Kinard	1983-89	27	574	21.3	2
8. Terry Jackson	1978-83	24	282	11.8	2
9. Frank Reagan	1941, 46-48	20	376	18.8	0
Howard Livingston	1944-47	20	375	18.8	1

1951
- B — John Cannady (1)
- QB — Charlie Connerly (1)
- T — Al De Rogatis (1)
- RB — Gene Roberts (1)
- DB — Em Tunnell (1)
- DB — Otto Schnellbacher (1)
- T — Arnie Weinmeister (1)

1952
- G — Jon Baker (1)
- QB — Charlie Conerly (2)
- T — Dewitt Coulter (1)
- T — Al De Rogatis (2)
- RB — Eddie Price (1)
- DB — Otto Schnelbacher (2)
- DB — Em Tunnell (2)
- T — Arnie Weinmeister (2)

1953
- G — Jon Baker (2)
- B — John Cannady (2)
- T — Dewitt Coulter (2)
- B-E — Frank Gifford (1)
- RB — Eddie Price (2)
- DB — Em Tunnell (3)
- T — Arnie Weinmeister (3)

1954
- G — Bill Austin (1)
- B-E — Frank Gifford (2)
- E — Kyle Rote (1)
- LB — Bill Svoboda (1)
- DB — Em Tunnell (4)

1955
- B-E — Frank Gifford (3)
- DB — Tom Landry (1)
- E — Kyle Rote (2)
- G-T — Jack Stroud (1)
- DB — Em Tunnell (5)
- C — Ray Wietecha (1)

1956
- T — Rosey Brown (1)
- B-E — Frank Gifford (4)
- DE — Andy Robustelli (1)
- E — Kyle Rote (3)
- DB — Em Tunnell (6)

1957
- T — Rosey Brown (2)
- QB — Charlie Conerly (3)
- B-E — Frank Gifford (5)
- DT — Rosey Grier (1)
- E — Kyle Rote (4)
- DE — Andy Robustelli (2)
- G-T — Jack Stroud (2)
- DB — Em Tunnell (7)

1958
- T — Rosey Brown (3)
- B-E — Frank Gifford (6)
- LB — Sam Huff (1)
- E — Bob Schnelker (1)
- RB — Alex Webster (1)
- C — Ray Wietecha (2)

1959
- T — Rosey Brown (4)
- DB — Lindon Crow (1)
- B-E — Frank Gifford (7)
- LB — Sam Huff (2)
- DB — Jim Patton (1)
- DE — Andy Robustelli (3)
- E — Bob Schnelker (2)

1960
- T — Rosey Brown (5)
- DT — Rosey Grier (2)
- LB — Sam Huff (3)
- DB — Jim Patton (2)
- DE — Andy Robustelli (4)
- G-T — Jack Stroud (3)
- C — Ray Wietecha (3)

1961
- DB — Erich Barnes (1)
- T — Rosey Brown (6)
- LB — Sam Huff (4)
- DE — Jim Katcavage (1)
- DB — Jim Patton (3)
- DE — Andy Robustelli (5)
- E — Del Shofner (1)
- QB — Y.A. Tittle (1)
- RB — Alex Webster (2)

1962
- DB — Erich Barnes (2)
- T — Rosey Brown (7)
- G — Darrell Dess (1)
- DE — Jim Katcavage (2)
- E — Del Shofner (2)
- QB — Y.A. Tittle (2)
- DB — Jim Patton (4)
- C — Ray Wietecha (4)

1963
- DB — Erich Barnes (3)
- G — Darrell Dess (2)
- B-E — Frank Gifford (8)
- DE — Jim Katcavage (3)
- DT — John Lovetere (1)
- DB — Dick Lynch (1)
- E — Del Shofner (3)
- QB — Y.A. Tittle (3)

1964
- DB — Erich Barnes (4)
- T — Rosey Brown (8)
- E — Aaron Thomas (1)

1965
- T — Rosey Brown (9)
- RB — Tucker Frederickson (1)

1966
- DB — Carl Lockhart (1)

1967
- E — Homer Jones (1)
- RB — Ernie Koy (1)
- QB — Fran Tarkenton (1)

1968
- E — Homer Jones (2)
- C — Greg Larson (1)
- DB — Carl Lockhart (2)
- QB — Fran Tarkenton (2)

1969
- QB — Fran Tarkenton (3)
- DB — Willie Williams (1)

1970
- RB — Ron Johnson (1)
- QB — Fran Tarkenton (4)

1972
- DE — Jack Gregory (1)
- RB — Ron Johnson (2)
- QB — Norm Snead (1)

1976
- LB — Brad Van Pelt (1)

1977
- LB — Brad Van Pelt (2)

1978
- LB — Harry Carson (1)
- P — Dave Jennings (1)
- LB — Brad Van Pelt (3)

1979
- LB — Harry Carson (2)
- P — Dave Jennings (2)
- LB — Brad Van Pelt (4)

1980
- P — Dave Jennings (3)
- LB — Brad Van Pelt (4)

1981
- LB — Harry Carson (3)
- LB — Lawrence Taylor (1)

1982
- LB — Harry Carson (4)
- P — Dave Jennings (4)
- LB — Lawrence Taylor (2)

1983
- LB — Harry Carson (5)
- PK — Ali Haji-Shiekh (1)
- DB — Mark Haynes (2)
- LB — Lawrence Taylor (3)

(DB — Mark Haynes (1))

1984
- LB — Harry Carson (6)
- DB — Mark Haynes (3)
- LB — Lawrence Taylor (4)

1985
- LB — Harry Carson (7)
- DE — Leonard Marshall (1)
- RB — Joe Morris (1)
- QB — Phil Simms (1)
- LB — Lawrence Taylor (5)

1986
- TE — Mark Bavaro (1)
- T — Brad Benson (1)
- DT — Jim Burt (1)
- LB — Harry Carson (8)
- P — Sean Landeta (1)
- DE — Leonard Marshall (2)
- RB — Joe Morris (2)
- LB — Lawrence Taylor (6)

1987
- LB — Carl Banks (1)
- TE — Mark Bavaro (2)
- LB — Harry Carson (9)
- LB — Lawrence Taylor (7)

1988
- DB — Terry Kinard (1)
- LB — Lawrence Taylor (8)

1989
- RB — David Meggett (1)
- LB — Lawrence Taylor (9)

1990
- DT — Erik Howard (1)
- LB — Pepper Johnson (1)
- P — Sean Landeta (2)
- C — Bart Oates (1)
- T — William Roberts (1)
- LB — Lawrence Taylor (10)
- DB — Reyna Thompson (1)

1991
- C — Bart Oates (2)

1992
- RB — Rodney Hampton (1)

1993
- RB — Rodney Hampton (2)
- T — John Elliott (1)
- C — Bart Oates (3)
- QB — Phil Simms (2)

GIANTS' ALL-NFL SELECTIONS, 1931-1992

- **1931** Morris Badgro (E); Denver Gibson (G)
- **1932** Ray Flanerty (E)
- **1933** Morris Badgro (E); Mel Hein (C); Harry Newman (QB)
- **1934** Denver Gibson (G); Mel Hein (C); Bill Morgan (T); Ken Strong (HB); Morris Badgro (E)
- **1935** Mel Hein (C); Bill Morgan (T); Ed Danowski (HB)
- **1936** Mel Hein (C); Tuffy Leemans (HB)
- **1937** Mel Hein (C)
- **1938** Mel Hein (C); Ed Danowski (HB); Ed Widseth (T)
- **1939** Tuffy Leemans (HB); Jim Poole (E); John Dell Isola (G); Mel Hein (C)
- **1940** Mel Hein (C)
- **1942** Bill Edwards (G)
- **1946** Jim White (T); Frank Filchock (HB)
- **1947** Len Younce (G)
- **1950** Arnie Weinmeister (DT)
- **1951** Arnie Weinmeister (DT); Dewitt Coulter (T); Eddie Price (HB); Al DeRogatis (DT); Jon Baker (G); Otto Schnelbacher (DB); Emlen Tunnell (DB)
- **1952** Eddie Price (HB); Arnie Weinmeister (DT); Emlen Tunnell (DB)
- **1953** Arnie Weinmeister (DT)
- **1954** Tom Landry (DB)
- **1955** Emlen Tunnell (DB); Bill Austin (G); Frank Gifford (HB)
- **1956** Emlen Tunnell (DB); Frank Gifford (HB); Roosevelt Brown (T); Andy Robustelli (DE); Roosevelt Grier (DT)
- **1957** Frank Gifford (HB); Roosevelt Brown (T); Andy Robustelli (DE)
- **1958** Roosevelt Brown (T); Andy Robustelli (DE); Ray Wietecha (C); Sam Huff (LB); Jim Patton (DB)
- **1959** Frank Gifford (HB); Roosevelt Brown (T); Andy Robustelli (DE); Sam Huff (LB); Jim Patton (DB)
- **1960** Roosevelt Brown (T); Andy Robustelli (DE); Jim Patton (DB)
- **1961** Roosevelt Brown (T); Jim Patton (DB); Del Shofner (E); Y.A. Tittle (QB); Jim Katcavage (DE); Erich Barnes (DB)
- **1962** Roosevelt Brown (T); Jim Patton (DB); Del Shofner (E); Y.A. Tittle (QB); Jim Katcavage (DE)
- **1963** Roosevelt Brown (T); Del Shofner (E); Y.A. Tittle (QB); Jim Katcavage (DE); Dick Lynch (DB)
- **1964** Erich Barnes (DB)
- **1967** Homer Jones (WR)
- **1970** Ron Johnson (RB)
- **1972** Bob Tucker (TE); Jack Gregory (DE)
- **1974** John Mendenhall (DT)
- **1976** Brad Van Pelt (LB), All-NFC
- **1977** Brad Van Pelt (LB), All-NFC
- **1978** Brad Van Pelt (LB), All-NFC; Harry Carson (LB); All-NFL; Dave Jennings (P), All-NFL
- **1979** Harry Carson (LB), All-NFL; All-NFC, Dave Jennings (P), All-NFL, All-NFC; Brad Van Pelt (LB), All-NFC
- **1980** Dave Jennings (P), All-NFL, All-NFC; Brad Van Pelt (LB), All-NFC
- **1981** Lawrence Taylor (LB), All-NFL; Harry Carson (LB), All-NFL; Mark Haynes (CB), All-NFL; Dave Jennings (P), All-NFL, (Second Team)
- **1982** Lawrence Taylor (LB), All-NFL; Dave Jennings (P), All-NFL; Mark Haynes (CB), All-NFL; Harry Carson (LB), All-NFL, (Second Team)
- **1983** Lawrence Taylor (LB); Ali Haji-Sheikh (PK); Mark Haynes (CB), (Second Team)
- **1984** Lawrence Taylor (LB); Mark Haynes (CB); Harry Carson (LB), (Second Team)
- **1985** Lawrence Taylor (LB); Leonard Marshall (DE); Joe Morris (RB); Harry Carson (LB)
- **1986** Lawrence Taylor (LB); Phil Simms (QB); Joe Morris (RB); Mark Bavaro (TE); Sean Landeta (P); Jim Burt (DT); Harry Carson (LB); Leonard Marshall (DE); Brad Benson (T)
- **1987** Mark Bavaro (TE); Carl Banks (LB); Lawrence Taylor (LB)
- **1988** Lawrence Taylor (LB)
- **1989** Lawrence Taylor (LB); Sean Landeta (P); David Meggett (RB); Mark Collins (CB)
- **1990** Lawrence Taylor (LB); Pepper Johnson (LB); Sean Landeta (P); David Megget (PR); Reyna Thompson (CB-ST)
- **1993** Michael Brooks (LB), All-NFL (Second Team), All-NFC; Mark Collins (CB), All-NFL (Second Team); William Roberts (G), All-NFC

STADIUM FACTS

Location: Giants Stadium is located in East Rutherford, Bergen County, New Jersey. It is bounded by Rte. 120, the Meadowlands Arena and the New Jersey Turnpike on the east, Route 3 on the south, Berry's Creek and Route 17 on the west and Paterson Plank Road on the north.

Seating Capacity:

Upper Tier	.32,791
Lower Tier	.34,824
Mezzanine Tier	.10,521
Total:	.78,136

Scoreboards: There are two Sony Jumbotron color video scoreboards at the top of each end of Giants Stadium. The scoreboards measure 32 x 24 feet and are supported by two Daktronics Matrix black and white scoreboards plus four auxiliary scoreboards.

Sound System: The Giants Stadium sound system has over 27,000 audio watts. There are 2,100 speakers in the entire system, fed by more than 47 miles of cable.

Playing Surface: Astroturf

Attendance Figures:

Opening Day, 10-10-76 vs Dallas	76,042
Largest Giants Stadium Crowd, 1-2-94 vs Dallas	77,356
Highest Home Attendance, 8 games, 1990	599,570

Notable Dates:

Groundbreaking, 11-19-72
Opening Day, 10-10-76, Giants vs Dallas
First College Game, 10-23-76, Rutgers vs Columbia

GIANTS RECORD BY THE DECADE

	Regular Season Home	Postseason Road	Home	Road	Total
Overall	279-182-16 (.602)	214-214-16 (.500)	11-6-0 (.647)	3-12-0 (.200)	507-414-32 (.549)
1920s	27-8-3 (.711)	17-9-2 (.607)	0-0	0-0	44-17-5 (.705)
1930s	47-15-4 (.727)	33-24-4 (.574)	2-0 (1.000)	0-3 (.000)	82-42-8 (.652)
1940s	34-26-3 (.563)	21-21-5 (.500)	0-3 (.000)	0-1 (.000)	55-51-8 (.518)
1950s	39-19-2 (.667)	37-22-1 (.625)	2-1 (.667)	0-2 (.000)	78-44-3 (.636)
1960s	35-31-3 (.529)	34-32-3 (.514)	0-1 (.000)	0-2 (.000)	69-66-6 (.511)
1970s	29-42-1 (.410)	21-51-0 (.292)	0-0	0-0	50-93-1 (.351)
1980s	46-31-0 (.597)	35-39-1 (.467)	4-1 (.800)	2-3 (.400)	87-74-1 (.540)
1990s	22-10-0 (.688)	16-16-0 (.500)	3-0 (1.000)	1-1 (.500)	42-27-0 (.609)

Super Bowl XXI and Super Bowl XXV count as Giants home games

GIANTS STADIUM FIRSTS

Preseason Game:	8-6-77	New England 19, Giants 3
Regular Season Game:	10-10-76	Dallas 24, Giants 14
Playoff Game:	12-28-85	Giants 17, San Francisco 3
Giants Victory:	11-14-76	Giants 12, Washington 9
Giants Loss:	10-10-76	Dallas 24, Giants 14
Giants Shutout:	12-10-78	Giants 17, St. Louis 0
Giants Shutout by Opponent:	10-24-76	Pittsburgh 27, Giants 0
Overtime Game:	12-18-77	Bears 12, Giants 9

GIANTS AT HOME

Home Stadium	Regular Season	Postseason	Total
Polo Grounds (1925-55)	130-62-11	2-3	132-65-11
Yankee Stadium (1956-Sept. 1973)	63-48-5	2-2	65-50-5
Yale Bowl (Oct. 1973-74)	1-11	0-0	1-11
Shea Stadium (1975)	2-5	0-0	2-5
Giants Stadium (1976-present)	83-56	5-1	88-57
Totals	**279-182-16**	**9-6**	**288-188-16**

MILESTONE GAMES IN GIANTS HISTORY

1st Game	10-11-25	at Providence	(L)	0-14
50th Game	12-8-28	at Frankford	(L)	0-7
100th Game	10-9-32	at Boston	(L)	6-14
200th Game	11-3-40	at Brooklyn	(W)	10-7
300th Game	11-20-49	vs Detroit	(L)	21-45
400th Game	9-28-58	at Chicago Cardinals	(W)	37-7
500th Game	11-14-65	at Cleveland	(L)	21-34
600th Game	11-26-72	at Philadelphia	(W)	62-10
700th Game	11-11-79	vs Atlanta	(W)	24-3
800th Game	10-12-86	vs Philadelphia	(W)	35-3
900th Game	11-22-92	vs Philadelphia	(L)	34-47

OFFENSE

SCORING

MOST POINTS
488 in 1963
399 in 1985
398 in 1962

MOST TOUCHDOWNS
57 in 1963
49 in 1967
49 in 1962

MOST TOUCHDOWNS
RUSHING
24 in 1985
22 in 1950
20 in 1992
18 in 4 seasons
PASSING
39 in 1963
35 in 1962
ON RETURNS
6 in 1947, 1949, 1963
5 in 1971, 1981
4 in 1955, 1966, 1978, 1988, 1990

MOST POINTS AFTER TOUCHDOWN
52 in 1963
47 in 1962

MOST FIELD GOAL ATTEMPTS
42 in 1983
41 in 1970
38 in 1989
38 in 1981

MOST FIELD GOALS
35 in 1983
29 in 1989

26 in 1993
26 in 1986
25 in 1970
24 in 1981, 1988, 1991
22 in 1985
21 in 1972, 1978, 1990

HIGHEST FIELD GOAL PERCENTAGE
83.3 in 1983
78.3 in 1992
76.5 in 1993
76.3 in 1989
75.8 in 1991
75.0 in 1951, 1990
72.4 in 1976

MOST SAFETIES
2 in 1950, 1953, 1961, 1989

FIRST DOWNS

MOST FIRST DOWNS
356 in 1985
324 in 1986
317 in 1988
310 in 1984
300 in 1993
296 in 1983
278 in 1963

RUSHING
138 in 1985
127 in 1993
127 in 1986
125 in 1978
124 in 1956

PASSING
198 in 1984
192 in 1985
171 in 1986

168 in 1988
164 in 1983
164 in 1963
160 in 1961

BY PENALTY
32 in 1992
30 in 1979
28 in 1983

MOST YARDS GAINED

5,884 in 1985
5,378 in 1986
5,292 in 1984
5,285 in 1983
5,145 in 1993
5,024 in 1963

RUSHING

MOST RUSHING ATTEMPTS
581 in 1985
580 in 1978
567 in 1950

MOST YARDS RUSHING
2,451 in 1985
2,336 in 1950
2,304 in 1978

MOST TOUCHDOWNS RUSHING
24 in 1985
21 in 1950
20 in 1992
18 in 4 seasons

PASSING

MOST PASSES ATTEMPTED
575 in 1983
535 in 1984

525 in 1988
514 in 1980
506 in 1981

MOST PASSES COMPLETED
290 in 1988
288 in 1984
284 in 1983
275 in 1985
268 in 1971
265 in 1987

HIGHEST COMPLETION PERCENTAGE
61.0 in 1991
60.6 in 1993
59.9 in 1972
58.0 in 1990
58.0 in 1971
57.1 in 1970
57.0 in 1963

MOST YARDS GAINED (NET)
3,632 in 1984
3,491 in 1983
3,433 in 1985
3,307 in 1962

MOST TOUCHDOWN PASSES
39 in 1963
35 in 1962

MOST PASSES HAD INTERCEPTED
34 in 1953
31 in 1966
31 in 1983

PUNTING

MOST PUNTS
104 in 1979
100 in 1977

MOST YARDS
4,445 in 1979
4,211 in 1980

HIGHEST PUNTING AVERAGE
46.6 in 1959
45.4 in 1964

PUNT RETURNS
MOST PUNT RETURNS
64 in 1981
55 in 1984
55 in 1983
55 in 1953

MOST YARDS GAINED
717 in 1941
675 in 1951
626 in 1938

HIGHEST RETURN AVERAGE
15.3 in 1941
14.1 in 1951
13.3 in 1943
kickoff returns

MOST KICKOFF RETURNS
80 in 1966
71 in 1983
71 in 1980

MOST YARDS GAINED
1,688 in 1964
1,616 in 1966

HIGHEST RETURN AVERAGE
27.4 in 1944
26.3 in 1953

FUMBLES
MOST FUMBLES
49 in 1960
44 in 1975
44 in 1964

MOST OWN FUMBLES RECOVERED
23 in 1960
21 in 1964

MOST OPPONENTS' FUMBLES RECOVERED
27 in 1950
26 in 1946
PENALTIES

PENALTIES
MOST PENALTIES
122 in 1979
113 in 1983

MOST YARDS PENALIZED
1,047 in 1979
1,020 in 1983

DEFENSE
SCORING
FEWEST POINTS ALLOWED
20 in 1927
72 in 1944

MOST POINTS ALLOWED
501 in 1966
425 in 1980

FEWEST TOUCHDOWNS ALLOWED
3 in 1927
9 in 1944

MOST TOUCHDOWNS
ALLOWED
66 in 1966
55 in 1980

AFTER TOUCHDOWN ALLOWED
64 in 1966
52 in 1948

MOST FIELD GOALS
ALLOWED
29 in 1991
25 in 1988
23 in 1987
22 in 1983
22 in 1981
22 in 1973
22 in 1971

MOST SAFETIES
BY OPPONENT
3 in 1984
2 in 1965

FIRST DOWNS
FEWEST FIRST DOWNS ALLOWED
116 in 1941
118 in 1943
MOST FIRST DOWNS ALLOWED
336 in 1980
322 in 1979

FEWEST FIRST DOWNS RUSHING ALLOWED
55 in 1982
60 in 1951
63 in 1943

MOST FIRST DOWNS RUSHING ALLOWED
156 in 1980
155 in 1978
137 in 1975

FEWEST FIRST DOWNS PASSING ALLOWED
47 in 1941
51 in 1943

MOST FIRST DOWNS PASSING ALLOWED
177 in 1986
174 in 1984
167 in 1983
161 in 1993
160 in 1980
NET YARDS

FEWEST YARDS ALLOWED
2,019 in 1935
2,029 in 1938

MOST YARDS ALLOWED
5,752 in 1980
5,378 in 1979

RUSHING
FEWEST ATTEMPTS, OPPONENT
301 in 1982
350 in 1986
366 in 1943
374 in 1944

MOST ATTEMPTS, OPPONENT
618 in 1979
584 in 1980
560 in 1976

FEWEST YARDS ALLOWED
913 in 1951
1,000 in 1944

MOST YARDS ALLOWED
2,656 in 1978
2,507 in 1980
2,452 in 1979
2,422 in 1975

FEWEST TOUCHDOWNS ALLOWED
1 in 1927
4 in 1944

MOST TOUCHDOWNS ALLOWED
31 in 1980
26 in 1948

PASSING
FEWEST ATTEMPTS, OPPONENT
149 in 1963
182 in 1937

MOST ATTEMPTS, OPPONENT
587 in 1986
566 in 1988
544 in 1981
535 in 1985
529 in 1984
514 in 1993
508 in 1987

FEWEST COMPLETIONS, OPPONENT
60 in 1936
68 in 1935

MOST COMPLETIONS, OPPONENT
334 in 1986
298 in 1993
294 in 1981 and 1988
292 in 1987
288 in 1984
283 in 1983

FEWEST YARDS ALLOWED (NET)
1,212 in 1941
1,290 in 1944

MOST YARDS ALLOWED (NET)
3,473 in 1986
3,375 in 1984
3,354 in 1993
3,327 in 1988
3,261 in 1983
3,245 in 1980

FEWEST TOUCHDOWNS ALLOWED
2 in 1927
3 in 1944

MOST TOUCHDOWNS ALLOWED
36 in 1966
28 in 1964
INTERCEPTIONS

MOST INTERCEPTIONS
41 in 1951
39 in 1948

FEWEST INTERCEPTIONS
12 in 1976, 1977, 1982 and 1991
13 in 1945

MOST YARDS, RETURNS
569 in 1941
561 in 1948

FEWEST YARDS, RETURNS
62 in 1976
91 in 1974
113 in 1980

MOST TOUCHDOWNS, RETURNS
5 in 1963

OFFENSE—INDIVIDUAL
RUSHING
MOST ATTEMPTS
33 Rodney Hampton (1-9-94 vs Minnesota)
33 Rob Carpenter (12-27-81 at Philadelphia)
29 Joe Morris (1-11-87 vs Washington)
28 Joe Morris (12-29-85 vs San Francisco)

MOST YARDS GAINED
161 Rodney Hampton (1-9-94 vs Minnesota)
161 Rob Carpenter (12-27-81 at Philadelphia)
159 Joe Morris (1-4-87 vs San Francisco)
141 Joe Morris (12-29-85 vs San Francisco)

MOST TOUCHDOWNS, RUSHING
2 Rodney Hampton (1-9-94 vs Minnesota)
2 Ken Strong (12-9-34 vs Chicago)
2 Alex Webster (12-30-56 vs Chicago)
2 Joe Morris (1-4-87 vs San Francisco)

PASSING
MOST ATTEMPTS
44 Phil Simms (12-29-84 at San Francisco)
41 Y.A. Tittle (12-30-62 vs Green Bay)
37 Scott Brunner (1-3-82 at San Francisco)
35 Charlie Conerly (12-27-59 at Baltimore)

MOST COMPLETIONS
25 Phil Simms (12-29-84 at San Francisco)
22 Phil Simms (12-23-84 at Rams)
22 Phil Simms (1-25-87 vs Denver)

MOST YARDS
290 Scott Brunner (1-3-82 at San Francisco)
268 Phil Simms (1-25-87 vs Denver)
234 Charlie Conerly (12-27-59 at Baltimore)

MOST TOUCHDOWN PASSES THROWN
4 Phil Simms (1-4-87 vs San Francisco)

MOST INTERCEPTIONS THROWN
4 Y.A. Tittle (12-31-61 at Green Bay)

RECEIVING
MOST RECEPTIONS
9 Bob Schnelker (12-27-59 at Green Bay)
7 Johnny Perkins (1-3-82 at San Francisco)
7 Rob Carpenter (12-23-84 at Rams)
7 Zeke Mowatt (12-23-84 at Rams)

MOST YARDS RECEIVING
178 Bob Schnelker (12-27-59 at Green Bay)
131 Frank Gifford (12-30-56 vs Chicago)
121 Johnny Perkins (1-3-82 at San Francisco)

MOST TOUCHDOWNS RECEIVING
2 Johnny Perkins (1-3-82 at San Francisco)

SCORING
MOST POINTS SCORED
16 Ken Strong (12-9-34 vs Chicago)
15 Matt Bahr (1-20-91 at San Francisco)

MOST TOUCHDOWNS
2 Ken Strong (12-9-34 vs Chicago)
2 Alex Webster (12-30-56 vs Chicago)
2 Johnny Perkins (1-3-82 at San Francisco)
2 Joe Morris (1-4-87 vs San Francisco)
2 Rodney Hampton (1-9-94 vs. Minnesota)

MOST FIELD GOALS
5 Matt Bahr (1-20-91 at San Francisco)

SPECIAL TEAMS

MOST SAFETIES RECORDED
1 George Martin (1-25-87 vs Denver)

MOST PUNTS
10 Len Younce (12-17-44 vs Green Bay)
9 Sean Landeta (1-5-86 vs Chicago)

MOST PUNT RETURNS
7 Phil McConkey (1-4-87 vs San Francisco)

LONGEST PLAYS

LONGEST TOUCHDOWN PASS
72 Scott Brunner to Earnest Gray
  (1-3-82 at San Francisco)
59 Scott Brunner to Johnny Perkins
  (1-3-82 at San Francisco)
42 Ed Danowski to Ken Strong
  (12-15-35 at Detroit)

LONGEST TOUCHDOWN RUN
51 Rodney Hampton (1-9-94 vs Minnesota)
45 Joe Morris (1-4-87 vs San Francisco)
42 Ken Strong (12-9-34 vs Chicago)

LONGEST FIELD GOAL
48 Joe Danelo (1-3-82 at San Francisco)
47 Eric Schubert (12-29-85 vs San Francisco)
47 Raul Allegre (1-11-87 vs Washington)

LONGEST PUNT
76 Ed Danowski (12-15-35 at Detroit)

SCORING—TEAM

MOST POINTS SCORED
49 1-4-87 vs San Francisco
47 12-30-56 vs Chicago
39 1-25-87 vs Denver

MOST POINTS ALLOWED
44 1-15-94 vs San Francisco
38 1-3-82 vs San Francisco
37 12-21-41 at Chicago
37 12-31-61 at Green Bay

FEWEST POINTS SCORED
0 12-10-39 at Green Bay (Milw.)
0 12-19-43 vs Washington
0 12-31-61 at Green Bay
0 1-6-86 at Chicago

FEWEST POINTS ALLOWED
0 12-21-58 vs Cleveland
0 1-11-87 vs Washington
3 12-29-85 vs San Francisco
3 1-4-87 vs San Francisco
3 1-13-91 vs Chicago

MOST POINTS SCORED BY BOTH TEAMS
62 1-3-82 vs San Francisco
  (SF 38, NYG 24)
59 1-25-87 vs Denver
  (NYG 39, DEN 20)
54 12-30-56 vs Chicago
  (NYG 47, CHI 7)

FEWEST POINTS SCORED BY BOTH TEAMS
10 12-21-58 vs Cleveland
  (NYG 10, CLE 0)
11 12-17-50 at Cleveland
  (CLE 8, NYG 3)
17 1-11-87 vs Washington
  (NYG 17, WAS 0)

MOST TOUCHDOWNS SCORED
7 1-4-87 vs San Francisco
6 12-30-56 vs Chicago
5 1-25-87 vs Denver

MOST TOUCHDOWNS ALLOWED
6 1-15-94 vs San Francisco
5 1-3-82 vs San Francisco
4 5 times; Last time: 12-31-61 at Green Bay

MOST TOUCHDOWNS RUSHING
3 12-9-34 vs Chicago
3 12-30-56 vs Chicago

MOST TOUCHDOWNS RUSHING ALLOWED
6 1-15-94 vs San Francisco
4 12-15-35 at Detroit
3 12-21-41 at Chicago
3 12-19-43 vs Washington
3 12-30-56 vs Chicago

MOST TOUCHDOWNS PASSING
4 1-4-87 vs San Francisco
3 1-3-82 at San Francisco
3 1-25-87 vs Denver

MOST TOUCHDOWNS PASSING ALLOWED
3 12-31-61 at Green Bay
3 12-29-84 vs San Francisco

MOST DEFENSIVE TOUCHDOWNS
1 5 times; Last time: 1-4-87 vs San Francisco

MOST DEFENSIVE TOUCHDOWNS ALLOWED
1 4 times; Last time: 1-3-82 vs San Francisco

MOST POINTS AFTER TOUCHDOWN
7 1-4-87 vs San Francisco
5 12-30-56 vs Chicago

MOST POINTS AFTER TOUCHDOWN ALLOWED
5 1-15-94 vs San Francisco
5 1-3-82 vs San Francisco

MOST FIELD GOALS
5 1-20-91 vs San Francisco

MOST FIELD GOALS ALLOWED
3 4 times; Last time: 12-30-62 vs Green Bay

MOST FIELD GOAL ATTEMPTS
6 1-20-91 vs San Francisco

FIRST DOWNS MOST FIRST DOWNS
24 1-25-87 vs Denver
24 1-27-91 vs Buffalo
23 1-13-91 vs Chicago

MOST FIRST DOWNS ALLOWED
27 12-28-58 vs Baltimore
26 1-7-90 vs Rams
25 1-15-94 vs San Francisco

FEWEST FIRST DOWNS
6 12-31-61 at Green Bay
10 12-17-44 vs Green Bay
10 1-5-86 at Chicago

FEWEST FIRST DOWNS ALLOWED
7 12-21-58 vs Cleveland
9 1-4-87 vs San Francisco
11 1-9-94 vs Minnesota
11 12-17-44 vs Green Bay
11 1-13-91 vs Chicago

MOST FIRST DOWNS RUSHING
16 1-13-91 vs Chicago
12 1-4-87 vs San Francisco
12 12-21-58 vs Cleveland

MOST FIRST DOWNS RUSHING ALLOWED
13 1-15-94 vs San Francisco
11 12-2-62 vs Green Bay
10 12-31-61 at Green Bay
9 1-5-86 at Chicago

FEWEST FIRST DOWNS RUSHING
1 12-31-61 at Green Bay
3 1-15-94 vs San Francisco
3 1-3-82 vs San Francisco
4 12-27-59 at Baltimore

FEWEST FIRST DOWNS RUSHING ALLOWED
0 1-13-91 vs Chicago
1 1-20-91 vs San Francisco
2 12-21-58 vs Cleveland

MOST FIRST DOWNS PASSING
13 1-25-87 vs Denver
13 1-27-91 vs Buffalo
11 12-27-59 vs Baltimore
11 12-2-62 vs Green Bay
11 1-20-91 vs San Francisco

MOST FIRST DOWNS PASSING ALLOWED
18 1-7-90 vs Rams
17 12-28-58 vs Baltimore
16 1-29-84 vs San Francisco
16 1-25-87 vs Denver

FEWEST FIRST DOWNS PASSING
3 12-10-39 at Green Bay
3 1-11-87 vs Washington
4 12-11-38 vs Green Bay
4 12-15-46 vs Chicago
4 12-31-61 at Green Bay

FEWEST FIRST DOWNS PASSING ALLOWED
3 12-17-44 vs Green Bay
4 12-10-39 at Green Bay

MOST FIRST DOWNS BY PENALTY
4 1-20-91 at San Francisco
3 1-15-94 vs San Francisco
3 1-4-87 vs San Francisco
3 12-23-84 vs Rams

MOST FIRST DOWNS BY PENALTY ALLOWED
3 1-11-87 vs Washington
3 12-23-84 vs Rams
3 12-27-81 at Philadelphia

NET YARDS

MOST NET YARDS GAINED
399 1-25-87 vs Denver
386 1-27-91 vs Buffalo
366 1-4-87 vs San Francisco

MOST NET YARDS ALLOWED
460 12-28-58 vs Baltimore
423 1-3-82 at San Francisco
413 1-15-94 vs San Francisco
412 12-29-84 vs San Francisco

FEWEST NET YARDS GAINED
130 12-31-61 at Green Bay
163 12-10-39 at Green Bay
173 1-7-90 vs Rams

FEWEST NET YARDS ALLOWED
86 12-21-58 vs Cleveland
167 12-9-34 vs Green Bay
184 1-4-87 vs San Francisco

RUSHING

MOST YARDS GAINED
216 1-4-87 vs San Francisco
211 12-21-58 vs Cleveland
194 1-13-91 vs Chicago

MOST YARDS ALLOWED
235 12-15-35 at Detroit
207 12-21-41 at Chicago
181 12-31-61 at Green Bay

FEWEST YARDS GAINED
31 12-31-61 at Green Bay
32 1-5-86 at Rams
40 12-23-84 vs Rams

FEWEST YARDS ALLOWED
24 12-21-58 vs Cleveland
27 1-13-91 vs Chicago
29 1-4-87 vs San Francisco

MOST RUSHING ATTEMPTS
54 12-21-58 vs Cleveland
48 1-13-91 vs Chicago
46 1-11-87 vs Washington

MOST RUSHING ATTEMPTS, OPPONENT
51 12-10-39 at Green Bay
46 12-11-38 vs Green Bay
46 12-30-62 vs Green Bay

FEWEST RUSHING ATTEMPTS
14 12-31-61 at Green Bay
14 1-5-86 vs Chicago
19 1-15-94 vs San Francisco

FEWEST RUSHING ATTEMPTS, OPPONENT
11 1-20-91 vs San Francisco
13 12-21-58 vs Cleveland
16 1-11-87 vs Washington
16 1-13-91 vs Chicago

PASSING

MOST YARDS GAINED
281 1-3-82 at San Francisco
263 1-25-87 vs Denver
222 12-30-56 vs Chicago

MOST YARDS ALLOWED
361 12-28-58 vs Baltimore
320 1-25-87 vs Denver
302 1-7-90 vs Rams

FEWEST YARDS GAINED
57 12-19-43 vs Washington
73 12-21-41 at Chicago
82 1-11-87 vs Washington

FEWEST YARDS ALLOWED
62 12-21-58 vs Cleveland
68 12-15-35 at Detroit
74 12-9-34 vs Chicago
74 12-17-44 vs Green Bay

MOST PASSES ATTEMPTED
44 12-29-84 at San Francisco
41 12-30-62 vs Green Bay
38 12-27-59 at Baltimore

MOST PASSES ATTEMPTED, OPPONENT
50 1-11-87 vs Washington
48 12-29-85 vs San Francisco
47 12-30-56 vs Chicago

FEWEST PASSES ATTEMPTED
13 12-9-34 vs Chicago
13 12-15-35 at Detroit

FEWEST PASSES ATTEMPTED, OPPONENT
5 12-15-35 at Detroit
10 12-10-39 at Green Bay
11 12-17-44 vs Green Bay

MOST PASS COMPLETIONS
25 12-29-84 at San Francisco
22 12-23-84 vs Rams
22 1-25-87 vs Denver

231

MOST PASS COMPLETIONS ALLOWED
26 12-28-58 at Baltimore
26 12-29-85 vs San Francisco
26 1-25-87 vs Denver

FEWEST PASS COMPLETIONS
3 12-21-41 at Chicago
4 12-15-35 at Detroit
4 12-19-43 vs Washington

FEWEST PASS COMPLETIONS ALLOWED
2 12-15-35 at Detroit
3 12-17-44 vs Green Bay

MOST PASSES HAD INTERCEPTED
5 12-29-63 at Chicago
4 12-31-61 at Green Bay
3 1-15-94 at San Francisco
3 12-27-59 vs Baltimore

MOST OPPONENT PASSES INTERCEPTED
3 5 times; Last time:
1-4-87 vs San Francisco

PUNTING MOST PUNTS
13 12-17-33 at Chicago
10 12-17-44 vs Green Bay
9 1-5-86 at Chicago

MOST PUNTS, OPPONENT
10 4 times; Last time: 1-4-87
vs San Francisco

FEWEST PUNTS
3 4 times; Last time: 1-20-91
at San Francisco

FEWEST PUNTS, OPPONENT
2 4 times; Last time: 1-13-91
vs Chicago

PENALTIES MOST PENALTIES
9 1-3-82 at San Francisco
6 12-30-56 vs Chicago
6 1-11-87 vs Washington
6 1-25-87 vs Denver

MOST PENALTIES, OPPONENT
14 1-3-82 at San Francisco
11 1-4-87 vs San Francisco
10 12-23-84 at Rams

FUMBLES MOST FUMBLES
6 12-21-58 vs Cleveland
6 12-28-58 vs Baltimore
5 12-31-61 at Green Bay

MOST FUMBLES, OPPONENT
5 12-27-81 at Philadelphia
4 12-11-38 vs Green Bay

MOST FUMBLES LOST
5 12-21-58 vs Cleveland
4 12-28-58 vs Baltimore
3 12-15-35 at Detroit
3 1-11-87 vs Washington

MOST FUMBLES LOST, OPPONENT
4 12-15-35 at Detroit
2 12-27-81 at Philadelphia
2 12-23-84 at Rams

GIANTS INDIVIDUAL RECORDS
SERVICE

MOST SEASONS, ACTIVE PLAYER
15 Phil Simms (1979-93)
15 Mel Hein (1931-45)
14 George Martin (1975-88)
14 Joe Morrison (1959-72)

14 Charlie Conerly (1948-61)
13 Lawrence Taylor (1981-93)
13 Harry Carson (1976-88)
13 Greg Larson (1961-73)
13 Jim Katcavage (1956-68)
13 Rosey Brown (1953-65)

MOST CONSECUTIVE GAMES PLAYED, CAREER
172 Mel Hein (1931-45)
165 Dave Jennings (1974-84)
140 Bart Oates (1985-93)
126 Emlin Tunnel (1948-58)
124 Ray Wietecha (1953-62)

MOST SEASONS, HEAD COACH
23 Steve Owen (1931-53)
8 Bill Parcells (1983-90)
8 Allie Sherman (1961-68)
7 Jim Lee Howell (1954-60)

MOST SEASONS LEADING LEAGUE
1 Don Chandler (1963)
1 Gene Roberts (1949) tied
1 Ken Strong (1933) tied

SCORING

MOST POINTS, CAREER
644 Pete Gogolak (1966-74)
(266-pat, 126-fg)
484 Frank Gifford (1950-60, 62-64)
(78-td, 10-pat, 2-fg)
482 Joe Danelo (1976-82)
(170-pat, 104-fg)
390 Joe Morrison (1959-71)
(65-td)

MOST POINTS, SEASON
127 Ali Haji-Sheikh 1983 (22-pat, 35-fg)
126 Joe Morris 1985 (21-tds)
107 Pete Gogolak 1970 (32-pat, 25-fg)
106 Don Chandler 1963 (52-pat, 18-fg)

MOST POINTS, ROOKIE SEASON
127 Ali Haji-Sheikh 1983 (22-pat, 35-fg)

MOST POINTS, GAME
24 Earnest Gray, at St. Louis
Sept. 7, 1980
24 Ron Johnson, at Philadelphia
Oct. 2, 1972
20 Joe Danelo, at Seattle
Oct. 18, 1981

TOUCHDOWNS

MOST CONSECUTIVE GAMES SCORING
61 Pete Gogolak (1969-73)
57 Ben Agajanian (1949, 54-57)
46 Pat Summerall (1958-61)

MOST SEASONS LEADING LEAGUE
2 Bill Paschal (1943 tied, 1944 tied)
1 Joe Morris (1985)
1 Homer Jones (1967)
1 Gene Roberts (1949)

MOST TOUCHDOWNS, CAREER
78 Frank Gifford (1952-60, 62-64)
65 Joe Morrison (1959-71)
56 Alex Webster (1955-64)

MOST TOUCHDOWNS, SEASON
21 Joe Morris (1985)
17 Gene Roberts (1949)
14 Rodney Hampton (1992)
14 Ottis Anderson (1989)
14 Joe Morris (1986)
14 Ron Johnson (1972)
14 Homer Jones (1967)
12 Ron Johnson (1970)

12 Del Shofner (1962)
12 Bill Paschal (1943)

MOST TOUCHDOWNS, ROOKIE SEASON
12 Bill Paschal (1943)

MOST TOUCHDOWNS, GAME
4 Earnest Gray, at St. Louis
Sept. 7, 1980
4 Ron Johnson, at Philadelphia
Oct. 2, 1972
3 by many players Last: **Rodney Hampton,** vs. Kansas
City Dec. 19, 1992

MOST CONSECUTIVE GAMES SCORING TOUCH-DOWNS
10 Frank Gifford (1957-58)
7 Kyle Rote (1959-60)
7 Bill Paschal (1944)
6 Frank Gifford (1953)

MOST SEASONS LEADING LEAGUE
1 Don Chandler (1963)
1 Pat Summerall (1961)
1 Ward Cuff (1938)

POINTS AFTER TOUCHDOWNS

MOST POINTS AFTER TOUCHDOWN ATTEMPT-ED, CAREER
277 Pete Gogolak (1966-74)
176 Joe Danelo (1976-82)
159 Ben Agajanian (1949, 54-57)

MOST POINTS AFTER TOUCHDOWN ATTEMPT-ED, SEASON
56 Don Chandler (1963)
48 Don Chandler (1962)
46 Pat Summerall (1961)

MOST POINTS AFTER TOUCHDOWN

(NO MISSES), GAME
8 Pete Gogolak, vs. Philadelphia
Nov. 26, 1972
7 by five players

MOST POINTS AFTER TOUCHDOWN, CAREER
268 Pete Gogolak (1966-74)
170 Joe Danelo (1976-82)
157 Ben Agajanian (1949, 54-57)

MOST POINTS AFTER TOUCHDOWN, SEASON
52 Don Chandler (1963)
47 Don Chandler (1962)
46 Pat Summerall (1961)

MOST POINTS AFTER TOUCHDOWN, GAME
8 Pete Gogolak, vs. Philadelphia
Nov. 26, 1972
7 Pete Gogolak, vs. St. louis
Dec. 7, 1969
7 Don Chandler, vs. Washington
Oct. 28, 1962
7 Pat Summerall, vs. Washington
Nov. 5, 1961
7 Ray Poole, at Baltimore
Nov. 19, 1950
7 Len Younce, at Green Bay
Nov. 21, 1948

MOST CONSECUTIVE POINTS AFTER TOUCH-DOWN
133 Pete Gogolak (1967-72)
126 Pat Summerall (1958-61)

(NO MISSES), SEASON
46 Pat Summerall (1961)
36 Pete Gogolak (1968)
35 Ben Agajanian (1954)

MOST SEASONS LEADING LEAGUE
3 Ward Cuff (1939, tied, 1939, 1943, tied)
1 Ali Haji-Sheikh (1983)
1 Pat Summerall (1959)
1 Ken Strong (1944)

MOST FIELD GOALS ATTEMPTED, CAREER
219 Pete Gogolak (1966-74)
176 Joe Danelo (1976-82)
112 Pat Summerall (1958-61)

MOST FIELD GOALS ATTEMPTED, SEASON
42 Ali Haji-Sheikh (1983)
41 Pete Gogolak (1970)
38 Joe Danelo (1981)
34 Pat Summerall (1961)
32 Raul Allegre (1986)
31 David Treadwell (1993)
31 Pete Gogolak (1972)

MOST FIELD GOALS ATTEMPTED, GAME
6 Raul Allegre, at Minnesota
Nov. 16, 1986
6 Ali Haji-Sheikh, at Washington
Dec. 17, 1983
6 Joe Danelo, at Seattle
Oct. 18, 1981
6 Pete Gogolak, at Philadelphia
Nov. 25, 1973
6 Ben Agajanian, vs. Philadelphia
Nov. 14, 1954

MOST FIELD GOALS, CAREER
126 Pete Gogolak (1966-74)
104 Joe Danelo (1976-82)
75 Raul Allegre (1986-90)
59 Pat Summerall (1958-61)

MOST FIELD GOALS, SEASON
35 Ali Haji-Sheikh (1983)
25 David Treadwell (1993)
25 Pete Gogolak (1970)
24 Raul Allegre (1986)
24 Joe Danelo (1981)
22 Matt Bahr (1991)
21 Joe Danelo (1978)
21 Pete Gogolak (1972)

MOST FIELD GOALS, GAME
6 Joe Danelo, at Seattle
Oct. 18, 1981
5 Raul Allegre, at Minnesota
Nov. 16, 1986
5 Eric Schubert, vs. Tampa Bay
Nov. 3, 1985
5 Ali Haji-Sheikh, at Washington
Dec. 17, 1983
4 David Treadwell, at Chicago
Sept. 5, 1993
4 Raul Allegre, at Philadelphia
Oct. 8, 1989
4 Raul Allegre, vs. Phoenix
Sept. 24, 1989
4 Raul Allegre, at Washington
Nov. 29, 1987
4 Raul Allegre, vs. Denver
Nov. 23, 1986
4 Ali Haji-Sheikh, at Dallas
Nov. 4, 1984
4 Ali Haji-Sheikh, vs. Seattle
Dec. 11, 1983
4 Joe Danelo, at Philadelphia
Jan. 2, 1983
4 Joe Danelo, vs. Washington
Nov. 14, 1976
4 Pete Gogolak, at Cleveland
Dec. 4, 1966
4 Pete Gogolak, vs. St. Louis
Oct. 9, 1966

4 Don Chandler, vs. Philadelphia
Nov. 18, 1962

MOST CONSECUTIVE GAMES
KICKING FIELD GOALS
18 Joe Danelo (1977-79)
15 Raul Allegre (1988-89)
15 Ali Haji-Sheikh (1983)
14 Pat Summerall (1960-61)
12 Matt Bahr (1990-91)
9 Pete Gogolak (1972)
7 Ali Haji-Sheikh (1984)
7 Pat Summerall (1959)
7 PAT SUMMERALL (1958-59)

LONGEST FIELD GOAL (IN YARDS)
56 Ali Haji-Sheikh, at Detroit
Nov. 7, 1983
56 Ali Haji-Sheikh, vs. Green Bay
Sept. 26, 1983
55 Joe Danelo, vs. New Orleans
Sept. 20, 1981
54 Brad Daluiso, vs. Phoenix
Nov. 28, 1993
54 Matt Bahr, vs. Houston
Dec. 21, 1991
54 Joe Danelo, at Seattle
Oct. 18, 1981
54 Pete Gogolak, vs. Dallas
Nov. 8, 1970
53 Raul Allegre, at Philadelphia
Nov. 15, 198
53 Don Chandler, at Dallas
Dec. 1, 1963
52 Raul Allegre, at Washington
Sept. 11, 1989
52 Raul Allegre, at Philadelphia
Nov. 15, 1987
52 Joe Danelo, at San Francisco
Nov. 29, 1981
52 Joe Danelo, vs. San Francisco
Sept. 24, 1978
51 Joe Danelo, at Dallas
Oct. 5, 1980
51 Joe Danelo, vs. Dallas
Nov. 6, 1977
50 Paul McFadden, vs. Dallas
Nov. 6, 1988
50 Joe Danelo, at Philadelphia
Sept. 22, 1980
50 Joe Danelo, at New Orleans
Oct. 29, 1978
50 Joe Danelo, vs. Washington
Nov. 14, 1976
50 Ben Agajanian, at Washington
Oct. 13, 1957

HIGHEST FIELD GOAL PERCENTAGE, CAREER
(50 ATTEMPTS)
75.3 Matt Bahr 55-73 (1990-92)
74.3 Raul Allegre 75-101 (1986-90)
67.5 Ali Haji-Sheikh 54-80 (1983-85)
59.0 Joe Danelo 104-176 (1976-82)
57.1 Pete Gogolak 126-219 (1966-74)
54.8 Ben Agajanian 46-84 (1949, 54-57)

HIGHEST FIELD GOAL PERCENTAGE, SEASON
(14 ATTEMPTS)
83.3 Ali Haji-Sheikh 35-42 (1983)
80.6 David Treadwell 25-31 (1993)
76.9 Raul Allegre 20-26 (1989)
76.2 Matt Bahr 16-21 (1992)
75.8 Matt Bahr 22-29 (1991)
75.0 Raul Allegre 24-32 (1986)
75.0 Ray Toole 12-16 (1951)
73.9 Matt Bahr 17-23 (1990)
73.7 Paul McFadden 21-29 (1978)
72.4 Joe Danelo 21-29 (1978)
69.0 Pat Summerall 20-29 (1959)

HIGHEST FIELD GOAL PERCENTAGE, GAME (4 ATTEMPTS)
100.0 David Treadwell, at Chicago
Sept. 5, 1993 (4-4)
100.0 Raul Allegre, at Washington
Nov. 29, 1987 (4-4)
100.0 Raul Allegre, vs. Denver
Nov. 23, 1986 (4-4)
100.0 Eric Schubert, vs. Tampa Bay
Nov. 3, 1985 (5-5)
100.0 Ali haji-Sheikh, at Dallas
Nov. 4, 1984 (4-4)
100.0 Joe Danelo, at Seattle
Oct. 18, 1981 (6-6)
100.0 Don Chandler, at Chicago
Dec. 2, 1962 (4-4)
83.3 Raul Allegre, at Minnesota
Nov. 16, 1986 (5-6)
83.3 Ali Haji-Sheikh, at Washington
Dec. 17, 1983 (5-6)
80.0 Ali Haji-Sheikh, vs. Seattle
Dec. 11, 1983 (4-5)
80.0 Joe Danelo, at Philadelphia
Jan. 2, 1983 (4-5)
80.0 Joe Danelo, vs. Washington
Nov. 14, 1976 (4-5)
80.0 Pete Gogolak, at Detroit
Nov. 17, 1974 (4-5)
80.0 Pete Gogolak, at St. Louis
Oct. 9, 1966 (4-5)
80.0 Don Chandler, at Cleveland
Oct. 27, 1963 (4-5)
80.0 Don Chandler, vs. Philadelphia
Nov. 18, 1962 (4-5)

SAFETIES

MOST SAFETIES, CAREER
3 Jim Katcavage (1956-68)
2 Leonard Marshall (1983-92)
1 by many players: last
Keith Hamilton (1993)

MOST SAFETIES, SEASON
1 By many players
Last: **Keith Hamilton** (1993)

MOST SAFETIES, GAME
1 by many players: last **Keith Hamilton**, at Miami
Dec. 5, 1993

RUSHING

MOST SEASONS LEADING LEAGUE
2 Bill Pascal (1943-44)
1 Tuffy Leemans (1936)
1 Eddie Price (1951)

MOST ATTEMPTS, CAREER
1,318 Joe Morris (1982-89)
1,196 Alex Webster (1955-64)
1,066 Ron Johnson (1970-75)
919 Tuffy Leemans (1936-43)

MOST ATTEMPTS, SEASON
341 Joe Morris (1986)
325 Ottis Anderson (1989)
307 Joe Morris (1988)
298 Ron Johnson (1972)
294 Joe Morris (1985)
292 Rodney Hampton (1993)
271 Eddie Price (1951)

MOST ATTEMPTS, GAME
43 Butch Woolfolk, at Philadelphia
Nov. 20, 1983
41 Rodney Hampton, vs. Rams
Sept. 19, 1993
38 Harry Newman, vs. Green Bay
Nov. 11, 1934

36 Joe Morris, vs. Pittsburgh
Dec. 21, 1985
36 Ron Johnson, at Philadelphia
Oct. 2, 1972
33 Rodney Hampton, vs. Indianapolis
Dec. 12, 1993
*33 Rob Carpenter, at Philadelphia
Dec. 27, 1981
32 Rodney Hampton, at Buffalo
Oct. 3, 1993
32 Joe Morris, vs. Phoenix
Dec. 4, 1988
32 Eddie Price, at Chicago Cardinals
Nov. 25, 1951
31 Joe Morris, vs. Kansas City
Dec. 11, 1988
31 Joe Morris, vs. Washington
oct. 27, 1986
30 Rodney Hampton, vs. Dallas
Jan. 2, 1994
30 Joe Morris, vs. San Diego
Sept. 14, 1986
30 Ron Johnson, vs. Philadelphia
Sept. 23, 1973
30 Eddie Price, at N.Y. Yankees
Dec. 16, 1951
30 Bill Paschal, vs. Washington
Dec. 3, 1944
*playoff game

MOST YARDS GAINED, CAREER
5,296 Joe Morris (1982-89)
4,638 Alex Webster (1955-64)
3,836 Ron Johnson (1970-75)
3,732 Rodney Hampton (1990-93)
3,609 Frank Gifford (1952-60, 62-64)

MOST YARDS GAINED, SEASON
1,516 Joe Morris (1986)
1,336 Joe Morris (1985)
1,182 Ron Johnson (1972)
1,141 Rodney Hampton (1992)
1,083 Joe Morris (1988)
1,077 Rodney Hampton (1993)
1,059 Rodney Hampton (1991)
1,027 Ron Johnson (1970)
1,023 Ottis Anderson (1989)
971 Eddie Price (1951)
928 Alex Webster (1961)

MOST YARDS GAINED, GAME
218 Gene Roberts, vs. Chicago Cardinals
Nov. 12, 1950
202 Joe Morris, vs. Pittsburgh
Dec. 21, 1985
188 Bill Paschal, vs. Washington
Dec. 5, 1943
181 Joe Morris, vs. Washington
Oct. 27, 1986
179 Joe Morris, vs. St. Louis
Dec. 14, 1986
173 Rodney Hampton, vs. Indianapolis
Dec. 12, 1993
171 Eddie Price, at Philadelphia
Dec. 9, 1951

MOST GAMES 100 YARDS OR MORE RUSHING, CAREER
19 Joe Morris (1982-89)
11 Rodney Hampton (1990-93)
11 Eddie Price (1950-55)
10 Ron Johnson (1970-73)
7 Rob Carpenter (1981-83)
5 Bill Paschal (1943-47)
5 Tuffy Leemans (1936-43)
4 Doug Kotar (1974-78)
4 Alex Webster (1955-64)
4 Gene Roberts (1947-50)

MOST GAMES, 100 YARDS OR MORE RUSHING, SEASON
8 Joe Morris (1986)
6 Joe Morris (1985)
5 Rodney Hampton (1993)
4 Rob Carpenter (1981)
4 Ron Johnson (1972)
4 Ron Johnson (1970)
4 Eddie Price (1952)
4 Eddie Price (1951)
3 Rodney Hampton (1991)
3 Joe Morris (1988)
3 Rob Carpenter (1983)
3 Eddie Price (1950)
3 Tuffy Leemans (1936)
2 Rodney Hampton (1992)
2 Billy Taylor (1979)
2 Doug Kotar (1976)
2 Ron Johnson (1973)
2 Gene Roberts (1949)
2 Ward Cuff (1944)
2 Bill Paschal (1944)
2 Bill Paschal (1943)

LONGEST RUN FROM SCRIMMAGE
91 Hap Moran, vs. Green Bay
Nov. 23, 1930
80 Eddie Price, at Philadelphia
Dec. 9, 1951
79 Frank Gifford, vs. Washington
Nov. 29, 1959
77 Bill Paschal, vs. Cleveland Rams
Nov. 4, 1945

HIGHEST AVERAGE GAIN, CAREER (500 ATTEMPTS)
4.30 Frank Gifford, 1952-60, 62-64
(840-3609)
4.14 Mel Triplett, 1955-60
(553-2289)
4.08 Rodney Hampton, 1990-93
(914-3732)
4.02 Joe Morris, 1982-88
(1318-5296)
3.88 Alex Webster, 1955-64
(1196-4638)
3.75 Doug Kotar, 1974-81
(900-3378)

HIGHEST AVERAGE GAIN, SEASON (QUALIFIERS)
5.58 Eddie Price 1950 (126-703)
5.15 Frank Gifford 1956 (159-819)
4.95 Alex Webster 1955 (128-634)

HIGHEST AVERAGE GAIN, GAME (10 ATTEMPTS)
13.30 Frank Reagan, vs. Los Angeles,
Dec. 1, 1946 (10-133)
12.23 Tuffy Leemans, vs. Green Bay
Nov. 20, 1938 (13-159)
11.43 Ernie Koy, at Washington
Oct. 1, 1967 (14-160)

MOST TOUCHDOWNS, CAREER
48 Joe Morris (1982-89)
39 Alex Webster (1955-64)
34 Frank Gifford (1952-60, 62-64)
33 Ron Johnson (1970-75)

MOST TOUCHDOWNS, SEASON
21 Joe Morris (1985)
14 Rodney Hampton (1992)
14 Ottis Anderson (1989)
14 Joe Morris (1986)
10 Rodney Hampton (1991)
10 Bill Paschal (1943)
9 Ron Johnson (1972)

9 Gene Roberts (1949)
9 Bill Paschal (1944)
8 Ottis Anderson (1988)
8 Ron Johnson (1970)
8 Frank Gifford (1958)

MOST TOUCHDOWNS, GAME
3 Rodney Hampton, vs. Kansas City
Dec. 19, 1992
3 Ottis Anderson, vs. Phoenix
Dec. 4, 1988
3 Joe Morris, vs. St. Louis
Dec. 14, 1986
3 Joe Morris, vs. Pittsburgh
Dec. 21, 1985
3 Joe Morris, at Houston
Dec. 8, 1985
3 Joe Morris, vs. Cleveland
Dec. 1, 1985
3 Joe Morris, at Washington
Nov. 18, 1985
3 Joe Morris, vs. Washington
Oct. 28, 1984
3 Charlie Evans, vs. San Diego
Nov. 7, 1971
3 Mel Triplett, at Chicago Cardinals
Oct. 7, 1956
3 Gene Roberts, at N.Y. Bulldogs
Sept. 30, 1949
3 Bill Paschal, vs. Cardinals-Pittsburgh
Oct. 22, 1944
2 by many players last: Lewis Tillman, vs. Philadelphia
Oct. 17, 1993

MOST CONSECUTIVE GAMES RUSHING FOR
TOUCHDOWNS
7 Bill Paschal (1944)
5 Rodney Hampton (1991)
5 Ottis Anderson (1989)
5 Bill Gaiters (1961)
4 Joe Morris (1985)
4 Ron Johnson (1970)
4 Bill Paschal (1943)
4 Ken Strong (1934)

PASSING

MOST SEASONS LEADING LEAGUE
2 Ed Danowski (1935, 1938)
1 Phil Simms (NFC, 1990)
1 Norm Snead (1972)
1 Y.A. Tittle (1963)
1 Charlie Conerly (1959)
1 Harry Newman (1933)

MOST PASSES ATTEMPTED, CAREER
4,647 Phil Simms (1979-93)
2,833 Charlie Conerly (1948-61)
1,898 Fran Tarkenton (1967-71)
1,308 Y.A. Tittle (1961-64)

MOST PASSES ATTEMPTED, SEASON
533 Phil Simms (1984)
495 Phil Simms (1985)
479 Phil Simms (1988)
468 Phil Simms (1986)
409 Fran Tarkenton (1969)
405 Phil Simms (1989)
402 Phil Simms (1980)
400 Phil Simms (1993)
389 Fran Tarkenton (1970)
386 Scott Brunner (1983)
386 Fran Tarkenton (1971)

MOST PASSES ATTEMPTED, GAME
62 Phil Simms, at Cincinnati
Oct. 13, 1985
53 Charlie Conerly, at Pittsburgh
Dec. 5, 1948
52 Jeff Rutledge, vs. Seattle

Dec. 11, 1983
51 Scott Brunner, vs. San Diego
Oct. 2, 1983
51 Scott Brunner, at St. Louis
Dec. 26, 1982
50 Phil Simms , at Dallas
Dec. 15, 1985
49 Phil Simms, vs. Rams
Sept. 25, 1988
49 Phil Simms, at Philadelphia
Sept. 22, 1980
48 Phil Simms, at San Francisco
Nov. 27, 1989
48 Phil Simms, at St. Louis
Dec. 13, 1987
47 Jeff Rutledge, at Washington
Dec. 17, 1983
47 Randy Johnson, vs. Philadelphia
Dec. 19, 1971

MOST PASSES COMPLETED, CAREER
2,576 Phil Simms (1979-93)
1,051 Fran Tarkenton (1967-71)
1,418 Charlie Conerly (1948-61)
731 Y.A. Tittle (1961-64)

MOST PASSES COMPLETED, SEASON
286 Phil Simms (1984)
275 Phil Simms (1985)
263 Phil Simms (1988)
259 Phil Simms (1986)
247 Phil Simms (1993)
228 Phil Simms (1989)
226 Fran Tarkenton (1971)
221 Y.A. Tittle (1963)
220 Fran Tarkenton (1969)

MOST PASSES COMPLETED, GAME
40 Phil Simms, at Cincinnati
Oct. 13, 1985
36 Charlie Conerly, at Pittsburgh
Dec. 5, 1948
31 Scott Brunner, vs. San Diego
Oct. 2, 1983
30 Phil Simms, at St. Louis
Dec. 13, 1987
30 Randy Johnson, vs. Philadelphia
Dec. 19, 1971
29 Phil Simms, vs. Rams
Sept. 25, 1988
29 Scott Brunner, at St.. Louis
Dec. 26, 1982
28 Jeff Hostetler, at Dallas
Sept. 29, 1991
28 Jeff Rutledge, vs. Seattle
Dec. 11, 1983
28 Phil Simms, vs . New Orleans
Sept. 20, 1981
28 Norm Snead, vs. New England
Sept. 22, 1974
28 Randy Johnson, at St. Louis
Oct. 28, 1973

MOST CONSECUTIVE PASSES COMPLETED
13 Phil Simms, at Cincinnati
Oct. 13, 1985
12 Y.A. Tittle, vs. Washington
Oct. 28, 1962

HIGHEST PASSING EFFICIENCY, CAREER (1000
ATTEMPTS)
55.89 Y.A. Tittle (731-1308, 1961-64)
55.43 Phil Simms (2576-4647, 1979-93)
55.37 Fran Tarkenton (1051-1898, 1967-71)
50.05 Charlie Conerly (1418-2833, 1948-61)

HIGHEST PASSING EFFICIENCY, SEASON
(QUALIFIERS)
62.81 Jeff Hostetler (179-285, 1991)
61.80 Phil Simms (247-400, 1993)

60.31 Norm Snead (196-325, 1972)
60.22 Y.A. Tittle (221-367, 1963)
59.20 Phil Simms (184-311, 1990)
58.55 Fran Tarkenton (226-386, 1971)
58.25 Charlie Conerly (113-194, 1959)

HIGHEST PASSING EFFICIENCY, GAME (20
ATTEMPTS)
88.00 Phil Simms, vs. Denver *
82.35 Jeff Hostetler, at Dallas
Sept. 29, 1991 (28-34)
80.95 Phil Simms, at Indianapolis
Nov. 5, 1990 (17-21)
80.95 Phil Simms, vs. St. Louis
Oct. 25, 1987 (17-21)
80.76 Phil Simms, vs. Green Bay
Dec. 19, 1987 (21-26)
80.00 Norm Snead, vs. New England
Sept. 22, 1974 (28-35)
80.00 Fran Tarkenton, vs. San Diego
Nov. 7, 1971 (16-20)
80.00 Y.A. Tittle, vs. Philadelphia
Nov. 10, 1963 (16-20)
77.80 Phil Simms, vs. Rams
Sept. 19, 1993 (21-27)
77.27 Bob Clatterbuck, vs. Pittsburgh
Dec. 5, 1954 (17-22)
76.92 Phil Simms, vs. Detroit
Sept. 17, 1989 (20-26)
76.70 Phil Simms, vs. Philadelphia
Sept. 2, 1984 (23-30)
76.19 Phil Simms, at Dallas
Sept. 16, 1990 (16-21)
75.00 Norm Snead, vs. Green Bay
Oct. 7, 1973 (21-28)
75.00 Y.A. Tittle, vs. Philadelphia
Nov. 12, 1961 (18-24)
*Superbowl xxi

MOST YARDS PASSING, CAREER
33,462 Phil Simms (1979-93)
19,488 Charlie Conerly (1948-61)
13,905 Fran Tarkenton (1967-71)
10,439 Y.A. Tittle (1961-64)

MOST YARDS PASSING, SEASON
4,044 Phil Simms (1984)
3,829 Phil Simms (1985)
3,487 Phil Simms (1986)
3,359 Phil Simms (1988)
3,224 Y.A. Tittle (1962)
3,145 Y.A. Tittle (1963)
3,088 Fran Tarkenton (1967)

MOST YARDS PASSING, GAME
513 Phil Simms, at Cincinnati
Oct. 13, 1985
505 Y.A. Tittle, vs. Washington
Oct. 28, 1962
432 Phil Simms, vs. Dallas
Oct. 6, 1985
409 Phil Simms, vs. Philadelphia
Sept. 2, 1984
395 Scott Brunner, vs. San Diego
Oct. 2, 1983
388 Phil Simms, at San Francisco
Dec. 1, 1986
372 Randy Johnson, at Dallas
Dec. 19, 1971
368 Jeff Hostetler, at Dallas
Sept. 29, 19913
63 Charlie Conerly, at Pittsburgh
Dec. 5, 1948

MOST GAMES, 300 YARDS OR MORE PASS-
ING, CAREER
21 Phil Simms (1979-93)
9 Y.A. Tittle (1961-64)
4 Scott Brunner (1980-83)
4 Fran Tarkenton (1967-71)

3 Jeff Rutledge (1983)
3 Charlie Conerly (1948-61)

MOST GAMES, 300 YARDS OR MORE PASS-
ING, SEASON
4 Phil Simms (1986)
4 Phil Simms (1984)
4 Y.A. Tittle (1962)
3 Phil Simms (1988)
3 Phil Simms (1985)
3 Jeff Rutledge (1983)
3 Y.A. Tittle (1961)
2 Scott Brunner (1983)
2 Scott Brunner (1982)
2 Phil Simms (1980)
2 Y.A. Tittle (1963)

LONGEST PASS COMPLETION (IN YARDS)
98 Earl Morrall (to homer jones)
at Pittsburgh, Sept. 11, 1966
94 Norm Snead (to Rich Houston)
vs. Dallas, Sept. 24, 1972
89 Earl Morrall (to Homer Jones)
vs. Philadelphia, Oct. 17, 1965
88 Frank Reagan (to George Franck)
vs. Washington, Oct. 12, 1947

MOST TOUCHDOWN PASSES, CAREER
199 Phil Simms (1979-93)
173 Charlie Conerly (1948-61)
103 Fran Tarkenton (1967-71)
96 Y.A. Tittle (1961-64)

MOST TOUCHDOWN PASSES, SEASON
36 Y.A. Tittle (1963)
33 Y.A. Tittle (1962)
29 Fran Tarkenton (1967)

MOST TOUCHDOWN PASSES, GAME
7 Y.A. Tittle, vs. Washington
Oct. 28, 1962
6 Y.A. Tittle, vs. Dallas
Dec. 16, 1962
5 Phil Simms at St. Louis
Sept. 7, 1980
5 Fran Tarkenton, vs. St. Louis
Oct. 25, 1970

MOST CONSECUTIVE GAMES TOUCHDOWN
PASSES
13 Y.A. Tittle (1963-64)
10 Phil Simms (1988-89)
10 phil Simms (1986-87)
10 Charlie Conerly (1948-49)
9 Earl Morrall (1965-66)

FEWEST PASSES HAD INTERCEPTED, CAREER
(1000 ATTEMPTS)
68 Y.A. Tittle (1308, 1961-64)
72 Fran Tarkenton (1898, 1967-71)
157 Phil Simms (4647, 1979-93)
167 Charlie Conerly (2833, 1948-61)

FEWEST PASSES HAD INTERCEPTED, SEASON
(QUALIFIERS)
3 Gary Wood (1964)
4 Jeff Hostetler (1991)
4 Phil Simms (1990)
4 Charlie Conerly (1959)
4 Ed Danowski (1937)

FEWEST PASSES HAD INTERCEPTED, GAME
(MOST ATTEMPTS)
0 Phil Simms, vs. Phoenix
Nov. 28, 1993 (41 attempts)
0 Scott Brunner, vs. St. Louis
Dec. 26, 1982 (51 attempts)
0 Fran Tarkenton, at Dallas
Oct. 11, 1971 (46 attempts)
0 Fran Tarkenton, vs. Dallas

Dec. 15, 1968 (43 attempts)
0 Y.A. Tittle, vs. Washington
Oct. 28, 1962 (39 attempts)

MOST PASSES HAD INTERCEPTED, CAREER
167 Charlie Conerly (1949-61)
157 Phil Simms (1979-93)
72 Fran Tarkenton (1967-71)
68 Y.A. Tittle (1961-64)

MOST PASSES HAD INTERCEPTED, SEASON
25 Charlie Conerly (1953)
25 Frank Filchock (1946)
23 Joe Pisarcik (1978)
22 Phil Simms (1986)
22 Scott Brunner (1983)
22 Norm Snead (1973)
22 Y.A. Tittle (1964)
22 Charlie Conerly (1951)

MOST PASSES HAD INTERCEPTED, GAME
5 Harry Newman, at Portsmouth
Sept. 24, 1933
5 Frank Filchock, at Washington
Oct. 13, 1946
5 Charlie Conerly, vs. Chicago Cardinals
Oct. 14, 1951
5 Charlie Conerly, vs. Detroit
Dec. 13, 1953
5 Jeff Rutledge, at New Orleans
Nov. 22, 1987
4 by many players last: Phil Simms, at Seattle
Oct. 19, 1986

LOWEST PERCENTAGE PASSES HAD INTER-CEPTED, CAREER (1000 ATTEMPTS)
3.38 Phil Simms (157-4647, 1979-93)
3.79 Fran Tarkenton (72-1898, 1967-71)
5.20 Y.A. Tittle (68-1308, 1961-64)
5.89 Charlie Conerly (167-2833, 1948-61)

LOWEST PERCENTAGE PASSES HAD INTER-CEPTED, SEASON (QUALIFIERS)
1.28 Phil Simms (4-311, 1990)
1.40 Jeff Hostetler (4-285, 1991)
1.96 Fran Tarkenton (8-409, 1969)
2.06 Charlie Conerly (4-194, 1959)
2.10 Gary Wood (3-143, 1964)

PASS RECEPTIONS

MOST SEASONS LEADING LEAGUE
1 Earnest Gray (1983)
1 Bob Tucker (1971)
1 Tod Goodwin (1935)

MOST PASS RECEPTIONS, CAREER
395 Joe Morrison (1959-72)
367 Frank Giiford (1952-60, 62-64)
327 Bob Tucker (1970-77)

MOST PASS RECEPTIONS, SEASON
78 Earnest Gray (1983)
68 Del Shofner (1961)
66 Mark Bavaro (1986)
65 Lionel Manuel (1988)
64 Del Shofner (1963)
59 Bob Tucker (1971)
58 Mark Jackson (1993)

MOST PASS RECEPTIONS, GAME
12 Mark Bavaro, at Cincinnati
Oct. 13, 1985
11 Mark Bavaro, at St. Louis
Dec. 13, 1987
11 Gary Shirk, vs. New Orleans
Sept. 20, 1981
11 Billy Taylor, at Tampa Bay
Nov. 2, 1980
11 Doug Kotar, at St. Louis

Oct. 3, 1976
11 Del Shofner, vs. Washington
Oct. 28, 1962
11 Frank Gifford, vs. San Francisco
dec. 1, 1957
10 George Adams, vs. Rams
Sept. 25, 1988
10 Ron Johnson, vs. New England
Sept. 22, 1974
10 Tucker Frederickson, vs. Washington
Nov. 15, 1970
10 Alex Webster, vs. Dallas
Dec. 16, 1962
9 by many players last: Mark Bavaro, at Philadelphia
Oct. 10, 1988

MOST CONSECUTIVE GAMES, PASS RECEP-TIONS
45 David Meggett (1989-92)
45 Bob Tucker (1970-73)
32 Homer Jones (1965-67)
26 Homer Jones (1968-69)
25 Earnest Gray (1982-84)
23 Joe Morrison (1964-65)
23 Kyle Rote (1956-58)
21 Mark Bavaro (1986-87)

MOST YARDS GAINED, CAREER
5,434 Frank Gifford (1952-60, 62-64)
4,993 Joe Morrison (1959-72)
4,845 Homer Jones (1964-69)

MOST YARDS GAINED, SEASON
1,209 Homer Jones (1967)
1,181 Del Shofner (1963)
1,139 Earnest Gray (1983)
1,133 Del Shofner (1962)

MOST YARDS GAINED, GAME
269 Del Shofner, vs. Washington
Oct. 28, 1962
212 Gene Roberts, at Green Bay
Nov. 13, 1949
201 Gene Roberts, vs. Chicago Bears
Oct. 23, 1949

LONGEST PASS RECEPTION (IN YARDS)
98 Homer Jones (from Earl Morrall)
at Pittsburgh, Sept. 11, 1966
94 Rich Houston (from Norm Snead)
vs. Dallas, Sept. 24, 1972
89 Homer Jones (from Earl Morrall)
vs. Philadelphia, Oct. 17, 1965
88 George Franck (from Frank Reagan)
at Washington, Oct. 12, 1947

HIGHEST AVERAGE GAIN, CAREER (200 MINIMUM)
22.6 Homer Jones (214-4845, 1964-69)
18.1 Del Shofner (239-4315, 1961-67)
17.2 Aaron Thomas (247-4253, 1962-70)

HIGHEST AVERAGE GAIN, SEASON (QUALI-FIERS)
24.7 Homer Jones (49-1209, 1967)
23.5 Homer Jones (45-1057, 1968)
21.8 Homer Jones (48-1044, 1966)

HIGHEST AVERAGE GAIN, GAME (4 MINIMUM)
50.3 Gene Roberts, vs. Chicago Bears
Oct. 23, 1949 (4-201)
49.0 Homer Jones, at Washington
Oct. 1, 1967 (4-196)
37.5 Frank Liebel, vs. Detroit
Nov. 18, 1945 (4-150)

MOST TOUCHDOWNS, CAREER
48 Kyle Rote (195!-61)
47 Joe Morrison (1959-71)
43 Frank Gifford (1952-60, 62-64)

MOST TOUCHDOWNS, SEASON
13 Homer Jones (1967)
12 Del Shofner (1962)
11 Del Shofner (1961)

MOST TOUCHDOWNS, GAME
4 Earnest Gray, at St. Louis
Sept. 7, 1980
3 Earnest Gray, vs. Green Bay
Nov. 16, 1980
3 Billy Taylor, at St. Louis
Dec. 9, 1979
3 Ron Johnson, at Philadelphia
Oct. 2, 1972
3 Rich Houston, at Green Bay
Sept. 19, 1971
3 Joe Walton, vs. Dallas
Dec. 16, 1962
3 Del Shofner, at Washington
Nov. 25, 1962
3 Del Shofner, at Dallas
Nov. 11, 1962
3 Joe Walton, vs. Washington
Oct. 28, 1962
3 Del Shofner, at Philadelphia
Dec. 10, 1961
3 Del Shofner, vs. Washington
Nov. 5, 1961
3 Bob Schnelker, at Washington
Oct. 10, 1954
3 Gene Roberts, at Green Bay
Nov. 13, 1949
3 Gene Roberts, vs. Chicago Bears
Oct. 23, 1949
3 Frank Liebel, vs. Philadelphia
Dec. 2, 1945

MOST CONSECUTIVE GAMES, TOUCHDOWN RECEPTION
7 Kyle Rote (1959-60)
5 Aaron Thomas (1967)
5 Joe Morrison (1966)
5 Homer Jones (1966)
5 Del Shofner (1963)
5 Frank Liebel (1945)
4 by many players
last: Mark Bavar (1987)

INTERCEPTIONS

MOST SEASONS LEADING LEAGUE
2 Dick Lynch (1961, 1963)

MOST INTERCEPTIONS BY, CAREER
74 Emlen Tunnell (1948-58)
52 Jimmy Patton (1955-66)
41 Carl Lockhart (1965-75)

MOST INTERCEPTIONS BY, SEASON
11 Jimmy Patton (1958)
11 Otto Schelbacher (1951)
10 Willie Williams (1968)
10 Emlen Tunnell (1949)
10 Frank Reagan (1947)
9 by five players last: Dick Lynch (1963)

MOST INTERCEPTIONS BY, GAME
3 Terry Kinard, vs. Dallas
Sept. 20, 1987
3 Carl Lockhart, at Cleveland
Dec. 4, 1966
3 Dick Lynch, at Philadelphia
Sept. 29, 1963
3 Jimmy Patton, at Chicago
Dec. 2, 1962
3 Dick Lynch, vs. Philadelphia
Nov. 12, 1961
3 Dick Lynch, at St. Louis
Oct. 8, 1961
3 Emlen Tunnell, at Chicago Cardinals
Nov. 24, 1957

3 Tom Landry, vs. Philadelphia
Nov. 14, 1954
3 Emlen Tunnell, at Pittsburgh
Nov. 7, 1954
3 Otto Schellbacher, vs. Cleveland
Oct. 22, 1950
3 Emlen Tunnell, at Washington
Oct. 9, 1949
3 Frank Reagan, vs. Boston Burlldogs??????
Nov. 28, 1948
3 Emlen Tunnell, at Green Bay
Nov. 21, 1948
3 Art Faircloth, at Boston
Sept. 23, 1948
3 Frank Reagan, vs. Green Bay
Nov. 23, 1947
3 Frank Reagan, at Detroit
Nov. 2, 1947
3 Howard Livingston, at Brooklyn
Oct. 15, 1944
3 Ward Cuff, at Philadelphia
Sept. 13, 1941

MOST CONSECUTIVE GAMES, INTERCEPTIONS BY
6 Willie Williams (1968)
5 Carl Lockhart (1969-70)
5 Emlen Tunnell (1954-55)
4 by many players last: Terry Jackson (1978)

MOST YARDS GAINED, CAREER
1,240 Emlen Tunnell (1948-58)
712 Jimmy Patton (1955-66)
574 Terry Kinard (1983-89)
568 Dick Lynch (1959-66)
475 Carl Lockhart (1965-75)

MOST YARDS GAINED, SEASON
251 Dick Lynch (1963)
251 Emlen Tunnell (1949)
203 Frank Reagan (1947)
195 Erich Barnes (1961)

MOST YARDS GAINED, GAME
109 Ward Cuff, at Philadelphia
Sept. 13, 1941
104 George Cheverko, at Washington
Oct. 3, 1948
102 Erich Barnes, at Dallas
Oct. 15, 1961

LONGEST GAIN (IN YARDS)
102 Erich Barnes, at Dallas
OCT. 15, 1961 (TD)
101 Henry Carr, at Rams
Nov. 13, 1966 (TD)
97 Lawrence Taylor, at Detroit
Nov. 25, 1982 (TD)
89 Bruce Maher, at Dallas
Nov. 10, 1968

MOST TOUCHDOWNS, CAREER
4 Dick Lynch (1959-66)
4 Emlen Tunnell (1948-58)
3 George Martin (1975-86)
3 Carl Lockhart (1965-72)
3 Jerry Hillebrand (1963-66)
3 Erich Barnes (1961-64)
3 Tom Landry (1950-55)
2 Lawrence Taylor (1981-93)
2 Pepper Johnson (1986-92)
2 Terry Kinard (1983-89)
2 Terry Jackson (1978-82)
2 Jimmy Patton (1955-66)
2 Tom Scott (1959-64)
2 Otto Schnellbacher (1950-51)
2 Bill Petrilas (1944-45)

MOST TOUCHDOWNS, SEASON
3 Dick Lynch (1963)
2 Carll lockhart (1968)

2 Erich Barnes (1961)
2 Tom Landry (1961)
2 Otto Schnellbacher (1951)
2 Emlen Tunnell (1949)
2 Bill Petrilas (1944)

MOST TOUCHDOWNS, GAME
1 by many players
last: Mark Collins, vs. Rams Sept. 19, 1993

MOST CONSECUTIVE GAMES, TOUCHDOWNS
2 Carl Lockhart, at Philadelphia, Sept. 22--vs. Washington, Sept. 29, 1968
2 Dick Lynch, vs. Cleveland, Oct. 13--vs. Dallas, Oct. 20, 1963
2 Tom Landry, at Cleveland, Oct. 28--vs. N.Y. Yankees, Nov. 4, 1951

PUNTING

MOST SEASONS LEADING LEAGUE
2 Sean Landeta (NFC, 1986, 1990)
1 Dave Jennings (1979, 1980)
1 Don Chandler (1957)

MOST PUNTS, CAREER
931 Dave Jennings (1974-84)
526 Sean Landeta (1985-93)
525 Don Dhandler (1956-64)

MOST PUNTS, SEASON
104 Dave Jennings (1979)
100 Dave Jennings (1977)
97 Dave Jennings (1981)
95 Dave Jennings (1978)
94 Dave Jennings (1980)

MOST PUNTS, GAME
14 Carl Kinschef, at Detroit
Nov. 7, 1943
11 Dave Jennings, at Atlanta
Oct. 25, 1981
11 Dave Jennings, at Washington
Sept. 13, 1981
11 Don Chandler, at St. Louis
Oct. 8, 1961
11 Charlie Conerly, vs. Cleveland
Nov. 18, 1951
11 Tom Landry, vs. Philadelphia
Nov. 26, 1950

MOST YARDS, CAREER
38,792 Dave Jennings (1974-84)
23,019 Don Chandler (1956-64)
22,804 Sean Landeta (1985-93)

MOST YARDS, SEASON
4,445 Dave Jennings (1979)
4,211 Dave Jennings (1980)
4,198 Dave Jennings (1981)
3,995 Dave Jennings (1978)\
3,993 Dave Jennings (1977)

MOST YARDS, GAME
583 Carl Kinschef, at Detroit
Nov. 7, 1943 (14 punts)
511 Dave Jennings, at Washington
Sept. 13, 1981 (11 punts)
485 Don Chandler, at St. Louis
Oct. 8, 1961 (11 punts)
470 Len Barnum, vs. Green Bay
Nov. 17, 1940 (10 punts)

LONGEST PUNT
74 Len Younce, vs. Chicago Bears
Nov. 14, 1943
74 Don Chandler, at Dallas
Oct. 11, 1964
73 Dave Jennings, vs. Houston
Dec. 5, 1982

72 Dave Jennings, vs. Dallas
Nov. 4, 1979
72 Len Younce, at Brooklyn
Oct. 15, 1944
72 Carl Kinscherf, at Philadelphia-Pittsburgh
Oct. 9, 1943
71 Sean Landeta, vs. Green Bay
Nov. 8, 1992
71 Sean Landeta, vs. Philadelphia
Dec. 3, 1989

HIGHEST AVERAGE, CAREER (150 PUNTS)
43.8 Don Chandler (525 punts, 1956-64)
43.4 Sean Landeta (526 punts, 1985-93)
41.8 Tom Blanchard (171 punts, 1971-73)
41.7 Dave Jennings (931 punts, 1974-84)

HIGHEST AVERAGE SEASON (35 PUNTS)
46.6 Don Chandler (55 punts, 1959)
45.6 Don Chandler (73 punts, 1964)
44.9 Don Chandler (59 punts, 1963)

HIGHEST AVERAGE, GAME (4 PUNTS)
55.3 Dave Jennings, vs. Houston
Dec. 5, 1982 (4 punts)
54.1 Don Chandler, at Cleveland
Oct. 11, 1959 (8 punts)
54.0 Dave Jennings, at Dallas
Oct. 5, 1980 (5 punts)
53.1 Dave Jennings, at Dallas
Nov. 15, 1992
52.4 Sean Landeta, at Denver
Nov. 15, 1992
52.1 Dave Jennings, vs. Kansas City
Sept. 17, 1978 (7 punts)
52.1 Don Chandler, vs. Pittsburgh
Nov. 15, 1959 (7 punts)

PUNT RETURNS

MOST PUNT RETURNS, CAREER
257 Emlen Tunnell (1948-58)
213 Phil McConkey (1984-88)
176 David Meggett (1989-93)
106 Leon Bright (1981-83)
62 Carl Lockhart (1965-71)

MOST PUNT RETURNS, SEASON
53 Phil McConkey (1985)
52 Leon Bright (1981)
46 David Meggett (1989)
46 Phil McConkey (1984)
43 David Meggett (1990)
42 Phil McConkey (1987)
40 Phil McConkey (1988)
38 Emlen Tunnell (1953)
37 Leon Bright (1982)

MOST PUNT RETURNS, GAME
9 Phil McConkey, vs. Philadelphia
Dec. 6, 1987
9 Pete Shaw, at Philadelphia
Nov. 20, 1983
9 Leon Bright, vs. Philadelphia
Dec. 11, 1982
8 Phil McConkey, at Dallas
Nov. 4, 1984
8 Leon Bright, at Washington
Sept. 13, 1981
8 Emlen Tunnell, vs. N.Y. Yankees
Dec. 3, 1950
7 Phil McConkey, at St. Louis
Oct. 5, 1986
7 Phil McConkey, vs. Philadelphia
Sept. 8, 1985
7 Rondy Colbert, vs. New Orleans
Dec. 14, 1975
6 Pete Athas, at St. Louis
Dec. 15, 1974
6 Emlen Tunnell, at Philadelphia
Oct. 4, 1952

MOST FAIR CATCHES, SEASON
25 Phil McConkey (1988)
20 David Meggett (1993)
18 Phil McConkey (1985)
16 Bobby Duhon (1971)
15 Phil McConkey (1984)
14 David Meggett (1989)
14 Pete Athas (1973)
14 Bob Grim (1972)
14 Carl Lockhart (1969)

MOST FAIR CATCHES, CAREER
84 Phil McConkey (1984-88)
66 David Meggett (1989-93)
57 Carl Lockhart (1965-71)
40 Bobby Duhon (1968-72)

FEWEST FAIR CATCHES, GAME
0 Leon Bright (17 returns, 1983)
0 Leon Bright (37 returns, 1982)
0 Leon Bright (52 returns, 1981)

MOST FAIR CATCHES, GAME
5 Phil McConkey, vs. Philadelphia
Nov. 20, 1988
4 David Meggett, at Pittsburgh
Oct. 14, 1991
4 Phil McConkey, at Philadelphia
Sept. 29, 1985
4 Phil McConkey, at Rams
Sept. 30, 1984
4 Phil McConkey, at Washington
Sept. 16, 1984
4 Carl Lockhart, vs. Minnesota
Oct. 31, 1971
4 Eddie Dove, at Cleveland
Oct. 27, 1963
3 by nany players last: David Meggett, at Philadelphia
Dec. 27, 1992

MOST PUNT RETURNS, CAREER
2,206 Emlen Tunnell (1948-58)
1,907 David Meggett (1989-93)
1,708 Phil McConkey (1984-88)
752 Leon Bright (1981-82)
491 Bob Hammond (1976-78)
449 Pete Athas (1971-74)

MOST PUNT RETURN YARDS, SEASON
582 David Meggett (1989)
489 Emlen Tunnell (1951)
467 David Meggett (1990)
442 Phil McConkey (1985)

MOST PUNT RETURN YARDS, GAME
147 Emlen Tunnell, vs. Chicago Cardinals
Oct. 14, 1951
143 leon bright, vs. philadelphia
Dec. 11, 1982
114 David Meggett, vs. Raiders
Dec. 24, 1989
112 Phil McConkey, vs. Philadelphia
Dec. 6, 1987
107 David Meggett, at New Orleans
Dec. 20, 1993
106 Emlen Tunnell, vs. Washington
Dec. 7, 1952
103 Phil McConkey, vs. Philadelphia
Sept. 8, 1985
103 Rondy Colbert, vs. New Orleans
Dec. 14, 1975
101 Leon Bright, vs. Rams
Dec. 6, 1981

LONGEST PUNT RETURN
83 Eddie Dove, at Philadelphia
Sept. 29, 1963
81 Bosh Pritchard, at Chicago Cardinals
Nov. 25, 1951
81 Emlen Tunnel, vs. Chicago Cardinals

Oct. 14, 1951
76T David Meggett, vs. Raiders
Dec. 24, 1989
75T David Meggett, at New Orleans
Dec. 20, 1993
74 Emlen Tunnell, at N.Y. Yankees
Dec. 16, 1951

HIGHEST AVERAGE RETURN, CAREER (30 RETURNS)
10.8 David Meggett (176 returns, 1989-93)
9.1 Bob Hammond (54 returns, 1976-78)
8.8 Pete Athas (51 returns, 1971-74)
8.6 Emlen Tunnell (257 returns, 1948-58)
8.3 Leon Bright (106 returns, 1981-82)
8.2 Alvin Garrett (35 returns, 1980)
8.1 Phil McConkey (213 returns, 1984-88)

HIGHEST AVERAGE RETURN, SEASON (QUALIFIERS)
15.5 Merle Hapes (11 returns, 1942)
14.9 George Franck (13 returns, 1941)
14.4 Emlen Tunnell (34 returns, 1951)

MOST TOUCHDOWNS, CAREER
5 Emlen Tunnell (1948-58)
4 David Meggett (1989-93)
1 by many players

MOST TOUCHDOWNS, SEASON
3 Emlen Tunnell (1951)
1 by nany players last: David Meggett (1993)

MOST TOUCHDOWNS, GAME
1 David Meggett, at New Orleans
Dec. 20, 1993
1 David Meggett, at Tampa Bay
Nov. 24, 1991
1 David Meggett, vs. Philadelphia
Sept. 9, 1990
1 David Meggett, vs. Raiders
Dec. 24, 1989
1 Bob Hammond, at Dallas
Sept. 25, 1977
1 Rondy Colbert, vs. New Orleans
Dec. 14, 1975
1 Bobby Duhon, vs. Philadelphia
Oct. 11, 1970
1 Emlen Tunnell, vs. Philadelphia
Nov. 20, 1955
1 Jimmy Patton, vs. Washington
Oct. 30, 1955
1 Herb Johnson, vs. Cleveland
Nov. 28, 1954
1 Emlen Tunnell, at N.Y. Yankees
Dec. 16, 1951
1 Bosh Pritchard, at Chicago Cardinals
Nov. 25, 1951
1 Emlen Tunnell, vs. Philadelphia
Oct. 21, 1951
1 Emlen Tunnell, vs. Chicago Cardinals
Oct. 14, 1951
1 Emlen Tunnell, vs. N.Y. Bulldogs
Nov. 6, 1949
1 Vic Carroll, at Boston Bulldogs
Oct. 8, 1944

KICKOFF RETURNS

MOST SEASONS LEADING LEAGUE
1 Joe Scott (1948)
1 Clarence Childs (1964)
1 David Meggett (NFC, 1990)

MOST KICKOFF RETURNS, CAREER
126 Clarence Childs (1964-67)
117 David Meggett (1989-93)
65 Rocky Thompson (1971-72)
64 Phil McConkey (1984-86)
54 Joe Scott (1948-53)

MOST KICKOFF RETURNS, SEASON
36 Rocky Thompson (1971)
35 Ronnie Blye (1968)
34 Clarence Jones (1964, 66)

MOST KICKOFF RETURNS, GAME
7 Alvin Garrett, at San Diego
 Oct. 19, 1980
7 Gene Filipski, at Washington
 Nov. 18, 1956
6 Clarence Childs, at Cleveland
 Dec. 4, 1966
5 by many players

MOST KICKOFF RETURN YARDS, CAREER
3,163 Clarence Childs (1964-67)
2,441 David Meggett (1989-93)
1,768 Rocky Thompson (1971-72)
1,467 Joe Scott (1948-53)
1,246 Phil McConkey (1984-86)
1,215 Emlen Tunnell (1948-58)

MOST KICKOFF RETURN YARDS, SEASON
987 Clarence Childs (1964)
947 Rocky Thompson (1971)
855 Clarence Childs (1966)

MOST KICKOFF RETURN YARDS, GAME
207 Joe Scott, vs. Rams
 Nov. 14, 1948
198 Rocky Thompson, at Detroit
 Sept. 17, 1972
170 Clarence Childs, at Cleveland
 Dec. 4, 1966
158 Clarence Childs, vs. Cleveland
 Oct. 24, 1965

LONGEST KICKOFF RETURN
100 Clarence Childs, vs. Minnesota
 Dec. 6, 1964
100 Emlen Tunnell, vs. N.Y. Yankees
 Nov. 4, 1951
99 Joe Scott, vs. Rams
 Nov. 14, 1948
98 Jimmy Patton vs. Washington
 Oct. 30, 1955

HIGHEST AVERAGE RETURN, CAREER (40 RETURNS)
27.2 Rocky Thompson (65 returns, 1971-72)
27.2 Joe Scott (54 returns, 1948-53)
26.4 Emlen Tunnell (46 returns, 1948-58)
25.1 Clarence Childs (126 returns, 1964-67)

HIGHEST AVERAGE RETURN, SEASON (QUALI-FIERS)
31.6 John Salscheider (15 returns, 1949)
30.2 John Counts (26 returns, 1962)
29.0 Clarence Childs (34 returns, 1964)

HIGHEST AVERAGE RETURN, GAME (3 RETURNS)
51.8 Joe Scott, vs. Rams
 Nov. 14, 1948 (4 returns)
50.3 Ronnie Blye, at Pittsburgh
 Sept. 15, 1968 (3 returns)
49.5 Rocky Thompson, at Detroit
 Sept. 17, 1972 (4 returns)
44.3 Emlen Tunnell, at Chicago Cardinals
 Nov. 1, 1953 (3 returns)

MOST TOUCHDOWNS, CAREER
2 Rocky Thompson (1971-72)
 2 Clarence Childs (1964-67)
 1 by many players
 last: David Meggett (1989-93)

MOST TOUCHDOWNS, SEASON
by many players, see next item

MOST TOUCHDOWNS, GAME
1 David Meggett, vs. Philadelphia
 Nov. 22, 1992
1 Rocky Thompson, at Detroit
 Sept. 17, 1972
1 Rocky Thompson, at \St. Louis
 Oct. 3, 1971
1 Clarence Childs, at Cleveland
 Dec. 4, 1966
1 Clarence Childs, vs. Minnesota
 Dec. 6, 1964
1 John Counts, at Washington
 Nov. 25, 1962
1 Jimmy Patton, vs. Washington]
 Oct. 30, 1955
1 Emlen Tunnell, vs. N.Y. Yankees
 Nov. 4, 1951
1 Joe Scott, vs. Rams
 Nov. 14, 1948

FUMBLERS

MOST FUMBLES, CAREER
93 Phil Simms (1979-93)
54 Charlie Conerly (1948-61)
48 Frank Gifford (1952-60, 62-64)
34 Alex Webster (1955-64)

MOST FUMBLES, GAME
5 Charlie Conerly, vs. San Francisco
 Dec. 1, 1957
4 Y.A. Tittle, at Philadelphia
 Sept. 13, 1964
3 by many players

MOST FUMBLES, SEASON
16 Phil Simms (l985)
11 Y.A. Tittle (1964)
11 Bobby Gaiters (1961)
11 Charlie Conerly (1957)

OWN RECOVERIES

MOST RECOVERED, CAREER
30 Phil Simms (1979-93)
26 Charlie Conerly (1948-61)
16 Frank Gifford (1952-60, 62-64)
15 Joe Morrison (1959-72)

MOST RECOVERED, SEASON
6 Jeff Hostetler (1991)
5 Phil Simms (1993)
5 Phil Simms (1985)
5 Joe Wells (1961)
5 Frank Gifford (1958)
5 Charlie Conerly (1948, 57)
5 Emlen Tunnell (1952)
5 Gene Roberts (1950)
4 by many players

MOST RECOVERED, GAME
3 Jeff Hostetler, vs. Phoenix
 Oct. 21, 1990
2 by many players last: Ottis Anderson, at San Francisco
 Dec. 3, 1990

OPPONENTS' RECOVERIES
MOST RECOVERIES, CAREER
19 Jim Katcavage (1956-68)
17 Harry Carson (1976-88)
15 George Martin (1975-88)
13 Cliff Livingston (1954-61)
12 Lawrence Taylor (1981-93)
12 Brad Van Pelt (1973-82)
12 Jim Patton (1955-66)

MOST RECOVERED, SEASON
2 by mnay players last: Lawrence Taylor, vs. Dallas
 Nov. 17, 1991

MOST RECOVERED, SEASON
5 Ernie Jones (1978)
5 Troy Archer (1977)
5 Ray Poole (1950)
4 Andy Stynchula (1964)
4 Erich Barnes (1963)
4 Sam Huff (1959)
4 Arnie Weinmeister (1953)
4 Frank ope (1946)
3 by many players

TOTAL RECOVERIES

MOST RECOVERED, CAREER
28 Phil Simms (1979-93)
26 Charlie Conerly (1948-61)
19 Jim Katcavage (1956-68)
17 Harry Carson (1976-88)
16 Frank Gifford (1952-60, 62-64)
15 George Martin (1975-88)
15 Joe Morrison (1959-72)

MOST RECOVERED, SEASON
6 Jeff Hostetler (1991)
6 Emlen Tunnell (1952)
5 by many players

MOST RECOVERED, GAME
3 Jeff Hostetler, vs. Phoenix
 Oct. 21, 1990

YARDS RETURNING FUMBLES
LONGEST FUMBLE RETURN
81 Andy Headen, vs. Dallas
 Sept. 9, 1984 (TD)
72 Wendell Harris, at Pittsburgh
 Sept. 11, 1966 (TD)
71 Roy Hilton, vs. Dallas
 Oct. 27, 1974 (TD)
67 Horace Sherrod, vs. Washington
 Dec. 7, 1952
65 Lindon Crow, vs. St. Louis
 Oct. 30, 1960 (TD)

MOST TOUCHDOWNS, CAREER (TOTAL)
2 George Martin (1981, 2-opp)
2 Sam Huff (1959, 63, 2-opp)
2 Tom Landry (1950, 51 2-opp)
2 Al Derogatis (1949, 50, 2-opp)

MOST TOUCHDOWNS, SEASON (TOTAL)
2 George Martin, at Washington, Sept. 13, 1981 (8 yards) and at St Louis, Dec.
 3, 1981 (20 yards)

MOST TOUCHDOWNS, GAME (TOATL)
1 by many players last: Dave Duerson, at Indianapolis
 Nov. 5, 1990 (31 yards)

QUARTERBACK SACKS
(compiled only since 1982)
MOST SACKS, CAREER
132.5 Lawrence Taylor (1981-93)
79.5 Leonard Marshall (1983-92)
45.5 George Martin (1982-88)

MOST SACKS, SEASON
20.5 Lawrence Taylor (1986)
15.5 Lawrence Taylor (1988)
15.5 Leonard Marshall (1985)
15.0 Lawrence Taylor (1989)
13.5 Lawrence Taylor (1985)

MOST SACKS, GAME
4.5 Pepper Johnson, at Tampa Bay
 Nov. 24, 1991
4.0 Lawrence Taylor, vs. Philadelphia
 Oct. 12, 1986
4.0 Lawrence Taylor, vs. Tampa Bay
 Sept. 23, 1984

3.0 Keith Hamilton, vs. Tampa Bay
 Sept. 12, 1993
3.0 Lawrence Taylor, vs. Philadelphia
 Sept. 9, 1990
3.0 Lawrence Taylor, at Phoenix
 Nov. 5, 1989
3.0 Lawrence Taylor, at New Orleans
 Nov. 27, 1988
3.0 Lawrence Taylor, vs. Detroit
 Oct. 16, 1988
3.0 Lawrence Taylor, at Washington
 Dec. 7, 1986
3.0 Lawrence Taylor, at Philadelphia
 Nov. 9, 1986
3.0 Lawrence Taylor, vs. Washington
 Oct. 27, 1986
3.0 Lawrence Taylor, vs. Dallas
 Sept. 9, 1984
3.0 Lawrence Taylor, at Washington
 Dec. 17, 1983
3.0 Lawrence Taylor, vs. Philadelphia
 Dec. 11, 1982
3.0 Leonard Marshall, at St. Louis
 Nov. 24, 1985
3.0 Leonard Marshall, at Philadelphia
 Sept. 29, 1985
3.0 Leonard Marshall, vs. Philadelphia
 Sept. 8, 1985

FIELD GOALS
MOST SEASONS LEADING LEAGUE
3 Ward Cuff (1938, tied, 1939, 1943, tied)
1 Ali Haji-Sheikh (1983)
1 Pat Summerall (1959)
1 Ken Strong (1944)

MOST FIELD GOALS ATTEMPTED, CAREER
219 Pete Gogolak (1966-74)
176 Joe Danelo (1976-82)
112 Pat Summerall (1958-61)

MOST FIELD GOALS ATTEMPTED, SEASON
42 Ali Haji-Sheikh (1983)
41 Pete Gogolak (1970)
38 Joe Danelo (1981)
34 Pat Summerall (1961)
32 Raul Allegre (1986)
31 David Treadwell (1993)
31 Pete Gogolak (1972)

MOST FIELD GOALS ATTEMPTED, GAME
6 Raul Allegre, at Minnesota
 Nov. 16, 1986
6 Ali Haji-Sheikh, at Washington
 Dec. 17, 1983
6 Joe Danelo, at Seattle
 Oct. 18, 1981
6 Pete Gogolak, at Philadelphia
 Nov. 25, 1973
6 Ben Agajanian, vs. Philadelphia
 Nov. 14, 1954

MOST FIELD GOALS, CAREER
126 Pete Gogolak (1966-74)
104 Joe Danelo (1976-82)
75 Raul Allegre (1986-90)
59 Pat Summerall (1958-61)

MOST FIELD GOALS, SEASON
35 Ali Haji-Sheikh (1983)
25 David Treadwell (1993)
25 Pete Gogolak (1970)
24 Raul Allegre (1986)
24 Joe Danelo (1981)
22 Matt Bahr (1991)
21 Joe Danelo (1978)
21 Pete Gogolak (1972)

MOST FIELD GOALS, GAME
6 Joe Danelo, at Seattle
Oct. 18, 1981
5 Raul Allegre, at Minnesota
Nov. 16, 1986
5 Eric Schubert, vs. Tampa Bay
Nov. 3, 1985
5 Ali Haji-Sheikh, at Washington
Dec. 17, 1983
4 David Treadwell, at Chicago
Sept. 5, 1993
4 Raul Allegre, at Philadelphia
Oct. 8, 1989
4 Raul Allegre, vs. Phoenix
Sept. 24, 1989
4 Raul Allegre, at Washington
Nov. 29, 1987
4 Raul Allegre, vs. Denver
Nov. 23, 1986
4 Ali Haji-Sheikh, at Dallas
Nov. 4, 1984
4 Ali Haji-Sheikh, vs. Seattle
Dec. 11, 1983
4 Joe Danelo, at Philadelphia
Jan. 2, 1983
4 Joe Danelo, vs. Washington
Nov. 14, 1976
4 Pete Gogolak, at Cleveland
Dec. 4, 1966
4 Pete Gogolak, vs. St. Louis
Oct. 9, 1966
4 Don Chandler, vs. Philadelphia
Nov. 18, 1962

MOST CONSECUTIVE GAMES KICKING FIELD GOALS
18 Joe Danelo (1977-79)
15 Raul Allegre (1988-89)
15 Ali Haji-Sheikh (1983)
14 Pat Summerall (1960-61)
12 Matt Bahr (1990-91)
9 Pete Gogolak (1972)
7 Ali Haji-Sheikh (1984)
7 Pat Summerall (1959)
7 Pat Summerall (1958-59)

LONGEST FIELD GOAL (IN YARDS)
56 Ali Haji-Sheikh, at Detroit
Nov. 7, 1983
56 Ali Haji-Sheikh, vs. Green Bay
Sept. 26, 1983
55 Joe Danelo, vs. New Orleans
Sept. 20, 1981
54 Brad Daluiso, vs. Phoenix
Nov. 28, 1993
54 Matt Bahr, vs. Houston
Dec. 21, 1991
54 Joe Danelo, at Seattle
Oct. 18, 1981
54 Pete Gogolak, vs. Dallas
Nov. 8, 1970
53 Raul Allegre, at Philadelphia
Nov. 15, 198
53 Don Chandler, at Dallas
Dec. 1, 1963
52 Raul Allegre, at Washington
Sept. 11, 1989
52 Raul Allegre, at Philadelphia
Nov. 15, 1987
52 Joe Danelo, at San Francisco
Nov. 29, 1981
52 Joe Danelo, vs. San Francisco
Sept. 24, 1978
51 Joe Danelo, at Dallas
Oct. 5, 1980
51 Joe Danelo, vs. Dallas
Nov. 6, 1977
50 Paul McFadded, vs. Dallas
Nov. 6, 1988
50 Joe Danelo, at Philadelphia
Sept. 22, 1980
50 Joe Danelo, at New Orleans
Oct. 29, 1978
50 Joe Danelo, vs. Washington
Nov. 14, 1976
50 Ben Agajanian, at Washington
Oct. 13, 1957

HIGHEST FIELD GOAL PERCENTAGE, CAREER (50 ATTEMPTS)
75.3 Matt Bahr 55-73 (1990-92)
74.3 Raul Allegre 75-101 (1986-90)
67.5 Ali Haji-Sheikh 54-80 (1983-85)
59.0 Joe Danelo 104-176 (1976-82)
57.1 Pete Gogolak 126-219 (1966-74)
54.8 Ben Agajanian 46-84 (1949, 54-57)

HIGHEST FIELD GOAL PERCENTAGE, SEASON (14 ATTEMPTS)
83.3 Ali Haji-Sheikh 35-42 (1983)
80.6 David Treadwell 25-31 (1993)
76.9 Raul Allegre 20-26 (1989)
76.2 Matt Bahr 16-21 (1992)
75.8 Matt Bahr 22-29 (1991)
75.0 Raul Allegre 24-32 (1986)
75.0 Ray Toole 12-16 (1951)
73.9 Matt Bahr 17-23 (1990)
73.7 Paul McFadded 21-29 (1978)
72.4 Joe Danelo 21-29 (1978)
69.0 Pat Summerall 20-29 (1959)

HIGHEST FIELD GOAL PERCENTAGE, GAME (4 ATTEMPTS)
100.0 David Treadwell, at Chicago
Sept. 5, 1993 (4-4)
100.0 Raul Allegre, at Washington
Nov. 29, 1987 (4-4)
100.0 Raul Allegre, vs. Denver
Nov. 23, 1986 (4-4)
100.0 Eric Schubert, vs. Tampa Bay
Nov. 3, 1985 (5-5)
100.0 Ali haji-Sheikh, at Dallas
Nov. 4, 1984 (4-4)
100.0 Joe Danelo, at Seattle
Oct. 18, 1981 (6-6)
100.0 Don Chandler, at Chicago
Dec. 2, 1962 (4-4)
83.3 Raul Allegre, at Minnesota
Nov. 16, 1986 (5-6)
83.3 Ali Haji-Sheikh, at Washington
Dec. 17, 1983 (5-6)
80.0 Ali Haji-Sheikh, vs. Seattle
Dec. 11, 1983 (4-5)
80.0 Joe Danelo, at Philadelphia
Jan. 2, 1983 (4-5)
80.0 Joe Danelo, vs. Washington
Nov. 14, 1976 (4-5)
80.0 Pete Gogolak, at Detroit
Nov. 17, 1974 (4-5)
80.0 Pete Gogolak, at St. Louis
Oct. 9, 1966 (4-5)
80.0 Don Chandler, at Cleveland
Oct. 27, 1963 (4-5)
80.0 Don Chandler, vs. Philadelphia
Nov. 18, 1962 (4-5)

MOST FIELD GOALS, GAME
6 Joe Danelo, at Seattle
Oct. 18, 1981
5 Raul Allegre, at Minnesota
Nov. 16, 1986
5 Eric Schubert, vs. Tampa Bay
Nov. 3, 1985
5 Ali Haji-Sheikh, at Washington
Dec. 17, 1983
4 David Treadwell, at Chicago
Sept. 5, 1993
4 Raul Allegre, at Philadelphia
Oct. 8, 1989
4 Raul Allegre, vs. Phoenix
Sept. 24, 1989
4 Raul Allegre, at Washington
Nov. 29, 1987
4 Raul Allegre, vs. Denver
Nov. 23, 1986
4 Ali Haji-Sheikh, at Dallas
Nov. 4, 1984
4 Ali Haji-Sheikh, vs. Seattle
Dec. 11, 1983
4 Joe Danelo, at·Philadelphia
Jan. 2, 1983
4 Joe Danelo, vs. Washington
Nov. 14, 1976
4 Pete Gogolak, at Cleveland
Dec. 4, 1966
4 Pete Gogolak, vs. St. Louis
Oct. 9, 1966
4 Don Chandler, vs. Philadelphia
Nov. 18, 1962

MOST CONSECUTIVE GAMES KICKING FIELD GOALS
18 Joe Danelo (1977-79)
15 Raul Allegre (1988-89)
15 Ali Haji-Sheikh (1983)
14 Pat Summerall (1960-61)
12 Matt Bahr (1990-91)
9 Pete Gogolak (1972)
7 Ali Haji-Sheikh (1984)
7 Pat Summerall (1959)
7 Pat Summerall (1958-59)

LONGEST FIELD GOAL (IN YARDS)
56 Ali Haji-Sheikh, at Detroit
Nov. 7, 1983
56 Ali Haji-Sheikh, vs. Green Bay
Sept. 26, 1983
55 Joe Danelo, vs. New Orleans
Sept. 20, 1981
**54 Brad Daluiso, vs. Phoenix
Nov. 28, 1993**
54 Matt Bahr, vs. Houston
Dec. 21, 1991
54 Joe Danelo, at Seattle
Oct. 18, 1981
54 Pete Gogolak, vs. Dallas
Nov. 8, 1970
53 Raul Allegre, at Philadelphia
Nov. 15, 1987
53 Don Chandler, at Dallas
Dec. 1, 1963
52 Raul Allegre, at Washington
Sept. 11, 1989
52 Raul Allegre, at Philadelphia
Nov. 15, 1987
52 Ali Haji-Sheikh, at Green Bay
Sept. 15, 1985
52 Joe Danelo, at San Francisco
Nov. 29, 1981
52 Joe Danelo, vs. San Francisco
Sept. 24, 1978
51 Joe Danelo, at Dallas
Oct. 5, 1980
51 Joe Danelo, vs. Dallas
Nov. 6, 1977
50 Paul McFadden, vs. Dallas
Nov. 6, 1988
50 Joe Danelo, at Philadelphia
Sept. 22, 1980
50 Joe Danelo, at New Orleans
Oct. 29, 1978
50 Joe Danelo, vs. Washington
Nov. 14, 1976
50 Ben Agajanian, at Washington
Oct. 13, 1957

HIGHEST FIELD GOAL PERCENTAGE, CAREER (50 ATTEMPTS)
75.3 Matt Bahr 55-73 (1990-92)
74.3 Raul Allegre 75-101 (1986-90)
67.5 Ali Haji-Sheikh 54-80 (1983-85)
59.0 Joe Danelo 104-176 (1976-82)
57.1 Pete Gogolak 126-219 (1966-74)
54.8 Ben Agajanian 46-84 (1949, 54-57)

HIGHEST FIELD GOAL PERCENTAGE, SEASON (14 ATTEMPTS)
83.3 Ali Haji-Sheikh 35-42 (1983)
80.6 David Treadwell 25-31 (1993)
76.9 Raul Allegre 20-26 (1989)
76.2 Matt Bahr 16-21 (1992)
75.8 Matt Bahr 22-29 (1991)
75.0 Raul Allegre 24-32 (1986)
75.0 Ray Poole 12-16 (1951)
73.9 Matt Bahr 17-23 (1990)
73.7 Paul McFadden 14-19 (1978)
72.4 Joe Danelo 21-29 (1978)
69.0 Pat Summerall 20-29 (1959)

HIGHEST FIELD GOAL PERCENTAGE, GAME (4 ATTEMPTS)
100.0 David Treadwell, at Chicago
Sept. 5, 1993 (4-4)
100.0 Raul Allegre, at Washington
Nov. 29, 1987 (4-4)
100.0 Raul Allegre, vs. Denver
Nov. 23, 1986 (4-4)
100.0 Eric Schubert, vs. Tampa Bay
Nov. 3, 1985 (5-5)
100.0 Ali Haji-Sheikh, at Dallas
Nov. 4, 1984 (4-4)
100.0 Joe Danelo, at Seattle
Oct. 18, 1981 (6-6)
100.0 Don Chandler, at Chicago
Dec. 2, 1962 (4-4)
83.3 Raul Allegre, at Minnesota
Nov. 16, 1986 (5-6)
83.3 Ali Haji-Sheikh, at Washington
Dec. 17, 1983 (5-6)
80.0 Ali Haji-Sheikh, vs. Seattle
Dec. 11, 1983 (4-5)
80.0 Joe Danelo, at Philadelphia
Jan. 2, 1983 (4-5)
80.0 Joe Danelo, vs. Washington
Nov. 14, 1976 (4-5)

80.0 Pete Gogolak, at Detroit
Nov. 17, 1974 (4-5)
80.0 Pete Gogolak, at St. Louis
Oct. 9, 1966 (4-5)
80.0 Don Chandler, at Cleveland
Oct. 27, 1963 (4-5)
80.0 Don Chandler, vs. Philadelphia
Nov. 18, 1962

SAFETIES

MOST SAFETIES, CAREER
3 Jim Katcavage (1956-68)
2 Leonard Marshall (1983-92)
1 by many players: Last
Keith Hamilton (1992-1993))

MOST SAFETIES, SEASON
1 by many players Last: **Keith Hamilton (1993)**

MOST SAFETIES, GAME
1 by many players:
Last **Keith Hamilton**, at Miami Dec. 5, 1993

RUSHING

MOST SEASONS LEADING LEAGUE
2 Bill Pascal (1943-44)
1 Eddie Price (1951)
1 Tuffy Leemans (1936)

MOST ATTEMPTS, CAREER
1,318 Joe Morris (1982-89)
1,196 Alex Webster (1955-64)
1,066 Ron Johnson (1970-75)
919 Tuffy Leemans (1936-43)

MOST ATTEMPTS, SEASON
341 Joe Morris (1986)
325 Ottis Anderson (1989)
307 Joe Morris (1988)
298 Ron Johnson (1972)
294 Joe Morris (1985)
292 Rodney Hampton (1993)
271 Eddie Price (1951)

MOST ATTEMPTS, GAME
43 Butch Woolfolk, at Philadelphia
Nov. 20, 1983
**41 Rodney Hampton, vs. Rams
Sept. 19, 1993**
38 Harry Newman, vs. Green Bay
Nov. 11, 1934
36 Joe Morris, vs. Pittsburgh
Dec. 21, 1985
36 Ron Johnson, at Philadelphia
Oct. 2, 1972
**33 Rodney Hampton, vs. Indianapolis
Dec. 12. 1993**
**32 Rodney Hampton, at Buffalo
Oct. 3, 1993**
32 Joe Morris, vs. Phoenix
Dec. 4, 1988
32 Eddie Price, at Chicago Cardinals
Nov. 25, 1951
31 Joe Morris, vs. Kansas City
Dec. 11, 1988
31 Joe Morris, vs. Washington
Oct. 27, 1986
**30 Rodney Hampton, vs. Dallas
Jan. 2, 1994**
30 Joe Morris, vs. San Diego
Sept. 14, 1986
30 Ron Johnson, vs. Philadelphia
Sept. 23, 1973
30 Eddie Price, at N.Y. Yankees
Dec. 16, 1951
30 Bill Paschal, vs. Washington
Dec. 3, 1944

MOST YARDS GAINED, CAREER
5,296 Joe Morris (1982-89)
4,638 Alex Webster (1955-64)
3,836 Ron Johnson (1970-75)
3,732 Rodney Hampton (1990-93)
3,609 Frank Gifford (1952-60, 62-64)

MOST YARDS GAINED, SEASON
1,516 Joe Morris (1986)
1,336 Joe Morris (1985)
1,182 Ron Johnson (1972)
1,141 Rodney Hampton (1992)
1,083 Joe Morris (1988)
1,077 Rodney Hampton (1993)
1,059 Rodney Hampton (1991)
1,027 Ron Johnson (1970)
1,023 Ottis Anderson (1989)
971 Eddie Price (1951)
928 Alex Webster (1961)

MOST YARDS GAINED, GAME
218 Gene Roberts, vs. Chicago Cardinals
Nov. 12, 1950
202 Joe Morris, vs. Pittsburgh
Dec. 21, 1985
188 Bill Paschal, vs. Washington
Dec. 5, 1943
181 Joe Morris, vs. Washington
Oct. 27, 1986
179 Joe Morris, vs. St. Louis
Dec. 14, 1986
**173 Rodney Hampton, vs. Indianapolis
Dec. 12, 1993**
171 Eddie Price, at Philadelphia
Dec. 9, 1951

MOST GAMES 100 YARDS OR MORE RUSHING, CAREER
19 Joe Morris (1982-89)
11 Rodney Hampton (1990-93)
11 Eddie Price (1950-55)
10 Ron Johnson (1970-73)
7 Rob Carpenter (1981-83)
5 Bill Paschal (1943-47)
5 Tuffy Leemans (1936-43)
4 Doug Kotar (1974-78)
4 Alex Webster (1955-64)
4 Gene Roberts (1947-50)

MOST GAMES, 100 YARDS OR MORE RUSHING, SEASON
8 Joe Morris (1986)
6 Joe Morris (1985)
5 Rodney Hampton (1993)
4 Rob Carpenter (1981)
4 Ron Johnson (1972)
4 Ron Johnson (1970)
4 Eddie Price (1952)
4 Eddie Price (1951)
3 Rodney Hampton (1991)
3 Joe Morris (1988)
3 Rob Carpenter (1983)
3 Eddie Price (1950)
3 Tuffy Leemans (1936)
2 Rodney Hampton (1992)
2 Billy Taylor (1979)
2 Doug Kotar (1976)
2 Ron Johnson (1973)
2 Gene Roberts (1949)
2 Ward Cuff (1944)
2 Bill Paschal (1944)
2 Bill Paschal (1943)

LONGEST RUN FROM SCRIMMAGE
91 Hap Moran, vs. Green Bay
Nov. 23, 1930
80 Eddie Price, at Philadelphia
Dec. 9, 1951
79 Frank Gifford, vs. Washington
Nov. 29, 1959

77 Bill Paschal, vs. Cleveland Rams
Nov. 4, 1945

HIGHEST AVERAGE GAIN, CAREER (500 ATTEMPTS)
4.30 Frank Gifford, 1952-60, 62-64
(840-3609)
4.14 Mel Triplett, 1955-60
(553-2289)
4.08 Rodney Hampton, 1990-93
(914-3732)
4.02 Joe Morris, 1982-88
(1318-5296)
3.88 Alex Webster, 1955-64
(1196-4638)
3.75 Doug Kotar, 1974-81
(900-3378)

HIGHEST AVERAGE GAIN, SEASON (QUALIFIERS)
5.58 Eddie Price 1950 (126-703)
5.15 Frank Gifford 1956 (159-819)
4.95 Alex Webster 1955 (128-634)

HIGHEST AVERAGE GAIN, GAME (10 ATTEMPTS)
13.30 Frank Reagan, vs. Los Angeles,
Dec. 1, 1946 (10-133)
12.23 Tuffy Leemans, vs. Green Bay
Nov. 20, 1938 (13-159)
11.43 Ernie Koy, at Washington
Oct. 1, 1967 (14-160)

MOST TOUCHDOWNS, CAREER
48 Joe Morris (1982-89)
39 Alex Webster (1955-64)
34 Frank Gifford (1952-60, 62-64)
33 Ron Johnson (1970-75)

MOST TOUCHDOWNS, SEASON
21 Joe Morris (1985)
14 Rodney Hampton (1992)
14 Ottis Anderson (1989)
14 Joe Morris (1986)
10 Rodney Hampton (1991)
10 Bill Paschal (1943)
9 Ron Johnson (1972)
9 Gene Roberts (1949)
9 Bill Paschal (1944)
8 Ottis Anderson (1988)
8 Ron Johnson (1970)
8 Frank Gifford (1958)

MOST TOUCHDOWNS, GAME
3 Rodney Hampton, vs. Kansas City
Dec. 19, 1992
3 Ottis Anderson, vs. Phoenix
Dec. 4, 1988
3 Joe Morris, vs. St. Louis
Dec. 14, 1986
3 Joe Morris, vs. Pittsburgh
Dec. 21, 1985
3 Joe Morris, at Houston
Dec. 8, 1985
3 Joe Morris, vs. Cleveland
Dec. 1, 1985
3 Joe Morris, at Washington
Nov. 18, 1985
3 Joe Morris, vs. Washington
Oct. 28, 1984
3 Charlie Evans, vs. San Diego
Nov. 7, 1971
3 Mel Triplett, at Chicago Cardinals
Oct. 7, 1956
3 Gene Roberts, at N.Y. Bulldogs
Sept. 30, 1949
3 Bill Paschal, vs. Cardinals-Pittsburgh
Oct. 22, 1944
2 by many players
last: Lewis Tillman, vs. Philadelphia
Oct. 17, 1993

MOST CONSECUTIVE GAMES RUSHING FOR TOUCHDOWNS
7 Bill Paschal (1944)
5 Rodney Hampton (1991)
5 Ottis Anderson (1989)
5 Bill Gaiters (1961)
4 Joe Morris (1985)
4 Ron Johnson (1970)
4 Bill Paschal (1943)
4 Ken Strong (1934)

MOST GAMES 100 YARDS+

RUSHING, CAREER
19 Joe Morris (1982-89)
11 Rodney Hampton (1990-93)
11 Eddie Price (1950-55)
10 Ron Johnson (1970-73)
7 Rob Carpenter (1981-83)
5 Bill Paschal (1943-47)
5 Tuffy Leemans (1936-43)
4 Doug Kotar (1974-78)
4 Alex Webster (1955-64)
4 Gene Roberts (1947-50)

RUSHING, SEASON
8 Joe Morris (1986)
6 Joe Morris (1985)
5 Rodney Hampton (1993)
4 Rob Carpenter (1981)
4 Ron Johnson (1972)
4 Ron Johnson (1970)
4 Eddie Price (1952)
4 Eddie Price (1951)
3 Rodney Hampton (1991)
3 Joe Morris (1988)
3 Rob Carpenter (1983)
3 Eddie Price (1950)
3 Tuffy Leemans (1936)
2 Rodney Hampton (1992)
2 Billy Taylor (1979)
2 Doug Kotar (1976)
2 Ron Johnson (1973)
2 Gene Roberts (1949)
2 Ward Cuff (1944)
2 Bill Paschal (1944)
2 Bill Paschal (1943)

LONGEST RUN FROM SCRIMMAGE
91 Hap Moran, vs. Green Bay
Nov. 23, 1930
80 Eddie Price, at Philadelphia
Dec. 9, 1951
79 Frank Gifford, vs. Washington
Nov. 29, 1959
77 Bill Paschal, vs. Cleveland Rams
Nov. 4, 1945

HIGHEST AVERAGE GAIN, CAREER (500 ATTEMPTS)
4.30 Frank Gifford, 1952-60, 62-64
(840-3609)
4.14 Mel Triplett, 1955-60
(553-2289)
**4.08 Rodney Hampton, 1990-93
(914-3732)**
4.02 Joe Morris, 1982-88
(1318-5296)
3.88 Alex Webster, 1955-64
(1196-4638)
3.75 Doug Kotar, 1974-81
(900-3378)

HIGHEST AVERAGE GAIN, SEASON (QUALIFIERS)
5.58 Eddie Price 1950 (126-703)
5.15 Frank Gifford 1956 (159-819)
4.95 Alex Webster 1955 (128-634)

HIGHEST AVERAGE GAIN, GAME (10 ATTEMPTS)

13.30 Frank Reagan, vs. Rams
Dec. 1, 1946 (10-133)
12.23 Tuffy Leemans, vs. Green Bay
Nov. 20, 1938 (13-159)
11.43 Ernie Koy, at Washington
Oct. 1, 1967 (14-160)

MOST RUSHING TOUCHDOWNS, CAREER

48 Joe Morris (1982-89)
39 Alex Webster (1955-64)
34 Frank Gifford (1952-60, 62-64)
33 Ron Johnson (1970-75)

MOST RUSHING TOUCHDOWNS, SEASON

21 Joe Morris (1985)
14 Rodney Hampton (1992)
14 Ottis Anderson (1989)
14 Joe Morris (1986)
11 Ottis Anderson (1990)
10 Rodney Hampton (1991)
10 Bill Paschal (1943)
9 Ron Johnson (1972)
9 Gene Roberts (1949)
9 Bill Paschal (1944)
8 Ottis Anderson (1988)
8 Ron Johnson (1970)
8 Frank Gifford (1958)

MOST RUSHING TOUCHDOWNS, GAME

3 Rodney Hampton, vs. Kansas City
Dec. 19, 1992
3 Ottis Anderson, vs. Phoenix
Dec. 4, 1988
3 Joe Morris, vs. St. Louis
Dec. 14, 1986
3 Joe Morris, vs. Pittsburgh
Dec. 21, 1985
3 Joe Morris, at Houston
Dec. 8, 1985
3 Joe Morris, vs. Cleveland
Dec. 1, 1985
3 Joe Morris, at Washington
Nov. 18, 1985
3 Joe Morris, vs. Washington
Oct. 28, 1984
3 Charlie Evans, vs. San Diego
Nov. 7, 1971
3 Mel Triplett, at Chicago Cardinals
Oct. 7, 1956
3 Gene Roberts, at N.Y. Bulldogs
Sept. 30, 1949
3 Bill Paschal, vs. Cardinals-Pittsburgh
Oct. 22, 1944
2 by many players
Last: Lewis Tillman, vs. Philadelphia
Oct. 17, 1993

MOST CONSECUTIVE GAMES RUSHING FOR TOUCHDOWNS

7 Bill Paschal (1944)
5 Rodney Hampton (1991)
5 Ottis Anderson (1989)
5 Bill Gaiters (1961)
4 Joe Morris (1985)
4 Ron Johnson (1970)
4 Bill Paschal (1943)
4 Ken Strong (1934)

MOST SEASONS LEADING LEAGUE

2 Ed Danowski (1935, 1938)
1 Phil Simms (NFC, 1990)
1 Norm Snead (1972)
1 Y.A. Tittle (1963)
1 Charlie Conerly (1959)
1 Harry Newman (1933)

MOST PASSES ATTEMPTED, CAREER

4,647 Phil Simms (1979-93)
2,833 Charlie Conerly (1948-61)
1,898 Fran Tarkenton (1967-71)
1,308 Y.A. Tittle (1961-64)

MOST PASSES ATTEMPTED, SEASON

533 Phil Simms (1984)
495 Phil Simms (1985)
479 Phil Simms (1988)
468 Phil Simms (1986)
409 Fran Tarkenton (1969)
405 Phil Simms (1989)
402 Phil Simms (1980)
400 Phil Simms (1993)
389 Fran Tarkenton (1970)
386 Scott Brunner (1983)
386 Fran Tarkenton (1971)

MOST PASSES ATTEMPTED, GAME

62 Phil Simms, at Cincinnati
Oct. 13, 1985
53 Charlie Conerly, at Pittsburgh
Dec. 5, 1948
52 Jeff Rutledge, vs. Seattle
Dec. 11, 1983
51 Scott Brunner, vs. San Diego
Oct. 2, 1983
51 Scott Brunner, at St. Louis
Dec. 26, 1982
50 Phil Simms , at Dallas
Dec. 15, 1985
49 Phil Simms, vs. Rams
Sept. 25, 1988
49 Phil Simms, at Philadelphia
Sept. 22, 1980
48 Phil Simms, at San Francisco
Nov. 27, 1989
48 Phil Simms, at St. Louis
Dec. 13, 1987
47 Jeff Rutledge, at Washington
Dec. 17, 1983
47 Randy Johnson, vs. Philadelphia
Dec. 19, 1971

MOST PASSES COMPLETED, CAREER

2,576 Phil Simms (1979-93)
1,051 Fran Tarkenton (1967-71)
1,418 Charlie Conerly (1948-61)
731 Y.A. Tittle (1961-64)

MOST PASSES COMPLETED, SEASON

286 Phil Simms (1984)
275 Phil Simms (1985)
263 Phil Simms (1988)
259 Phil Simms (1986)
247 Phil Simms (1993)
228 Phil Simms (1989)
226 Fran Tarkenton (1971)
221 Y.A. Tittle (1963)
220 Fran Tarkenton (1969)

MOST PASSES COMPLETED, GAME

40 Phil Simms, at Cincinnati
Oct. 13, 1985
36 Charlie Conerly, at Pittsburgh
Dec. 5, 1948
31 Scott Brunner, vs. San Diego
Oct. 2, 1983
30 Phil Simms, at St. Louis
Dec. 13, 1987
30 Randy Johnson, vs. Philadelphia
Dec. 19, 1971
29 Phil Simms, vs. Rams
Sept. 25, 1988
29 Scott Brunner, at St.. Louis
Dec. 26, 1982
28 Jeff Hostetler, at Dallas
Sept. 29, 1991
28 Jeff Rutledge, vs. Seattle
Dec. 11, 1983

28 Phil Simms, vs . New Orleans
Sept. 20, 1981
28 Norm Snead, vs. New England
Sept. 22, 1974
28 Randy Johnson, at St. Louis
Oct. 28, 1973

MOST CONSECUTIVE PASSES COMPLETED

13 Phil Simms, at Cincinnati
Oct. 13, 1985
12 Y.A. Tittle, vs. Washington
Oct. 28, 1962

HIGHEST PASSING EFFICIENCY, CAREER (1000 ATTEMPTS)

55.89 Y.A. Tittle (731-1308, 1961-64)
55.43 Phil Simms (2576-4647, 1979-93)
55.37 Fran Tarkenton (1051-1898, 1967-71)
50.05 Charlie Conerly (1418-2833, 1948-61)

HIGHEST PASSING EFFICIENCY, SEASON (QUALIFIERS)

62.81 Jeff Hostetler (179-285, 1991)
61.80 Phil Simms (247-400, 1993)
60.31 Norm Snead (196-325, 1972)
60.22 Y.A. Tittle (221-367, 1963)
59.20 Phil Simms (184-311, 1990)
58.55 Fran Tarkenton (226-386, 1971)
58.25 Charlie Conerly (113-194, 1959)

HIGHEST PASSING EFFICIENCY, GAME (20 ATTEMPTS)

* 88.00 Phil Simms, vs. Denver
Jan. 25, 1987 (22-25)
82.35 Jeff Hostetler, at Dallas
Sept. 29, 1991 (28-34)
80.95 Phil Simms, at Indianapolis
Nov. 5, 1990 (17-21)
80.95 Phil Simms, vs. St. Louis
Oct. 25, 1987 (17-21)
80.76 Phil Simms, vs. Green Bay
Dec. 19, 1987 (21-26)
80.00 Norm Snead, vs. New England
Sept. 22, 1974 (28-35)
80.00 Fran Tarkenton, vs. San Diego
Nov. 7, 1971 (16-20)
80.00 Y.A. Tittle, vs. Philadelphia
Nov. 10, 1963 (16-20)
77.80 Phil Simms, vs. Rams
Sept. 19, 1993 (21-27)
77.27 Bob Clatterbuck, vs. Pittsburgh
Dec. 5, 1954 (17-22)
76.92 Phil Simms, vs. Detroit
Sept. 17, 1989 (20-26)
76.70 Phil Simms, vs. Philadelphia
Sept. 2, 1984 (23-30)
76.19 Phil Simms, at Dallas
Sept. 16, 1990 (16-21)
75.00 Norm Snead, vs. Green Bay
Oct. 7, 1973 (21-28)
75.00 Y.A. Tittle, vs. Philadelphia
Nov. 12, 1961 (18-24)
*superbowl xxi

MOST YARDS PASSING, CAREER

33,462 Phil Simms (1979-93)
19,488 Charlie Conerly (1948-61)
13,905 Fran Tarkenton (1967-71)
10,439 Y.A. Tittle (1961-64)

MOST YARDS PASSING, SEASON

4,044 Phil Simms (1984)
3,829 Phil Simms (1985)
3,487 Phil Simms (1986)
3,359 Phil Simms (1988)
3,224 Y.A. Tittle (1962)
3,145 Y.A. Tittle (1963)
3,088 Fran Tarkenton (1967)

MOST YARDS PASSING, GAME

513 Phil Simms, at Cincinnati
Oct. 13, 1985
505 Y.A. Tittle, vs. Washington
Oct. 28, 1962
432 Phil Simms, vs. Dallas
Oct. 6, 1985
409 Phil Sinms, vs. Philadelphia
Sept. 2, 1984
395 Scott Brunner, vs. San Diego
Oct. 2, 1983
388 Phil Simms, at San Francisco
Dec. 1, 1986
372 Randy Johnson, at Dallas
Dec. 19, 1971
368 Jeff Hostetler, at Dallas
Sept. 29, 1991
363 Charlie Conerly, at Pittsburgh
Dec. 5, 1948

MOST GAMES, 300 YARDS OR MORE PASSING, CAREER

21 Phil Simms (1979-93)
9 Y.A. Tittle (1961-64)
4 Scott Brunner (1980-83)
4 Fran Tarkenton (1967-71)
3 Jeff Rutledge (1983)
3 Charlie Conerly (1948-61)

MOST GAMES, 300 YARDS OR MORE PASSING, SEASON

4 Phil Simms (1986)
4 Phil Simms (1984)
4 Y.A. Tittle (1962)
3 Phil Simms (1988)
3 Phil Simms (1985)
3 Jeff Rutledge (1983)
3 Y.A. Tittle (1961)
2 Scott Brunner (1983)
2 Scott Brunner (1982)
2 Phil Simms (1980)
2 Y.A. Tittle (1963)

PASSING

MOST SEASONS LEADING LEAGUE

2 Ed Danowski (1935,1938)
1 Phil Simms (NFC, 1990)
1 Norm Snead (1972)
1 Y.A. Tittle (1963)
1 Charlie Conerly (1959)
1 Harry Newman (1933)

MOST PASSES ATTEMPTED, CAREER

4,647 Phil Simms (1979-93)
2,833 Charlie Conerly (1948-61)
1,898 Fran Tarkenton (1967-71)
1,308 Y.A. Tittle (1961-64)

MOST PASSES ATTEMPTED, SEASON

533 Phil Simms (1984)
495 Phil Simms (1985)
479 Phil Simms (1988)
468 Phil Simms (1986)
409 Fran Tarkenton (1969)
405 Phil Simms (1989)
402 Phil Simms (1980)
400 Phil Simms (1993)
389 Fran Tarkenton (1970)
386 Scott Brunner (1983)
386 Fran Tarkenton (1971)

MOST PASSES ATTEMPTED, GAME

62 Phil Simms, at Cincinnati
Oct. 13, 1985
53 Charlie Conerly, at Pittsburgh
Dec. 5, 1948
52 Jeff Rutledge, vs. Seattle
Dec. 11, 1983

240

51 Scott Brunner, vs. San Diego
Oct. 2, 1983
51 Scott Brunner, at St. Louis
Dec. 26, 1982
50 Phil Simms , at Dallas
Dec. 15, 1985
49 Phil Simms, vs. Rams
Sept. 25, 1988
49 Phil Simms, at Philadelphia
Sept. 22, 1980
48 Phil Simms, at San Francisco
Nov. 27, 1989
48 Phil Simms, at St. Louis
Dec. 13, 1987
47 Jeff Rutledge, at Washington
Dec. 17, 1983
47 Randy Johnson, vs. Philadelphia
Dec. 19, 1971

MOST PASSES COMPLETED, CAREER
2,576 Phil Simms (1979-93)
1,051 Fran Tarkenton (1967-71)
1,418 Charlie Conerly (1948-61)
731 Y.A. Tittle (1961-64)

MOST PASSES COMPLETED, SEASON
286 Phil Simms (1984)
275 Phil Simms (1985)
263 Phil Simms (1988)
259 Phil Simms (1986)
247 Phil Simms (1993)
228 Phil Simms (1989)
226 Fran Tarkenton (1971)
221 Y.A. Tittle (1963)
220 Fran Tarkenton (1969)

MOST PASSES COMPLETED, GAME
40 Phil Simms, at Cincinnati
Oct. 13, 1985
36 Charlie Conerly, at Pittsburgh
Dec. 5, 1948
31 Scott Brunner, vs. San Diego
Oct. 2, 1983
30 Phil Simms, at St. Louis
Dec. 13, 1987
30 Randy Johnson, vs. Philadelphia
Dec. 19, 1971
29 Phil Simms, vs. Rams
Sept. 25, 1988
29 Scott Brunner, at St.. Louis
Dec. 26, 1982
28 Jeff Hostetler, at Dallas
Sept. 29, 1991
28 Jeff Rutledge, vs. Seattle
Dec. 11, 1983
28 Phil Simms, vs . New Orleans
Sept. 20, 1981
28 Norm Snead, vs. New England
Sept. 22, 1974
28 Randy Johnson, at St. Louis
Oct. 28, 1973

MOST CONSECUTIVE PASSES COMPLETED
13 Phil Simms, at Cincinnati
Oct. 13, 1985
12 Y.A. Tittle, vs. Washington
Oct. 28, 1962

HIGHEST PASSING EFFICIENCY, CAREER (1000 ATTEMPTS)
55.89 Y.A. Tittle (731-1308, 1961-64)
55.43 Phil Simms (2576-4647, 1979-93)
55.37 Fran Tarkenton (1051-1898, 1967-71)
50.05 Charlie Conerly (1418-2833, 1948-61)

HIGHEST PASSING EFFICIENCY, SEASON (QUALIFIERS)
62.81 Jeff Hostetler (179-285, 1991)
61.80 Phil Simms (247-400, 1993)
60.31 Norm Snead (196-325, 1972)

60.22 Y.A. Tittle (221-367, 1963)
59.20 Phil Simms (184-311, 1990)
58.55 Fran Tarkenton (226-386, 1971)
58.25 Charlie Conerly (113-194, 1959)

HIGHEST PASSING EFFICIENCY, GAME (20 ATTEMPTS)
82.35 Jeff Hostetler, at Dallas
Sept. 29, 1991 (28-34)
80.95 Phil Simms, at Indianapolis
Nov. 5, 1990 (17-21)
80.95 Phil Simms, vs. St. Louis
Oct. 25, 1987 (17-21)
80.76 Phil Simms, vs. Green Bay
Dec. 19, 1987 (21-26)
80.00 Norm Snead, vs. New England
Sept. 22, 1974 (28-35)
80.00 Fran Tarkenton, vs. San Diego
Nov. 7, 1971 (16-20)
80.00 Y.A. Tittle, vs. Philadelphia
Nov. 10, 1963 (16-20)
77.80 Phil Simms, vs. Rams
Sept. 19, 1993 (21-27)
77.27 Bob Clatterbuck, vs. Pittsburgh
Dec. 5, 1954 (17-22)
76.92 Phil Simms, vs. Detroit
Sept. 17, 1989 (20-26)
76.70 Phil Simms, vs. Philadelphia
Sept. 2, 1984 (23-30)
76.19 Phil Simms, at Dallas
Sept. 16, 1990 (16-21)
75.00 Norm Snead, vs. Green Bay
Oct. 7, 1973 (21-28)
75.00 Y.A. Tittle, vs. Philadelphia
Nov. 12, 1961 (18-24)

MOST YARDS PASSING, CAREER
33,462 Phil Simms (1979-93)
19,488 Charlie Conerly (1948-61)
13,905 Fran Tarkenton (1967-71)
10,439 Y.A. Tittle (1961-64)

MOST YARDS PASSING, SEASON
4,044 Phil Simms (1984)
3,829 Phil Simms (1985)
3,487 Phil Simms (1986)
3,359 Phil Simms (1988)
3,224 Y.A. Tittle (1962)
3,145 Y.A. Tittle (1963)
3,088 Fran Tarkenton (1967)

MOST YARDS PASSING, GAME
513 Phil Simms, at Cincinnati
Oct. 13, 1985
505 Y.A. Tittle, vs. Washington
Oct. 28, 1962
432 Phil Simms, vs. Dallas
Oct. 6, 1985
409 Phil Simms, vs. Philadelphia
Sept. 2, 1984
395 Scott Brunner, vs. San Diego
Oct. 2, 1983
388 Phil Simms, at San Francisco
Dec. 1, 1986
372 Randy Johnson, vs. Philadelphia
Dec. 19, 1971
368 Jeff Hostetler, at Dallas
Sept. 29, 1991
363 Charlie Conerly, at Pittsburgh
Dec. 5, 1948

MOST GAMES, 300 YARDS OR MORE PASSING, CAREER
21 Phil Simms (1979-93)
9 Y.A. Tittle (1961-64)
4 Scott Brunner (1980-83)
4 Fran Tarkenton (1967-71)
3 Jeff Rutledge (1983)
3 Charlie Conerly (1948-61)

MOST GAMES, 300 YARDS OR MORE PASSING, SEASON
4 Phil Simms (1986)
4 Phil Simms (1984)
4 Y.A. Tittle (1962)
3 Phil Simms (1988)
3 Phil Simms (1985)
3 Jeff Rutledge (1983)
3 Y.A. Tittle (1961)
2 Scott Brunner (1983)
2 Scott Brunner (1982)
2 Phil Simms (1980)
2 Y.A. Tittle (1963)

LONGEST PASS COMPLETION (IN YARDS)
98 Earl Morrall (to Homer Jones)
at Pittsburgh, Sept. 11, 1966
94 Norm Snead (to Rich Houston)
vs. Dallas, Sept. 24, 1972
89 Earl Morrall (to Homer Jones)
vs. Philadelphia, Oct. 17, 1965
88 Frank Reagan (to George Franck)
vs. Washington, Oct. 12, 1947

MOST TOUCHDOWN PASSES, CAREER
199 Phil Simms (1979-93)
173 Charlie Conerly (1948-61)
103 Fran Tarkenton (1967-71)
96 Y.A. Tittle (1961-64)

MOST TOUCHDOWN PASSES, SEASON
36 Y.A. Tittle (1963)
33 Y.A. Tittle (1962)
29 Fran Tarkenton (1967)

MOST TOUCHDOWN PASSES, GAME
7 Y.A. Tittle, vs. Washington
Oct. 28, 1962
6 Y.A. Tittle, vs. Dallas
Dec. 16, 1962
5 Phil Simms at St. Louis
Sept. 7, 1980
5 Fran Tarkenton, vs. St. Louis
Oct. 25, 1970

MOST CONSECUTIVE GAMES TOUCHDOWN PASSES
13 Y.A. Tittle (1963-64)
10 Phil Simms (1988-89)
10 Phil Simms (1986-87)
10 Charlie Conerly (1948-49)
9 Earl Morrall (1965-66)

FEWEST PASSES HAD INTERCEPTED, CAREER (1000 ATTEMPTS)
68 Y.A. Tittle (1308, 1961-64)
72 Fran Tarkenton (1898, 1967-71)
157 Phil Simms (4647, 1979-93)
167 Charlie Conerly (2833, 1948-61)

FEWEST PASSES HAD INTERCEPTED, SEASON (QUALIFIERS)
3 Gary Wood (1964)
4 Jeff Hostetler (1991)
4 Phil Simms (1990)
4 Charlie Conerly (1959)
4 Ed Danowski (1937)

FEWEST PASSES HAD INTERCEPTED, GAME (MOST ATTEMPTS)
0 Phil Simms, vs. Phoenix
Nov. 28, 1993 (41 attempts)
0 Scott Brunner, vs. St. Louis
Dec. 26, 1982 (51 attempts)
0 Fran Tarkenton, at Dallas
Oct. 11, 1971 (46 attempts)
0 Fran Tarkenton, vs. Dallas
Dec. 15, 1968 (43 attempts)
0 Y.A. Tittle, vs. Washington
Oct. 28, 1962 (39 attempts)

MOST PASSES HAD INTERCEPTED, CAREER
167 Charlie Conerly (1949-61)
157 Phil Simms (1979-93)
72 Fran Tarkenton (1967-71)
68 Y.A. Tittle (1961-64)

MOST PASSES HAD INTERCEPTED, SEASON
25 Charlie Conerly (1953)
25 Frank Filchock (1946)
23 Joe Pisarcik (1978)
22 Phil Simms (1986)
22 Scott Brunner (1983)
22 Norm Snead (1973)
22 Y.A. Tittle (1964)
22 Charlie Conerly (1951)

MOST PASSES HAD INTERCEPTED, GAME
5 Jeff Rutledge, at New Orleans
Nov. 22, 1987
5 Charlie Conerly, vs. Detroit
Dec. 13, 1953
5 Charlie Conerly, vs. Chicago Cardinals
Oct. 14, 1951
5 Frank Filchock, at Washington
Oct. 13, 1946
5 Harry Newman, at Portsmouth
Sept. 24, 1933
4 by many players
Last: Phil Simms, at Seattle
Oct. 19, 1986

LOWEST PERCENTAGE PASSES HAD INTERCEPTED, CAREER (1000 ATTEMPTS)
3.38 Phil Simms (157-4647, 1979-93)
3.79 Fran Tarkenton (72-1898, 1967-71)
5.20 Y.A. Tittle (68-1308, 1961-64)
5.89 Charlie Conerly (167-2833, 1948-61)

LOWEST PERCENTAGE PASSES HAD INTERCEPTED, SEASON (QUALIFIERS)
1.28 Phil Simms (4-311, 1990)
1.40 Jeff Hostetler (4-285, 1991)
1.96 Fran Tarkenton (8-409, 1969)
2.06 Charlie Conerly (4-194, 1959)
2.10 Gary Wood (3-143, 1964)

MOST SEASONS LEADING LEAGUE
1 Earnest Gray (1983)
1 Bob Tucker (1971)
1 Tod Goodwin (1935)

PASS RECEPTIONS

MOST PASS RECEPTIONS, CAREER
395 Joe Morrison (1959-72)
367 Frank Gifford (1952-60, 62-64)
327 Bob Tucker (1970-77)

MOST PASS RECEPTIONS, SEASON
78 Earnest Gray (1983)
68 Del Shofner (1961)
66 Mark Bavaro (1986)
65 Lionel Manuel (1988)
64 Del Shofner (1963)
59 Bob Tucker (1971)
58 Mark Jackson (1993)

MOST PASS RECEPTIONS, GAME
12 Mark Bavaro, at Cincinnati
Oct. 13, 1985
11 Mark Bavaro, at St. Louis
Dec. 13, 1987
11 Gary Shirk, vs. New Orleans
Sept. 20, 1981
11 Billy Taylor, at Tampa Bay
Nov. 2, 1980
11 Doug Kotar, at St. Louis
Oct. 3, 1976
11 Del Shofner, vs. Washington
Oct. 28, 1962

11 Frank Gifford, vs. San Francisco
Dec. 1, 1957
10 George Adams, vs. Rams
Sept. 25, 1988
10 Ron Johnson, vs. New England
Sept. 22, 1974
10 Tucker Frederickson, vs. Washington
Nov. 15, 1970
10 Alex Webster, vs. Dallas
Dec. 16, 1962
9 by many players Last: Mark Bavaro, at Philadelphia
Oct. 10, 1988

MOST CONSECUTIVE GAMES, PASS RECEPTIONS
46 David Meggett (1989-93)
45 Bob Tucker (1970-73)
32 Homer Jones (1965-67)
26 Homer Jones (1968-69)
25 Earnest Gray (1982-84)
23 Joe Morrison (1964-65)
23 Kyle Rote (1956-58)
21 Mark Bavaro (1986-87)

MOST YARDS GAINED, CAREER
5,434 Frank Gifford (1952-60, 62-64)
4,993 Joe Morrison (1959-72)
4,845 Homer Jones (1964-69)

MOST YARDS GAINED, SEASON
1,209 Homer Jones (1967)
1,181 Del Shofner (1963)
1,139 Earnest Gray (1983)
1,133 Del Shofner (1962)

MOST YARDS GAINED, GAME
269 Del Shofner, vs. Washington
Oct. 28, 1962
212 Gene Roberts, at Green Bay
Nov. 13, 1949
201 Gene Roberts, vs. Chicago Bears
Oct. 23, 1949

LONGEST PASS RECEPTION (IN YARDS)
98 Homer Jones (from Earl Morrall)
at Pittsburgh, Sept. 11, 1966
94 Rich Houston (from Norm Snead)
vs. Dallas, Sept. 24, 1972
89 Homer Jones (from Earl Morrall)
vs. Philadelphia, Oct. 17, 1965
88 George Franck (from Frank Reagan)
at Washington, Oct. 12, 1947

HIGHEST AVERAGE GAIN, CAREER (200 MINIMUM)
22.6 Homer Jones (214-4845, 1964-69)
18.1 Del Shofner (239-4315, 1961-67)
17.2 Aaron Thomas (247-4253, 1962-70)

HIGHEST AVERAGE GAIN, SEASON (QUALIFIERS)
24.7 Homer Jones (49-1209, 1967)
23.5 Homer Jones (45-1057, 1968)
21.8 Homer Jones (48-1044, 1966)

HIGHEST AVERAGE GAIN, GAME (4 MINIMUM)
50.3 Gene Roberts, vs. Chicago Bears
Oct. 23, 1949 (4-201)
49.0 Homer Jones, at Washington
Oct. 1, 1967 (4-196)
37.5 Frank Liebel, vs. Detroit
Nov. 18, 1945 (4-150)

MOST TOUCHDOWNS, CAREER
48 Kyle Rote (1951-61)
47 Joe Morrison (1959-71)
43 Frank Gifford (1952-60, 62-64)

MOST TOUCHDOWNS, SEASON
13 Homer Jones (1967)
12 Del Shofner (1962)
11 Del Shofner (1961)

MOST TOUCHDOWNS, GAME
4 Earnest Gray, at St. Louis
Sept. 7, 1980
3 Earnest Gray, vs. Green Bay
Nov. 16, 1980
3 Billy Taylor, at St. Louis
Dec. 9, 1979

3 Ron Johnson, at Philadelphia
Oct. 2, 1972
3 Rich Houston, at Green Bay
Sept. 19, 1971
3 Joe Walton, vs. Dallas
Dec. 16, 1962
3 Del Shofner, at Washington
Nov. 25, 1962
3 Del Shofner, at Dallas
Nov. 11, 1962
3 Joe Walton, vs. Washington
Oct. 28, 1962
3 Del Shofner, at Philadelphia
Dec. 10, 1961
3 Del Shofner, vs. Washington
Nov. 5, 1961
3 Bob Schnelker, at Washington
Oct. 10, 1954
3 Gene Roberts, at Green Bay
Nov. 13, 1949
3 Gene Roberts, vs. Chicago Bears
Oct. 23, 1949
3 Frank Liebel, vs. Philadelphia
Dec. 2, 1945

MOST CONSECUTIVE GAMES, TOUCHDOWN RECEPTION
7 Kyle Rote (1959-60)
5 Aaron Thomas (1967)
5 Joe Morrison (1966)
5 Homer Jones (1966)
5 Del Shofner (1963)
5 Frank Liebel (1945)
4 by many players Last: Mark Bavaro (1987)

INTERCEPTIONS

MOST SEASONS LEADING LEAGUE
2 Dick Lynch (1961, 1963)

MOST INTERCEPTIONS BY, CAREER
74 Emlen Tunnell (1948-58)
52 Jimmy Patton (1955-66)
41 Carl Lockhart (1965-75)

MOST INTERCEPTIONS BY, SEASON
11 Jimmy Patton (1958)
11 Otto Schellbacher (1951)
10 Willie Williams (1968)
10 Emlen Tunnell (1949)
10 Frank Reagan (1947)
9 by five players. Last: Dick Lynch (1963)

MOST INTERCEPTIONS BY, GAME
3 Terry Kinard, vs. Dallas
Sept. 20, 1987
3 Carl Lockhart, at Cleveland
Dec. 4, 1966
3 Dick Lynch, at Philadelphia
Sept. 29, 1963
3 Jimmy Patton, at Chicago
Dec. 2, 1962
3 Dick Lynch, vs. Philadelphia
Nov. 12, 1961
3 Dick Lynch, at St. Louis
Oct. 8, 1961
3 Emlen Tunnell, at Chicago Cardinals
Nov. 24, 1957
3 Tom Landry, vs. Philadelphia
Nov. 14, 1954
3 Emlen Tunnell, at Pittsburgh
Nov. 7, 1954
3 Otto Schellbacher, vs. Cleveland

Oct. 22, 1950
3 Emlen Tunnell, at Washington
Oct. 9, 1949
3 Frank Reagan, vs. Boston Bulldogs
Nov. 28, 1948
3 Emlen Tunnell, at Green Bay
Nov. 21, 1948

3 Art Faircloth, at Boston
Sept. 23, 1948
3 Frank Reagan, vs. Green Bay
Nov. 23, 1947
3 Frank Reagan, at Detroit
Nov. 2, 1947
3 Howard Livingston, at Brooklyn
Oct. 15, 1944
3 Ward Cuff, at Philadelphia
Sept. 13, 1941

MOST CONSECUTIVE GAMES, INTERCEPTIONS BY
6 Willie Williams (1968)
5 Carl Lockhart (1969-70)
5 Emlen Tunnell (1954-55)
4 by many players. Last: Terry Jackson (1978)

MOST YARDS GAINED, CAREER
1,240 Emlen Tunnell (1948-58)
712 Jimmy Patton (1955-66)
574 Terry Kinard (1983-89)
568 Dick Lynch (1959-66)
475 Carl Lockhart (1965-75)

MOST YARDS GAINED, SEASON
251 Dick Lynch (1963)
251 Emlen Tunnell (1949)
203 Frank Reagan (1947)
195 Erich Barnes (1961)

MOST YARDS GAINED, GAME
109 Ward Cuff, at Philadelphia
Sept. 13, 1941
104 George Cheverko, at Washington
Oct. 3, 1948
102 Erich Barnes, at Dallas
Oct. 15, 1961

LONGEST GAIN (IN YARDS)
102 Erich Barnes, at Dallas
Oct. 15, 1961 (TD)
101 Henry Carr, at Rams
Nov. 13, 1966 (TD)
97 Lawrence Taylor, at Detroit
Nov. 25, 1982 (TD)
89 Bruce Maher, at Dallas
Nov. 10, 1968

MOST TOUCHDOWNS, CAREER
4 Dick Lynch (1959-66)
4 Emlen Tunnell (1948-58)
3 George Martin (1975-86)
3 Carl Lockhart (1965-72)
3 Jerry Hillebrand (1963-66)
3 Erich Barnes (1961-64)
3 Tom Landry (1950-55)
2 Lawrence Taylor (1981-93)
2 Pepper Johnson (1986-92)
2 Terry Kinard (1983-89)
2 Terry Jackson (1978-82)
2 Jimmy Patton (1955-66)
2 Tom Scott (1959-64)
2 Otto Schnellbacher (1950-51)
2 Bill Petrilas (1944-45)

MOST TOUCHDOWNS, SEASON
3 Dick Lynch (1963)
2 Carl Lockhart (1968)
2 Erich Barnes (1961)
2 Tom Landry (1961)
2 Otto Schnellbacher (1951)

2 Emlen Tunnell (1949)
2 Bill Petrilas (1944)

MOST TOUCHDOWNS, GAME
1 by many players
Last: Mark Collins, vs. Rams Sept. 19, 1993

MOST CONSECUTIVE GAMES, TOUCHDOWNS
2 Carl Lockhart, at Philadelphia, Sept. 22--vs. Washington, Sept. 29, 1968
2 Dick Lynch, vs. Cleveland, Oct. 13--vs. Dallas, Oct. 20, 1963
2 Tom Landry, at Cleveland, Oct. 28--vs. N.Y. Yankees, Nov. 4, 1951

PUNTING

MOST SEASONS LEADING LEAGUE
2 Sean Landeta (NFC, 1986, 1990)
1 Dave Jennings (1979, 1980)
1 Don Chandler (1957)

MOST PUNTS, CAREER
931 Dave Jennings (1974-84)
526 Sean Landeta (1985-93)
525 Don Chandler (1956-64)

MOST PUNTS, SEASON
104 Dave Jennings (1979)
100 Dave Jennings (1977)
97 Dave Jennings (1981)
95 Dave Jennings (1978)
94 Dave Jennings (1980)

MOST PUNTS, GAME
14 Carl Kinschef, at Detroit
Nov. 7, 1943
11 Dave Jennings, at Atlanta
Oct. 25, 1981
11 Dave Jennings, at Washington
Sept. 13, 1981
11 Don Chandler, at St. Louis
Oct. 8, 1961
11 Charlie Conerly, vs. Cleveland
Nov. 18, 1951
11 Tom Landry, vs. Philadelphia
Nov. 26, 1950

MOST YARDS, CAREER
38,792 Dave Jennings (1974-84)
23,019 Don Chandler (1956-64)
22,804 Sean Landeta (1985-93)

MOST YARDS, SEASON
4,445 Dave Jennings (1979)
4,211 Dave Jennings (1980)
4,198 Dave Jennings (1981)
3,995 Dave Jennings (1978)
3,993 Dave Jennings (1977)

MOST YARDS, GAME
583 Carl Kinscherf, at Detroit
Nov. 7, 1943 (14 punts)
511 Dave Jennings, at Washington
Sept. 13, 1981 (11 punts)
485 Don Chandler, at St. Louis
Oct. 8, 1961 (11 punts)
470 Len Barnum, vs. Green Bay
Nov. 17, 1940 (10 punts)

LONGEST PUNT
74 Len Younce, vs. Chicago Bears
Nov. 14, 1943
74 Don Chandler, at Dallas
Oct. 11, 1964
73 Dave Jennings, vs. Houston
Dec. 5, 1982
72 Dave Jennings, vs. Dallas
Nov. 4, 1979
72 Len Younce, at Brooklyn
Oct. 15, 1944

72 Carl Kinscherf, at Philadelphia-Pittsburgh
Oct. 9, 1943
71 Sean Landeta, vs. Green Bay
Nov. 8, 1992
71 Sean Landeta, vs. Philadelphia
Dec. 3, 1989

HIGHEST AVERAGE, CAREER (150 PUNTS)
43.8 Don Chandler (525 punts, 1956-64)
43.4 Sean Landeta (526 punts, 1985-93)
41.8 Tom Blanchard (171 punts, 1971-73)
41.7 Dave Jennings (931 punts, 1974-84)

HIGHEST AVERAGE SEASON (35 PUNTS)
46.6 Don Chandler (55 punts, 1959)
45.6 Don Chandler (73 punts, 1964)
44.9 Don Chandler (59 punts, 1963)

HIGHE8T AVERAGE, GAME (4 PUNT8)
~5.3 DAVE JENNINGS, VS. HOUSTON
DEC. 5, 1982 (4 PUNTS)
DON CHANDLER, AT CLEVELAND
OCT. 11, 1959 (8 PUNTS)
DAVE JENNINGS, AT DALLAS
OCT. 5, 1980 (5 PUNTS)
DAVE JENNINGS, AT DALLAS
NOV. 15, 1992
SEAN LANDETA, AT DENVER
NOV. 15, 1992
DAVE JENNINGS, VS. KANSAS CITY
SEPT. 17, 1978 (7 PUNTS)
DON CHANDLER, VS. PITTSBURGH
NOV. 15, 1959 (7 PUNTS)

HIGHEST AVERAGE, GAME (4 PUNTS)
55.3 Dave Jennings, vs. Houston
Dec. 5, 1982 (4 punts)
54.1 Don Chandler, at Cleveland
Oct. 11, 1959 (8 punts)
54.0 Dave Jennings, at Dallas
Oct. 5, 1980 (5 punts)
53.1 Dave Jennings, at Dallas
Nov. 30, 1975 (7 punts)
52.4 Sean Landeta, at Denver
Nov. 15, 1992 (5 punts)
52.1 Dave Jennings, vs. Kansas City
Sept. 17, 1978 (7 punts)
52.1 Don Chandler, vs. Pittsburgh
Nov. 15, 1959 (7 punts)

PUNT RETURNS

MOST PUNT RETURNS, CAREER
257 Emlen Tunnell (1948-58)
213 Phil McConkey (1984-88)
176 David Meggett (1989-93)
106 Leon Bright (1981-83)
62 Carl Lockhart (1965-71)

MOST PUNT RETURNS, SEASON
53 Phil McConkey (1985)
52 Leon Bright (1981)
46 David Meggett (1989)
46 Phil McConkey (1984)
43 David Meggett (1990)
42 Phil McConkey (1987)
40 Phil McConkey (1988)
38 Emlen Tunnell (1953)
37 Leon Bright (1982)

MOST PUNT RETURNS, GAME
9 Phil McConkey, vs. Philadelphia
Dec. 6, 1987
9 Pete Shaw, at Philadelphia
Nov. 20, 1983
9 Leon Bright, vs. Philadelphia
Dec. 11, 1982
8 Phil McConkey, at Dallas
Nov. 4, 1984
8 Leon Bright, at Washington
Sept. 13, 1981

8 Emlen Tunnell, vs. N.Y. Yankees
Dec. 3, 1950
7 Phil McConkey, at St. Louis
Oct. 5, 1986
7 Phil McConkey, vs. Philadelphia
Sept. 8, 1985
7 Rondy Colbert, vs. New Orleans
Dec. 14, 1975
6 Pete Athas, at St. Louis
Dec. 15, 1974
6 Emlen Tunnell, at Philadelphia
Oct. 4, 1952

MOST FAIR CATCHES, SEASON
25 Phil McConkey (1988)
20 David Meggett (1993)
18 Phil McConkey (1985)
16 Bobby Duhon (1971)
15 Phil McConkey (1984)
14 David Meggett (1989)
14 Phil McConkey (1987)
14 Pete Athas (1973)
14 Bob Grim (1972)
14 Carl Lockhart (1969)

MOST FAIR CATCHES, CAREER
84 Phil McConkey (1984-88)
66 David Meggett (1989-93)
57 Carl Lockhart (1965-71)
40 Bobby Duhon (1968-72)

FEWEST FAIR CATCHES, GAME
0 Leon Bright (17 returns, 1983)
0 Leon Bright (37 returns, 1982)
0 Leon Bright (52 returns, 1981)

MOST FAIR CATCHES, GAME
5 Phil McConkey, vs. Philadelphia
Nov. 20, 1988
**4 David Meggett, at Pittsburgh
Oct. 14, 1991**
4 Phil McConkey, at Philadelphia
Sept. 29, 1985
4 Phil McConkey, at Rams
Sept. 30, 1984
4 Phil McConkey, at Washington
Sept. 16, 1984
4 Carl Lockhart, vs. Minnesota
Oct. 31, 1971
4 Eddie Dove, at Cleveland
Oct. 27, 1963
3 by many players. Last: **David Meggett**, at
Philadelphia, Dec. 27, 1992

MOST PUNT RETURNS YARDS, CAREER
2,206 Emlen Tunnell (1948-58)
1,907 David Meggett (1989-93)
1,708 Phil McConkey (1984-88)
752 Leon Bright (1981-82)
491 Bob Hammond (1976-78)
449 Pete Athas (1971-74)

MOST PUNT RETURN YARDS, SEASON
582 David Meggett (1989)
489 Emlen Tunnell (1951)
467 David Meggett (1990)
442 Phil McConkey (1985)

MOST PUNT RETURN YARDS, GAME
147 Emlen Tunnell, vs. Chicago Cardinals
Oct. 14, 1951
143 Leon Bright, vs. Philadelphia
Dec. 11, 1982
**114 David Meggett, vs. Raiders
Dec. 24, 1989**
112 Phil McConkey, vs. Philadelphia
Dec. 6, 1987
**107 David Meggett, at New Orleans
Dec. 20, 1993**
106 Emlen Tunnell, vs. Washington
Dec. 7, 1952

103 Phil McConkey, vs. Philadelphia
Sept. 8, 1985
103 Rondy Colbert, vs. New Orleans
Dec. 14, 1975
101 Leon Bright, vs. Rams
Dec. 6, 1981

LONGEST PUNT RETURN
83 Eddie Dove, at Philadelphia
Sept. 29, 1963
81 Bosh Pritchard, at Chicago Cardinals
Nov. 25, 1951
81 Emlen Tunnel, vs. Chicago Cardinals
Oct. 14, 1951
**76T David Meggett, vs. Raiders
Dec. 24, 1989**
**75T David Meggett, at New Orleans
Dec. 20, 1993**
74 Emlen Tunnell, at N.Y. Yankees
Dec. 16, 1951

HIGHEST AVERAGE RETURN, CAREER (30 RETURNS)
10.8 David Meggett (176 returns, 1989-93)
9.1 Bob Hammond (54 returns, 1976-78)
8.8 Pete Athas (51 returns, 1971-74)
8.6 Emlen Tunnell (257 returns, 1948-58)
8.3 Leon Bright (106 returns, 1981-82)
8.2 Alvin Garrett (35 returns, 1980)
8.1 Phil McConkey (213 returns, 1984-88)

HIGHEST AVERAGE RETURN, SEASON (QUALI- FIERS)
15.5 Merle Hapes (11 returns, 1942)
14.9 George Franck (13 returns, 1941)
14.4 Emlen Tunnell (34 returns, 1951)

HIGHEST AVERAGE RETURN, GAME (3 RETURNS)
36.8 Emlen Tunnell, vs. Chicago Cardinals
Oct. 14, 1951 (4 returns)
35.3 Emlen Tunnell vs. Washington
Dec. 7, 1952 (3 returns)
**32.7 David Meggett vs. Seattle
Nov. 19, 1989 (3 returns)**
31.0 Emlen Tunnell vs. Washington
Oct. 7, 1951 (3 returns)

MOST TOUCHDOWNS, CAREER
5 Emlen Tunnell (1948-58)
4 David Meggett (1989-93)
1 by many players

MOST TOUCHDOWNS, SEASON
3 Emlen Tunnell (1951)
**1 by many players
Last: David Meggett (1993)**

MOST TOUCHDOWNS, GAME
**1 David Meggett, at New Orleans
Dec. 20, 1993**
**1 David Meggett, at Tampa Bay
Nov. 24, 1991**
**1 David Meggett, vs. Philadelphia
Sept. 9, 1990**
**1 David Meggett, vs. Raiders
Dec. 24, 1989**
1 Bob Hammond, at Dallas
Sept. 25, 1977
1 Rondy Colbert, vs. New Orleans
Dec. 14, 1975
1 Bobby Duhon, vs. Philadelphia
Oct. 11, 1970
1 Emlen Tunnell, vs. Philadelphia
Nov. 20, 1955
1 Jimmy Patton, vs. Washington
Oct. 30, 1955
1 Herb Johnson, vs. Cleveland
Nov. 28, 1954

1 Emlen Tunnell, at N.Y. Yankees
Dec. 16, 1951
1 Bosh Pritchard, at Chicago Cardinals
Nov. 25, 1951
1 Emlen Tunnell, vs. Philadelphia
Oct. 21, 1951
1 Emlen Tunnell, vs. Chicago Cardinals
Oct. 14, 1951
1 Emlen Tunnell, vs. N.Y. Bulldogs
Nov. 6, 1949
1 Vic Carroll, at Boston Bulldogs
Oct. 8, 1944

KICKOFF RETURNS

MOST SEASONS LEADING LEAGUE
1 David Meggett (NFC, 1990)
1 Joe Scott (1948)
1 Clarence Childs (1964)

MOST KICKOFF RETURNS, CAREER
126 Clarence Childs (1964-67)
117 David Meggett (1989-93)
65 Rocky Thompson (1971-72)
64 Phil McConkey (1984-86)
54 Joe Scott (1948-53)

MOST KICKOFF RETURNS, SEASON
36 Rocky Thompson (1971)
35 Ronnie Blye (1968)
34 Clarence Jones (1964, 1966)

MOST KICKOFF RETURNS, GAME
7 Alvin Garrett, at San Diego
Oct. 19, 1980
7 Gene Filipski, at Washington
Nov. 18, 1956
6 Clarence Childs, at Cleveland
Dec. 4, 1966
5 by many players

MOST KICKOFF RETURN YARDS, CAREER
3,163 Clarence Childs (1964-67)
2,441 David Meggett (1989-93)
1,768 Rocky Thompson (1971-72)
1,467 Joe Scott (1948-53)
1,215 Emlen Tunnell (1948-58)

MOST KICKOFF RETURN YARDS, SEASON
987 Clarence Childs (1964)
947 Rocky Thompson (1971)
855 Clarence Childs (1966)

MOST KICKOFF RETURN YARDS, GAME
207 Joe Scott, vs. Rams
Nov. 14, 1948
198 Rocky Thompson, at Detroit
Sept. 17, 1972
170 Clarence Childs, at Cleveland
Dec. 4, 1966
158 Clarence Childs, vs. Cleveland
Oct. 24, 1965

LONGEST KICKOFF RETURN
100 Clarence Childs, vs. Minnesota
Dec. 6, 1964
100 Emlen Tunnell, vs. N.Y. Yankees
Nov. 4, 1951
99 Joe Scott, vs. Rams
Nov. 14, 1948
98 Jimmy Patton vs. Washington
Oct. 30, 1955

HIGHEST AVERAGE RETURN, CAREER (40 RETURNS)
27.2 Rocky Thompson (65 returns, 1971-72)
27.2 Joe Scott (54 returns, 1948-53)
26.4 Emlen Tunnell (46 returns, 1948-58)
25.1 Clarence Childs (126 returns, 1964-67)

HIGHEST AVERAGE RETURN, SEASON (QUALIFIERS)

31.6 John Salscheider (15 returns, 1949)
30.2 John Counts (26 returns, 1962)
29.0 Clarence Childs (34 returns, 1964)

HIGHEST AVERAGE RETURN, GAME (3 RETURNS)

51.8 Joe Scott, vs. Rams
  Nov. 14, 1948 (4 returns)
50.3 Ronnie Blye, at Pittsburgh
  Sept. 15, 1968 (3 returns)
49.5 Rocky Thompson, at Detroit
  Sept. 17, 1972 (4 returns)
44.3 Emlen Tunnell, at Chicago Cardinals
  Nov. 1, 1953 (3 returns)

MOST TOUCHDOWNS, CAREER

2 Rocky Thompson (1971-72)
2 Clarence Childs (1964-67)
1 by many players. Last: **David Meggett** (1989-93)

MOST TOUCHDOWNS, SEASON

by many players, see next item

MOST TOUCHDOWNS, GAME

1 David Meggett, vs. Philadelphia
Nov. 22, 1992
1 Rocky Thompson, at Detroit
  Sept. 17, 1972
1 Rocky Thompson, at St. Louis
  Oct. 3, 1971
1 Clarence Childs, at Cleveland
  Dec. 4, 1966
1 Clarence Childs, vs. Minnesota
  Dec. 6, 1964
1 John Counts, at Washington
  Nov. 25, 1962
1 Jimmy Patton, vs. Washington
  Oct. 30, 1955
1 Emlen Tunnell, vs. N.Y. Yankees
  Nov. 4, 1951
1 Joe Scott, vs. Rams
  Nov. 14, 1948

FUMBLES

MOST FUMBLES, CAREER

93 Phil Simms (1979-93)
54 Charlie Conerly (1948-61)
48 Frank Gifford (1952-60, 62-64)
34 Alex Webster (1955-64)

MOST FUMBLES, GAME

5 Charlie Conerly, vs. San Francisco
  Dec. 1, 1957
4 Y.A. Tittle, at Philadelphia
  Sept. 13, 1964
3 by many players

MOST FUMBLES, SEASON

16 Phil Simms (1985)
11 Y.A. Tittle (1964)
11 Bobby Gaiters (1961)
11 Charlie Conerly (1957)

OWN RECOVERIES

MOST RECOVERED, CAREER

30 Phil Simms (1979-93)
26 Charlie Conerly (1948-61)
16 Frank Gifford (1952-60, 62-64)
15 Joe Morrison (1959-72)

MOST RECOVERED, SEASON

6 Jeff Hostetler (1991)
5 Phil Simms (1993)
5 Phil Simms (1985)
5 Joe Wells (1961)
5 Frank Gifford (1958)
5 Charlie Conerly (1948, 57)
5 Emlen Tunnell (1952)
5 Gene Roberts (1950)
4 by many players

MOST RECOVERED, GAME

3 Jeff Hostetler, vs. Phoenix
  Oct. 21, 1990
2 by many players
  Last: Ottis Anderson, at San Francisco Dec. 3, 1990

OPPONENTS' RECOVERIES

MOST RECOVERIES, CAREER

19 Jim Katcavage (1956-68)
17 Harry Carson (1976-88)
15 George Martin (1975-88)
13 Cliff Livingston (1954-61)
12 Lawrence Taylor (1981-93)
12 Brad Van Pelt (1973-82)
12 Jim Patton (1955-66)

MOST RECOVERED, GAME

2 by many players. Last: Lawrence Taylor, vs. Dallas
  Nov. 17, 1991

MOST RECOVERED, SEASON

5 Ernie Jones (1978)
5 Troy Archer (1977)
5 Ray Poole (1950)
4 Andy Stynchula (1964)
4 Erich Barnes (1963)
4 Sam Huff (1959)
4 Arnie Weinmeister (1953)
4 Frank Cope (1946)
3 by many players
26 Charlie Conerly (1948-61)
19 Jim Katcavage (1956-68)
17 Harry Carson (1976-88)

16 Frank Gifford (1952-60, 62-64)
15 George Martin (1975-88)
15 Joe Morrison (1959-72)

MOST RECOVERED, SEASON

6 Jeff Hostetler (1991)
6 Emlen Tunnell (1952)
5 by many players

MOST RECOVERED, GAME

3 Jeff Hostetler, vs. Phoenix
  Oct. 21, 1990

TOTAL RECOVERIES

MOST RECOVERED, CAREER

28 Phil Simms (1979-93)
26 Charlie Conerly (1948-61)
19 Jim Katcavage (1956-68)
17 Harry Carson (1976-88)
16 Frank Gifford (1952-60, 62-64)
15 George Martin (1975-88)
15 Joe Morrison (1959-72)

MOST RECOVERED, SEASON

6 Jeff Hostetler (1991)
6 Emlen Tunnell (1952)
5 by many players

MOST RECOVERED, GAME

3 Jeff Hostetler, vs. Phoenix
  Oct. 21, 1990

YARDS RETURNING FUMBLES

LONGEST FUMBLE RETURN

81 Andy Headen, vs. Dallas
  Sept. 9, 1984 (td)
72 Wendell Harris, at Pittsburgh
  Sept. 11, 1966 (td)
71 Roy Hilton, vs. Dallas
  Oct. 27, 1974 (td)
67 Horace Sherrod, vs. Washington
  Dec. 7, 1952
65 Lindon Crow, vs. St. Louis
  Oct. 30, 1960 (td)

MOST TOUCHDOWNS, CAREER (TOTAL)

2 George Martin (1981, 2-opp)
2 Sam Huff (1959, 63, 2-opp)
2 Tom Landry (1950, 51 2-opp)
2 Al De Rogatis (1949, 50, 2-opp)

MOST TOUCHDOWNS, SEASON (TOTAL)

2 George Martin, at Washington,
Sept. 13, 1981 (8 yards) and at St. Louis,
Dec. 13, 1981 (20 yards)

MOST TOUCHDOWNS, GAME (TOTAL)

1 by many players. Last: Dave Duerson, at Indianapolis
Nov. 5, 1990 (31 yards)

QUARTERBACK SACKS (SINCE 1982)

MOST SACKS, CAREER

132.5 Lawrence Taylor (1981-93)
79.5 Leonard Marshall (1983-92)
45.5 George Martin (1982-88)

MOST SACKS, SEASON

20.5 Lawrence Taylor (1986)
15.5 Lawrence Taylor (1988)
15.5 Leonard Marshall (1985)
15.0 Lawrence Taylor (1989)
13.5 Lawrence Taylor (1985)

MOST SACKS, GAME

4.5 Pepper Johnson, at Tampa Bay
  Nov. 24, 1991
4.0 Lawrence Taylor, vs. Philadelphia
  Oct. 12, 1986
4.0 Lawrence Taylor, vs. Tampa Bay
  Sept. 23, 1984
3.0 Keith Hamilton, vs. Tampa Bay
Sept. 12, 1993
3.0 Lawrence Taylor, vs. Philadelphia
  Sept. 9, 1990
3.0 Lawrence Taylor, at Phoenix
  Nov. 5, 1989
3.0 Lawrence Taylor, at New Orleanns
  Nov. 27, 1988
3.0 Lawrence Taylor, vs. Detroit
  Oct. 16, 1988
3.0 Lawrence Taylor, at Washington
  Dec. 7, 1986
3.0 Lawrence Taylor, at Philadelphia
  Nov. 9, 1986
3.0 Lawrence Taylor, vs. Washington
  Oct. 27, 1986
3.0 Leonard Marshall, at St. Louis
  Nov. 24, 1985
3.0 Leonard Marshall, at Philadelphia
  Sept. 29, 1985
3.0 Leonard Marshall, vs. Philadelphia
  Sept. 8, 1985
3.0 Lawrence Taylor, vs. Dallas
  Sept. 9, 1984
3.0 Lawrence Taylor, at Washington
  Dec. 17, 1983
3.0 Lawrence Taylor, vs. Philadelphia
  Dec. 11, 1982

A

PLAYER	POSITION	SCHOOL	GIANT SEASONS
Abrams, Bobby	LB	Michigan	1990-1992
Adamchik, Ed	C	Pittsburgh	1965
Adams, George	RB	Kentucky	1985-89
Adams, O'Neal	E	Arkansas	1941-45
Adams, Verlin	T	Morris Harvey	1942-45
Agajanian, Ben	K	New Mexico	1949, 54-57
Albright, Bill	G	Wisconsin	1951-54
Alexakos, Steve	G	San Jose State	1971
Alexander, Joe	G	Texas A&M	1928
Alexander, John	T	Rutgers	1926
Allegre, Raul	K	Texas	1986-91
Allison, Jim	E	Texas A&M	1928
Almodobar, Beau	WR	Norwich	1987
Amberg, John	B	Kansas	1951-52
Anderson, Bob	B	Army	1963
Anderson, Bruce	DE	Williamette	1967-69
Anderson, Cliff	E	Indiana	1953
Anderson, Ottis	RB	Miami	1986-92
Anderson, Roger	DT	Virginia Union	1965-68
Anderson, Winston	E	Colgate	1936
Apuna, Ben	LB	Arizona State	1980
Ard, Billy	G	Wake Forest	1981-88
Archer, Troy	DT	Colorado	1976-78
Artman, Corwan	T	Stanford	1931
Armstead, Jessie	LB	Miami (Fla)	1993
Ashburn, Cliff	G	Nebraska	1929
Athas, Pete	DB	Tennessee	1971-74
Atkinson, Jess	K	Maryland	1985
Atwood, John	B	Wisconsin	1948
Austin, Bill	G	Oregon St.	49-50, 53-57
Avedisian, Charles	G	Providence	1942-44
Averno, Sisto	G	Muhlenberg	1951
Avery, Ken	LB	So. Mississippi	1967-68
Avinger, Clarence	B	Alabama	1953

B

PLAYER	POSITION	SCHOOL	GIANT SEASONS
Badgro, Morris	E	USC	1927-35
Bahr, Matt	PK	Penn State	1990-1992
Bailey, Carlton	LB	North Carolina	1993
Bain, Bill	T	USC	1978
Baker, Ed	OB	Lafayette	1970-71
Baker, John	DE	Norfolk State	1970
Baker, Jon	G	California	1949-52
Baker, Stephen	WR	Fresno State	1987-92
Baldinger, Rich	OT	Wake Forest	1982-83
Ballman, Gary	TE	Michigan State	1973
Banks, Carl	LB	Michigan State	1984-92
Banks, Willie	G	Alcorn A&M	1970
Barasich, Carl	DT	Princeton	1981
Barber, Ernie	C	San Francisco	1945
Barbour, Wes	QB	Wake Forest	1945
Barker, Hubert	B	Arkansas	1942-45
Barnard, Charles	E	Edmond St.	1938
Bames, Erich	DB	Purdue	1961-64
Barnum, Len	QB	W. Va Wesleyan	1938-40
Barrett, Emmet	C	Portland	1942-44
Barry, Al	G	USC	1958-59
Bavaro, Mark	TE	Notre Dame	1985-90
Barzilauskas, F	G	Yale	1951
Bauer, John	G	Illinois	1954
Beamon, Wille	CB	Northern Iowa	1993
Beck, Ray	G	Georgia Tech	1952, 55-57
Beckman, Brad	TE	Neb. Omaha	1988
Bednar, Al	G	Lafayette	1925-26
Beeble, Keith	B	Occidental	1944
Beecham, Earl	RB	Bucknell	1987
Belcher, Kevin	G	Texas El-Paso	1983-85
Beil, Lawrence	T	Portland	1948
Bell, Gordon	RB	Michigan	1976-77
Bell, Kay	T	Wash. State	1942
Bellinger, Bob	T	Gonzaga	1934-35
Benkert, Harry	B	Rutgers	1925
Benners, Fred	QB	SMU	1952
Benson, Brad	G	Penn State	1977-87
Bennett, Lewis	WR	Flonda A&M	1987
Benyola, George	PK	Louisiana Tech	1987
Berry, Wayne	B	Wash. State	1954
Berthusen, Bill	DE	Iowa State	1987
Besana, Fred	QB	Califomia	1978
Best, Art	RB	Kent State	1980
Biggs, Riley	C	Baylor	1926-27
Biscaha, Joe	E	Richmond	1959
Bishop, Greg	T	Pacific	1993
Black, Mike	T	Cal State-Sac	1987
Blanchard, Tom	P-QB	Oregon	1971-73
Blazine, Anthony	T	Georgetown	1942-44
Bloodgood, Elbert	B	Nebraska	1928
Blount, Tony	S	Virginia	1980
Blozis, Al	T	Georgetown	1942-44
Blumenstock, Jim	B	Fordham	1947
Bly, Ron	B	Notre Dame	1968
Boggan, Rex	T	Mississippi	1955
Bookman, John	DB	Miami	1962-67
Bohovich, Reed	T	Lehigh	1962-63
Bolin, Booke	G	Mississippi	1955
Boll, Don	T	Nebraska	1960
Bomar, Lynn	E	Vanderbilt	1925-26
Bonness, Rik	LB	Nebraska	1980
Borcky, Dennis	DT	Memphis State	1987
Borden, Les	E	Fordham	1935
Boston, McKinley	DE	Minnesota	1968-69
Bowdoin, Jim	G	Alabama	1932
Bowman, Steve	B	Alabama	1966
Boyle, Bill	T	No College	1934
Brackett, M.L.	G	Auburn	1958
Brahm, Larry	G	Temple	1943
Brandes, John	TE	Cameron	1992
Brennan, Matt	B	Lafayette	1925
Brenner, Al	DB	Michigan St.	1969-70
Bnght, Leon	RB	Flonda State	1981-83
Broadstone, Manon	T	Nebraska	1931
Brooks, Bobby	DB	Bishop College	1974-76
Brooks, Michael	LB	LSU	1993
Brossard, Fred	C	N.W. Louisiana	1955
Brovarney, Casimir	T	Detroit	1941
Brown, Barry	LB	Flonda	1968
Brown, Boyd	TE	Alcorn State	1977
Brown, Dave	B	Alabama	1943, 46-47
Brown, Dave	QB	Duke	1992-93
Brown, Derek	TE	Notre Dame	1992-93
Brown, Donald	CB	Maryland	1987
Brown, Otto	DB	Praine View	1970-73
Brown, Roger	DB	Virginia Tech.	1990-1991
Brown, Rosey	T	Morgan State	1953-65
Browning, Greg	E	Denver	1947
Brunner, Scott	QB	Delaware	1980-83
Bryant, Bill	DB	Grambling	1976-78
Buckley, Marcus	LB	Texas A&M	1993
Bucklin, Tom	B	Idaho	1931
Buetow, Bart	G	Minnesota	1973
Buffington, Harry	G	Oklahoma A&M	1942
Buford, Maury	P	Texas Tech	1968
Buggs, Danny	WR	West Virginia	1975-76
Bunch, Jarrod	RB	Michigan	1991-93
Bundra, Mike	DT	USC	1965
Burgess, Charlie	LB	Carson-Newman	1987
Burkhardt, Art	G	Rutgers	1928
Bumett, Dale.	B	Kansas Teachers	1930-39
Burnine, Hal	E	Missouri	1956
Burt, Jim	DT	Miami	1981-88
Busch, Mike	QB	So Dakota State	1987
Butkus, Carl	T	George Washington	1949
Butler, Skip	K	Texas, Arlington	1971
Buzin, Dick	T	Penn State	1969-70
Byers, Ken	G	Cincinnati	1962-64
Byler, Joe	T	Nebraska	1946
Byrd, Boris	CB	Austin, Peay	1987

C

PLAYER	POSITION	SCHOOL	GIANT SEASONS
Cagle, Chris	B	Army	1930-1932
Caldwell, Alan	CB	No. Carolina	1979
Caldwell, Bruce	B	Yale	1928
Calligaro, Len	B	Wisconsin	1944-45
Calloway, Chris	WR	Michigan	1992-93
Campbell, Carter	LB	Weber State	1972-73
Campbell, Glen	E	Kansas Teachers	1929-33
Campbell, Jesse	S	N. Carolina St.	1992-93
Campfield, Billy	RB	Kansas	1983
Cancik, Phil	LB	No. Anzona	1980
Cannady, John	B	Indiana	1947-54
Cannella, John	T	Fordham	1933-34
Cantor, Leo	B	UCLA	1942
Capps, Wilbur	B	Okla. St. Central	1929
Caranci, Roland	T	Colorado	1944
Carney, Art	G	Navy	1925-26
Carpenter, Brian	DB	Michigan	1982
Carpenter, Rob	RB	Miami, Ohio	1981-85
Carr, Henry	DB	Arizona State	1965-67
Carr, Reggie	DE	Jackson State	1987
Carrocio, Russ	G	Virginia	1954-55
Carroll, Jim	LB	Notre Dame	1965-66
Carroll, Vic	T	Nevada	1943-47
Carson, Harry	LB	So. Carolina St.	1976-88
Carthon, Maurice	RB	Arkansas St.	1985-91
Case, Pete	G	Georgia	1965-70
Cavanaugh, Matt	QB	Pittsburgh	1990-91
Cephous, Frank	RB	UCLA	1984
Ceppetelli, Gene	C	Villanova	1969
Chandler, Don	K	Flonda	1956-64
Chandler, Karl	C	Princeton	1974-77
Chatman, Cliff	RB	Central State (Okla)	1982
Chemerko, George	B	Fordham	1947-48
Chickerneo, John	B	Pittsburgh	1942
Childs, Clarence	DB	Flonda A&M	1964-67
Christensen, Todd	RB	Brigham Young	1979
Cicolella, Mike	LB	Dayton	1966-68
Clack, Jim	C	Wake Forest	1978-80
Clancy, Stuart	B	Holy Cross	1933-35
Clatterbuck, Bob	QB	Houston	1954-57
Clay, Randy	B	Texas	1950-53
Clay, Roy	B	Colorado	1944
Clayton, Harvey	CB	Florida State	1987
Clements, Vin	RB	Connecticut	1972-73
Clune, Don	WR	Penn	1974-75
Coates, Ray	B	LSU	1948-49
Coffey, Junior	RB	Washington	1969-71
Coffield, Randy	LB	Florida State	1978-79
Colbert, Rondy	DB	Lamar University	1974-76
Cole, Pete	G	Trinity (Texas)	1937-40
Coleman, Charles	TE	Alcorn State	1987
Colhouer, Jake	G	Oklahoma	1949
Collier, Jim	E	Arkansas	1962-63
Collins, Mark	CB	Cal. St. Fullerton	1986-93
Collins, Ray	T	LSU	1954
Colvin, Jim	DT	Houston	1967
Comstock, Rudy	G	Georgetown	1930
Condren, Glen	DE	Oklahoma	1965-67
Conerly, Charlie	QB	Mississippi	1948-61
Contoulis, John	DT	Connecticut	1964
Cook, Charles	DT	Miami	1983
Cooks, Johnie	LB	Mississippi St.	1988-90
Cope Frank	T	Santa Clara	1938-47
Coppens, Gus	T	UCLA	1979
Cooper, Joe	K	California	1986
Cordileone, Lou	G	Clemson	1960
Corgan, Charles	E	Arkansas	1927
Corzine, Lester	B	Davis-Elkins	1934-37
Coulter, Dewitt	T	Army	194652
Costello, Tom	LB	Dayton	1964-65
Costello, Vince	LB	Ohio University	1967
Counts, John	B	Illinois	1962-63
Cousino, Brad	LB	Miami (Ohio)	1976
Covington, Jamie	RB	Syracuse	1987
Cox, Greg	S	San Jose State	1989
Crane, Dennis	T	USC	1970
Crawford, Bill	G	British Columbia	1960
Crawford, Ed	B	Mississippi	1957
Crawford, Keith	WR	Howard Payne	1993
Crespino, Bob	E	Mississippi	1964-68
Crist Chuck	DB	Penn State	1972-74
Crocicchia, Jim	QB	Pennsylvania	1987
Crosby, Steve	RB	Fort Hays	1974-75
Cross, Howard	TE	Alabama	1989-93
Crow, Lindon	B	USC	1958-60
Crutcher, Tommy	LB	TCU	1968-69
Csonka, Larry	RB	Syracuse	1976-77
Cuff, Ward	B	Marquette	1937-45
Culwell, Val	G	Oregon	1942
Culbreath, Jim	RB	Oklahoma	1980
Cummings, Mack	WR	East Tenn. State	1987
Curcio, Mike	LB	Temple	1982
Currier, Bill	S	South Carolina	1981-85

D

PLAYER	POSITION	SCHOOL	GIANT SEASONS
Daluiso, Brad	PK	UCLA	1993
Damiani, Francis	T	Manhattan	1944
Danelo, Joe	K	Washington State	1976-82
Daniel, Kenny	DB	San Jose State	1984
Danowski, Ed	QB	Fordham	1934-41
Davis, Chris	LB	San Diego State	1987
Davis, Don	DT	L.A. State	1966-67
Davis, Gains	G	Texas Tech	1936
Davis, Henry	LB	Grambling	1968-69
Davis, Kelvin	G	Johnson Smith	1987
Davis, Paul	LB	North Carolina	1983
Davis, Roger	T	Syracuse	1965-66
Davis, Roosevelt	DE	Tennessee A&T	1965-67
Davis, Scott	G	Iowa	1993
Davis, Tyrone	CB	Clemson	1985-86
Dawkins, Joe	RB	Wisconsin	1974-75
Dean, Randy	QB	Northwestern	1977-79
DeFilippo, Lou	C	Fordham	1941, 45-48
DelGaizo, Jim	QB	Tampa	1974
Dell Isola, John	C	Fordham	1934-40
Dennerlien, Gerry	T	St. Mary's	1937-40
Dennery, Vince	E	Fordham	1941
Dennis, Mike	CB	Wyoming	1980-83
DeOssie, Steve	LB	Boston College	1989-93
DeRogatis, Al	T	Duke	1949-52
DeRose, Dan	LB	Southern Colorado	1987
Dess, Darrell	G	N.Carolina St.	1959-64, 66-69
Dillard, Stacey	DE	Oklahoma	1992-93
DiRenzo, Fred	RB	New Haven	1987
DiRico, Bob	RB	Kutztown State	1987
Dixon, Al	TE	Iowa State	1977-78
Dixon, Zach	RB	Temple	1979
Dobelstein, Bob	G	Tennessee	1946-48
Doggert, Keith	T	Wichita	1942
Doolan, John	B	Georgetown	1945-46
Doornink, Dan	RB	Washington State	1978
Dorsey, Eric	DE	Notre Dame	1986-92
Douglas, Everett	T	Florida	1953
Douglas, John	LB	Missouri	1970-73
Douglass, Paul	DB	Illinois	1953
Dove, Eddie	DB	Colorado	1963
Dryer, Fred	DE	San Diego State	1969-71
Dubinski, Tom	QB	Utah	1958
Dubinski, Walt	G	Boston College	1943
Dubzinsky, Maurice	G	Georgetown	1932
Duckens, Mark	DE	Arizona State	1989
Duden, Dick	E	Navy	1949
Dudley, Paul	B	Arkansas	1962
Duerson, Dave	DB	Notre Dame	1990
Dugan, Bill	G	Penn State.	1987
Dugan, Leonard	C	Wichita	1936
Duggan, Gill	T	Oklahoma	1940
Duhon, Bobby	B	Tulane	1968-72
Dunaway, Dave	WR	Duke	1969
Duncan, Jim	E	Wake Forest	1950-53
Dunlap, Bob	B	Oklahoma	1936
Dvorak, Rick	LB	Wichita State	1974-76

E

Eakin, Kay	(B)	Arkansas	1940-41
Eaton, Lou	(T)	California	1945
Eaton, Scott	(DB)	Oregon State	1967-71
Echhardt, Oscar	(B)	Texas	1928
Eck, Keith	(C)	UCLA	1979
Eddings, Floyd	(WR)	California	1982-83
Edwards, Bill	(G)	Baylor	1941-42, 46
Epps, Bobby	(B)	Pittsburgh	1954-55, 57
Ellenbogen, Bill	(G)	Virginia Tech	1976-77
Elliott, John	(T)	Michigan	1988-93
Ellison, Mark	(G)	Dayton	1972-73
Enderle, Dick	(G)	Minnesota	1972-74
Erickson, Bill	(G)	Mississippi	1948
Eshmont, Len	(B)	Fordham	1940-41
Ettinger, Don	(G)	Kansas	1948-50
Evans, Charlie	(RB)	USC	1971-73

F

Faircloth, Art	(B)	No. Carolina	1947-48
Falaschi, Nello	(B)	Santa Clara	1938-41
Falcon, Terry	(G)	Montana	1980
Feather, Erwin	(B)	Kansas St.	1929-30, 32-33
Felton, Eric	(DB)	Texas Tech	1980
Fennema, Carl	(C)	Washington	1948-49
Fields, Joe	(C)	Widener	1988
Filchock, Frank	(QB)	Indiana	1946
Files, Jim	(LB)	Oklahoma	1970-73
Filipowicz, Steve	(B)	Fordham	1945-46
Filipski, Gene	(B)	Villanova	1956-57
Fischer, Cletus	(B)	Nebraska	1949
Fitzgerald, Mike	(DB)	Iowa State	1967
Flaherty, Ray	(E)	Gonzaga	1928-35
Flenniken, Max	(B)	Geneva	1930-31
Flowers, Larry	(S)	Texas Tech	1981-85
Flowers, Richmond	(DB)	Tennessee	1971-73
Flynn, Tom	(S)	Pittsburgh	1986-88
Flythe, Mark	(DE)	Penn State	1993
Folsom, Steve	(TE)	Utah	1982
Foote, Chris	(C)	USC	1982-83
Ford, Charlie	(DB)	Houston	1975-76
Forte, Ike	(RB)	Arkansas	1981
Fox, Mike	(DE)	West Virginia	1990-93
Fox, Samuel	(E)	Ohio State	1945-46
Franck, George	(B)	Minnesota	1941,45-48
Franklin, George	(RB)	Texas A&I	1979
Franklin, Mal	(E)	St. Mary's	1934-35
Friede, Mike	(WR)	Indiana	1980
Friedman, Bennie.	(QB)	Michigan	1929-31
Frederickson, Tucker	(FB)	Auburn	1965-71
Freeman, Lorenzo	(DT)	Pittsburgh	1991
Frugonne, Jim	(B)	Syracuse	1925
Fuqua, John	(RB)	Morgan State	1969

G

Gaiters, Bobby	(B)	New Mexico St.	1961-62
Galazian, Stan	(C)	Villanova	1937-39
Galbreath, Tony	(RB)	Missouri	1984-87
Galiffa, Arnold	(QB)	Army	1953
Gallagher, Dave	(DE)	Michigan	1975-76
Gallagher, Ed	(T)	Wash. & Jefferson	1928
Garcia, Jim	(DE)	Purdue	1966
Garner, Bob	(G)	No College	1945
Garrett, Alvin	(RB)	Angelo State	1980
Garrett, Curtis	(DE)	Illinois State	1987
Garvey, Art	(G)	Notre Dame	1927-28
Garzoni, Mike	(G)	USC	1948
Gatewood, Tom	(WR)	Notre Dame	1972-73
Gehrke, Bruce	(E)	Columbia	1948
Gehrke, Fred	(B)	Utah	1948
Gelatka, Charles	(E)	Mississippi St.	1937-40
Gibbons, Mike	(T)	S.W. Oklahoma St.	1976-77
Giblin, Robert	(S)	Houston	1975-76
Gifford, Frank	(B-E)	USC	1952-60, 62-64
Gigson, Denver	(G)	Grove City	1930-34
Gildea, John	(B)	St. Bonaventure	1938
Gillard, Larry	(DE)	Mississippi State	1978
Gillette Walker	(WR)	Richmond	1974-76
Gladchuk Chet	(C)	Boston Coll.	1941,46-47
Glass, Chip	(TE)	Florida St.	1974
Glover, Rich	(DT)	Nebraska	1973
Godfrey, Chris	(G)	Michigan	1984-87
Gogolak, Pete	(K)	Cornell	1966-74
Goich, Dan	(DT)	California	1972-73
Golsteyn, Jerry	(QB)	No. Illinois	1976-78
Goode, Conrad	(T)	Missouri	1984-85
Goodwin, Tod	(E)	West Virginia	1935-36
Gorgone, Pete	(B)	Muhlenberg	1946
Gossage, Gene	(T)	Northwestern	1963
Governali, Paul	(QB)	Columbia	1947-48
Grandelius, Ev	(B)	Michigan St.	1953
Grant, Len.	(T)	NYU	1930-37
Grate, Carl	(C)	Georgia	1945
Gravelle, Gordon	(T)	Brigham Young	1977-78
Graham, Kent	(QB)	Ohio State	1992-93
Gray, Earnest	(WR)	Memphis State	1979-84
Green, Joe	(DB)	Bowling Green	1970-71
Green, Tony	(RB)	Florida	1979
Greene, A J.	(DB)	Wake Forest	1991
Greenhalgh, Bob	(B)	San Francisco	1949
Gregory, Jack	(DE)	Delta State	1972-78
Grier Rosey	(DT)	Penn St.	1955-56, 58-62
Griffing, Glynn	(QB)	Mississippi	1963
Griffith, Forrest	(B)	Kansas	1950-51
Grigg, Cecil	(B)	Austin	1926
Grim, Bob	(WR)	Oregon State	1972-74
Gross, Andy	(G)	Auburn	1967-68
Grosscup, Lee	(QB)	Utah	1960-62
Guggemos, Neal	(S)	St. Thomas (Mn)	1988
Guglielmi, Ralph	(QB)	Notre Dame	1962-63
Gunn, Jimmy	(LB)	Southern California	1975
Gursky, Al	(LB)	Penn State	1963
Gutowsky, Leroy	(B)	Oklahoma City	1931
Guy, Lou	(B)	Mississippi	1963
Guy, Melwood	(T)	Duke	1958
Guyon, Joe	(B)	Carlisle	1927
Guyton, Myron	(S)	Eastern Kentucky	1989-93

H

Hachten, Bill	(G)	Stanford	1947
Haden, John	(T)	Arkansas	1936-38
Haddix, Wayne	(CB)	Liberty Baptist	1987-88
Hagerty, John	(B)	Georgetown	1926-30
Haines, Henry	(B)	Penn State	1925-28
Haji-Sheikh, Ali	(PK)	Michigan	1983-85
Hall, H.	(C)	No College	1942
Hall John	(E)	Iowa	1955
Hall Pete	(E)	Marquette	1961-62
Hamilton, Keith	(DE)	Pittsburgh	1992-93
Hammond, Bob	(RB)	Morgan State	1976-78
Hampton, Rodney	(RB)	Georgia	1990-93
Hanken, Ray	(E)	Geo. Wash.	1937-38
Hannah, Herb	(T)	Alabama	1951
Hanson, Dick	(T)	No. Dakota St.	1971
Hapes, Merle	(B)	Mississippi	1942-46
Hardison, Dee	(DE)	North Carolina	1981-85
Hare, Cecil	(B)	Gonzaga	1946
Harms, Art	(T)	Vermont	1927
Harper, Charlie	(G)	Oklahoma State	1966-72
Harper, LaSalle	(LB)	Arkansas	1989
Harns, Don	(S)	Rutgers	1980
Harris, Oliver	(E)	Geneva	1926
Harris, Phil .	(DB)	Texas	1966
Harris, Wendell	(DB)	LSU	1966-67
Harrison, Ed	(E)	Boston College	1928
Harrison, Granville	(E)	Mississippi St.	1941
Harrison, Max	(E)	Auburn	1940
Hart, Harold	(HB)	Texas Southern	1977
Hasselbeck, Don	(TE)	Colorado	1985
Hathcock, Dave	(DB)	Memphis State	1967
Hartzog, Howard	(T)	Baylor	1928
Hasenohrl, George	(DT)	Ohio State	1974
Hauser, Art	(T)	Xavier	1959
Hayes, Larry	(LB)	Vanderbilt	1961
Haynes, Mark	(CB)	Colorado	1980-85
Hazeltine, Man	(LB)	California	1970
Headen, Andy	(LB)	Clemson	1983-88
Heap, Joe	(B)	Notre Dame	1955
Heater, Larry	(RB)	Arizona	1980-83
Hebert, Bud	(S)	Oklahoma	1980
Heck, Ralph	(LB)	Colorado	1969-71
Hein, Mel	(C)	Washington St.	1931-45
Heinrich, Don	(QB)	Washington	1954-59
Hendnan, Warren	(B)	Pittsburgh	1925
Henry, Steve	(DB)	Emporia State	1980
Henry, Wilbur	(T)	Wash. & Jefferson	1927
Hensley, Dick	(E)	Kentucky	1949
Herber, Arnie	(QB)	Regis	1944-45
Hermann, John	(B)	UCLA	1956
Hernon, Don	(B)	Ohio State	1960
Herrmann, Don	(WR)	Waynesburg	1969-74
Hickl, Ray	(LB)	Texas A&I	1969-70
Hicks, Eddie	(RB)	East Carolina	1979-80
Hicks, John	(G)	Ohio State	1974-77
Hienstra, Ed	(C)	Sterling	1942
Hill, Charles	(B)	No College	1926
Hill, John	(B)	Amherst	1926
Hill, Kenny	(DB)	Yale	1984-88
Hill, John	(T)	Lehigh	1972-74
Hill, Ralph	(C)	Florida A&M	1976-77
Hillebrand, Jerry	(LB)	Colorado	1963-66
Hilert Hal	(B)	Oklahoma City	1930
Hilton, Roy	(DE)	Jackson State	1974
Hinton, Chuck	(C)	Mississippi	1967-69
Hodel, Merwin	(B)	Colorado	1953
Hogan, Mike	(RB)	Tenn.-Chananooga	1980
Hogan, Paul	(B)	Wash. & Jefferson	1926
Holland, Vern	(T)	Tennessee	1980
Holifield, Jimmy	(DB)	Jackson St	1968-69
Horan, Mike	(P)	Long Beach State	1993
Horne, Richard	(G)	Oregon	1941
Horner, Sam	(B)	VMI	1962-63
Hornsby, Ron	(LB)	S. E. Louisiana	1971-74
Hostetler, Jeff	(QB)	West Virginia	1984-92
Houston, Dick	(WR)	Easl Texas St.	1969-73
Hovious, John	(B)	Mississippi	1945
Howard, Erik	(DT)	Washington St.	1986-93
Howard, Bob	(G)	Marietta	1929-30
Howell, Jim Lee	(E)	Arkansas	1937-42, 46-48
Howell, Lane	(T)	Grambling	1963-64
Hubbard, Cal	(T)	Geneva	1927-29, 36
Hudson, Bob	(E)	Clemson	1951-52
Huff, Sam	(LB)	West Virginia	1956-63
Hugger, Keith	(WR)	Connecticut	1983
Hughes, Ed	(B)	Tulsa	1956-58
Hughes, Ernie	(C)	Notre Dame	1981-83
Hughes, Pat	(LB)	Boston U	1970-76
Hunt, Byron	(LB)	SMU	1981-88
Hunt, George	(K)	Tennessee	1975
Hutchinson, Bill	(B)	Dartmouth	1942
Hutchinson, R.	(T)	Chattanooga	1949
Huth, Gerry	(G)	Wake Forest	1956
Hyland, Bob	(G)	Boston College	1971-75

I

Imlay, Talma	(B)	California	1927
Ingram, Mark	(WR)	Michigan State	1987-92
Irvin, Cecil	(T)	Davis-Elkins	1932-35
Iverson, Chris	(B)	Oregon	1947

J

Jackson, Bob	(B)	No. Carolina A&T	1950-51
Jackson, Cleveland	(TE)	Nevada-Las Vegas	1979
Jackson, Greg	(S)	LSU	1989-93
Jackson, Honor	(DB)	Pacific	1973-74
Jackson, Louis	(RB)	Cal Poly (SLO)	1981
Jackson, Mark	(WR)	Purdue	1993
Jackson, Terry	(CB)	San Diego State	1978-83
Jacobs, Allen	(FB)	Utah	1966-67
Jacobs, Proverb	(T)	California	1960
Jacobson, Larry	(DT)	Nebraska	1972-74
James, Dick	(B)	Oregon	1964
Janarette, Charlie	(T)	Penn State	1961-62
Jappe, Paul	(E)	Syracuse	1925, 27-28
Jelacic, Jon	(E)	Minnesota	1958
Jenkins, Eddie	(RB)	Holy Cross	1974
Jenkins, Izel	(CB)	N.C. State	1993
Jennings, Dave	(P)	St. Lawrence	1974-84
Jeter, Gary	(DT)	USC	1977-82
Jiles, Dwayne	(LB)	Texas Tech	1989
Johnson, Bill	(P)	Livingston	1970
Johnson, Bob	(WR)	Kansas	1984-86
Johnson, Curley	(K)	Houston	1969
Johnson, Damian	(G)	Kansas State	1986-89
Johnson, Dennis	(TE)	Mississippi St.	1980
Johnson, Gene	(DB)	Cincinnati	1961-62
Johnson, Herb	(B)	No College	1954
Johnson, Jon	(B)	Mississippi	1948
Johnson, Ken	(RB)	Miami	1979
Johnson, Larry	(C)	Haskell	1936-39
Johnson, Len	(G)	St. Cloud	1970
Johnson, Nate	(WR)	Hillsdale	1980
Johnson, Pepper	(LB)	Ohio State	1986-92
Johnson, Randy	(QB)	Texas A&I	1971-73
Johnson, Ron	(RB)	Michigan	1970-75
Johnston, Brian	(C)	North Carolina	1986-87
Jones, Chris	(C)	Delaware State	1987
Jones, Clarence	(T)	Maryland	1991-93
Jones, Ernie	(DB)	Miami	1977-79
Jones, Homer	(E)	Texas Southern	1964-69
Jones, James	(DE)	No. Carolina A&T	1987
Jones, Robbie	(LB)	Alabama	1984-87
Jones, Tom	(G)	Bucknell	1932-36
Jordan, David	(G)	Auburn	1984-86

K

Kab, Vyto	(TE)	Penn State	1985
Kane, Herb	(T)	Okla.Teachers	1944-45
Kanicki, Jim	(DT)	Michigan St.	1970-71
Kaplan, Bernie	(G)	West Maryland	1935-36
Karcis, John	(B)	Carnegie Tech	1938-39, 43
Karilivacz, Carl	(DB)	Syracuse	1958
Katcavage, Jim	(DE)	Dayton	1956-68
Keahy, Eulis	(G)	Geo. Washington	1942
Kearns, Tom	(T)	Miami	1945
Kelley, Brian	(LB)	California Lutheran	1973-83
Kelly, Ellison	(G)	Michigan State	1959
Kelly, John S.	(B)	Kentucky	1932
Kelly, Paul	(QB)	New Haven	1987
Kemp, Jackie	(QB)	Occidental	1958
Kendricks, Jim	(T)	Texas A&M	1927
Kennard, George	(G)	Kansas	1952-55
Kennedy, Tom	(QB)	L. A. State	1966-67
Kenyon, Bill	(B)	Georgetown	1925
Kerrigan, Tom	(G)	Columbia	1930
Kershaw, George	(E)	Colgate	1949
Ketzko, Alex	(T)	Michigan St.	1942
Keuper, Ken	(B)	Georgia	1948
Killenger, Glenn	(B)	Penn State	1926
Killett, Charlie	(B)	Memphis St.	1963
Kimball, Bruce	(G)	Massachusetts	1982
Kimber, Bill	(E)	Florida St.	1959-60
Kimmel, Jerry	(LB)	Syracuse	1987
Kinard, Terry	(S)	Clemson	1983-89
King, Gordon	(T)	Stanford	1978-85
King, Jerome	(DB)	Purdue	1980
King, Phil	(B)	Vanderbilt	1958-63
Kinscherf, Carl	(B)	Colgate	1943-44
Kirby, John	(LB)	Nebraska	1969-70
Kirouac, Lou	(G)	Boston College	1963
Kitzmiller, John	(B)	Oregon	1931
Klasoskus, Al	(T)	Holy Cross	1941-42
Kline, Harry	(E)	Kansas Teachers	1939-41
Klotovich, Mike	(B)	St. Mary's	1945
Knight, Pat	(B)	SMU	1952, 54-55
Kobrosky, Milt	(B)	Trinity (Conn.)	1937
Kolman, Ed	(T)	Temple	1949
Koontz, Joe	(E)	San Francisco St.	1968
Koppisch, Walter	(B)	Columbia	1925-26
Kotar, Doug	(RB)	Kentucky	1974-80
Kottie, Dick	(LB)	Wagner	1967, 69-72
Koy, Ernie	(B)	Texas	1965-70
Krahl, Jim	(DT)	Texas Tech	1978
Kratch, Bob	(G)	Iowa	1989-93
Krause, Max	(RB)	Gonzaga	1933-36
Krause, Ray	(T)	Maryland	1951-55
Kyles, Troy	(WR)	Howard	1990

L

Lacey, Bob	(E)	No. Carolina	1965
Lagod, Chester	(G)	Chattanooga	1953

Ladlaw, Scott	(RB)	Stanford	1980
Lakes, Roland	(DT)	Wichita	1971
Lalonde, Roger	(DT)	Muskingum	1965
Landeta, Sean	(P)	Towson State	1985-93
Landry, Tom	(DB)	Texas	1950-55
Landshell, Granville	(B)	USC	1940
Lane, Gary	(QB)	Missouri	1968
Lapka, Myron	(DT)	USC	1980
Larson, Greg	(C)	Minnesota	1961-73
Lascari, John	(E)	Georgetown	1942
Lasker, Greg	(S)	Arkansas	1986-88
Lasky, Frank	(T)	Florida	1964-65
Lasse, Dick	(LB)	Syracuse	1962-63
Lechner, Edgar	(T)	Minnesota	1942
Leemans, Tuffy	(B)	Geo. Washington	1936-43
Leo, Jim	(LB)	Cincinnati	1960
Levy, Harvey	(G)	Syracuse	1928
Lewis, Art	(T)	Ohio	1936
Lewis, Danny	(B)	Wisconsin	1966
Lieberum, Don	(B)	Manchester	1942
Lieble, Frank	(E)	Norwich	1942-47
Linnin, Chris	(DE)	Washington	1980
Lindahl, Virgil	(G)	Nebraska St.	1945
Little, Jim	(T)	Kentucky	1945
Livingston, Cliff	(LB)	UCLA	1954-61
Livingston, Howard	(B)	No College	1944-47
Lloyd, Dan	(LB)	Washington	1976-79
Lockhart, Carl	(DB)	No. Texas St	1965-75
Long, Bufford	(B)	Florida	1953-55
Longo, Tom	(DB)	Notre Dame	1969-70
Lott, Billy	(B)	Mississippi	1958
Love, Walter	(WR)	Westminster (Utah)	1973
Lovelady, Edwin	(WR)	Memphis State	1987
LoVetere, John	(DT)	Compton	1963-65
Lovuolo, Frank	(E)	St. Bonaventure	1949
Lummus, John	(E)	Baylor	1941
Lumpkin, Ron	(DB)	Arizona State	1973
Lunday, Ken	(C)	Arkansas	1937-41, 46-47
Lurtsema, Bob	(DT)	West Michigan	1967-71
Lynch, Dick	(DB)	Notre Dame	1959-66
Lyons, George	(T)	Kansas State	1929

M

MacAtee, Ken	(E)	Alabama	1954-58
Mackorell, John	(B)	Davidson	1935
Mackrides, Bill	(QB)	Nevada	1953
Maher, Bruce	(DB)	Detroit	1968-69
Maikkula, Ken	(E)	Connecticut	1942
Mallory, Larry	(DB)	Tennessee State	1976-78
Mallouf, Ray	(QB)	SMU	1949
Mangum, Pete	(LB)	Mississippi	1954
Manton, Tilly	(B)	TCU	1936-38
Manuel, Lionel	(WR)	Pacific	1984-90
Marefos, Andy	(B)	St. Mary's	1941-42
Marion, Frank	(LB)	Florida A&M	1977-83
Marone, John	(G)	Manhattan	1943
Maronic, Dusan	(G)	No College	1951
Markham. Dale	(DE)	North Dakota	1980
Marker. Cliff	(B)	Washington St.	1927
Marsh, Dick	(G)	Oklahoma	1933
Marshall, Ed	(WR)	Cameron State	1976-77
Marshall, Leonard	(DE)	LSU	1983-92
Martin, Frank	(B)	Alabama	1945
Martin, George	(DE)	Oregon	1975-88
Martinkovich, J.	(E)	Xavier	1957
Mastrangelo, John	(G)	Notre Dame	1950
Matthews, Bo	(RB)	Colorado	1980
Matan, Bill	(DE)	Kansas State	1966
Maynard, Don	(B)	Texas Western	1958
Mayock, Mike	(DB)	Boston College	1982-83
Maxon, Alvin	(RB)	SMU	1978
Mazurek, Ed	(B)	Xavier	1960
McBride, John	(B)	Syracuse	1925-28, 32-33
McCafferty, Don	(E)	Ohio State	1946
McCaffrey, Ed	(WR)	Stanford	1991-93
McCann, Jim	(P)	Arizona State	1973
McCann, Tim	(DT)	Princeton	1969
McConkey Phil	(WR)	Navy	1984-88
McCoy, Mike	(DT)	Notre Dame	1979
McChesney, Bob	(E)	Hardon-Simmons	1950
McClain, Clint	(B)	SMU	1941
McCreary, Loaird	(TE)	Tennessee State	1979
McDaniel, LeCharls	(CB)	Cal-Poly	1983-84
McDowell, John	(T)	St. John's (Minn)	1965
McElhenny, Hugh	(B)	Washington	1963
McFadden, Paul	(PK)	Youngstown	1988
McGee, Ed	(T)	Temple	1940
McGhee, Kanavis	(LB)	Colorado	1991-93
McGlasson, Ed	(C)	Youngstown State	1981
McGriff, Curtis	(DT)	Alabama	1980-86
McGinley, Ed	(T)	Penn	1925
McGowan, Reggie	(WR)	Abilene Christian	1987
McGrew, Lawrence	(LB)	USC	1990
McGriggs, Lamar	(DB)	Western Illinois	1991-92
McKinney, Odis	(DB)	Colorado	1978-79
McLaughlin, Joe	(LB)	Massachusetts	1980-84
McLaughry, John	(B)	Brown	1940
McLean, Ron	(DE)	Cal St-Fullerton	1988
McMullen, Dan	(G)	Nebraska	1929
McNeil, Clifton	(WR)	Grambling	1970-71
McQuay. Leon	(RB)	Tampa	1974
McRae, Bennie	(DB)	Michigan	1971
Mead, John	(E)	Wisconsin	1946-47
Meggett, David	(RB)	Towson State	1989-93
Meisner, Greg	(DT)	Pittsburgh	1991
Mellus, John	(T)	Villanova	1938-41
Menasco, Don	(B)	Texas	1952-53
Menefee, Hartwell	(E)	New Mexico St.	1966
Mendenhall, John	(DT)	Grambling	1972-79
Mercer, Jim	(QB)	Oregon State	1942-43
Mercein, Chuck	(FB)	Yale	1965-66
Merrill, Casey	(DE)	Cal-Davis	1983-85
Mertes, Bernie	(B)	Iowa	1949
Messner, Max	(L)	Cincinnati	1964
Meuth, Kevin	(T)	Southwest Texas St.	1987
Mietzner, Saul	(C)	Carnegie Tech	1929-30
Miklich, Bill	(B)	Idaho	1947-48
Mikolajczyk, Ron	(T)	Tampa	1976-79
Miles, Leo	(B)	Virginia St.	1953
Miller, Calvin	(DT)	Oklahoma State	1979
Miller, Corey	(LB)	South Carolina	1991-93
Miller, Ed	(B)	New Mexico	1939-40
Miller, Jim	(P)	Mississippi	1987
Miller, Mike	(WR)	Tennessee	1983
Miller, Solomon	(WR)	Utah State	1986
Milling, James	(WR)	Maryland	1991
Milner, Bill	(G)	Duke	1950
Milstead, Century	(T)	Yale	1925, 27-28
Minisi, Tony	(B)	Penn	1948
Minniear, Randy	(RB)	Purdue	1967-69
Mischak, Bob	(G)	Army	1958
Mistler, John	(WR)	Arizona State	1981-84
Mitchell, Grandville	(E)	Davis-Elkins	1935
Mitchell, Harold	(T)	UCLA	1952
Mitchell, Russell	(C)	Mississippi	1987
Modzelewski, D	(DT)	Maryland	1956-63
Molden, Frank	(DT)	Jackson State	1969
Molenda, John	(B)	Michigan	1932-35
Moore, Dana	(P)	So. Mississippi	1987
Moore, Eric	(G)	Indiana	1988-93
Moore, Henry	(B)	Arkansas	1956
Moore, Ken	(C)	W. Va. Wesleyan	1940
Moorehead, Emery	(WR)	Colorado	1977-79
Moran, Dale (Hap)	(B)	Carnegie Tech	1928-34
Moran, Jim	(T)	Idaho	1964-67
Morgan, Bill	(T)	Oregon	1933-36
Morgan, Dan	(G)	Penn State	1987
Morrall, Earl	(QB)	Michigan St.	1965-67
Morris, Joe	(RB)	Syracuse	1982-89
Morrison, Joe	(B-E)	Cincinnati	1959-72
Morrison, Pat	(DB)	So. Connecticut St.	1987
Morrow, Bob	(B)	Ill. Wesleyan	1945
Morton, Craig	(QB)	California	1974-76
Mote, Kelly	(E)	Duke	1950-52
Mowatt, Zeke	(TE)	Florida State	1983-89,90
Mrosko, Bob	(TE)	Penn State	1990
Mullady, Tom	(TE)	Rhodes College	1979-84
Mullen, Tom	(G)	So. West Mo. State	1974-77
Mulleaneaux, Lee	(B)	Arizona	1932
Mullins, Noah	(B)	Kentucky	1949
Munday, George	(T)	Kansas Teachers	1931-32
Munn, Lyle	(E)	Kansas State	1929
Murdock, Les	(K)	Florida State	1967
Murray, Earl	(G)	Purdue	1951
Murtaugh, George	(C)	Georgetown	1926-32
Myers, Tom	(B)	Fordham	1925-26

N

Nash, Bob	(T)	Rutgers	1925
Neill, Bill	(DT)	Pittsburgh	1981-83
Neill, Jim	(B)	Texas Tech	1937
Nelson, Andy	(DB)	Memphis St.	1964
Nelson, Karl	(T)	Iowa State	1984-88
Nesser, AL	(E)	No College	1926-28
Nettles, Doug	(DB)	Vanderbilt	1980
Neville, Tom	(T)	Mississippi State	1979
Newman, Harry	(QB)	Michigan	1933-35
Nicholson, Frank	(LB)	Delaware State	1987
Nielsen, Walter	(B)	Arizona	1940
Niles, Gary	(B)	Iowa	1946-47
Nittmo, Bjorn	(K)	Appalachian State	1989
Nix, Emery	(QB)	TCU	1943-46
Nolan, Dick	(DB)	Maryland	1954-57, 59-61
Norby, John	(B)	Idaho	1934
Nordstrom, Harry	(G)	Trinity (Conn.)	1925
Norris, Jimmy	(CB)	Upsala	1987
Norton, Jim	(DT)	Washington	1970
Nutt, Richard	(B)	TexasState	1949

O

Oates, Bart	(C)	Brigham Young	1985-93
O'Brien, Dave	(G)	Boston College	1965
Obradovich, Jim	(TE)	Southern California	1975
Odom, Steve	(WR)	Utah	1979
Olander, Cliff	(DB)	New Mexico State	1980
Oldershaw, Doug	(G)	Santa Barbara	1939-41
Oldham, Ray	(S)	Middle Tennessee	1979
Orduna, Joe	(RB)	Nebraska	1972-73
Ostendarp, Jim	(B)	Bucknell	1950-51
Owen, Alton	(B)	Mercer	1939-41
Owen, Steve	(T)	Phillips	1926-36
Owen, Tom	(QB)	Wichita State	1983
Owen, Vilas	(QB)	Wisconsin Teachers	1942
Owen, William	(T)	Oklahoma A&M	1929-37
Owens, R. C.	(E)	Idaho	1964

P

Palazzi, Lou	(C)	Penn State	1946-47
Palm, Mike	(B)	Penn State	1925-26
Park, Kaulana	(RB)	Stanford	1987
Parker, Frank	(DT)	Oklahoma State	1969
Parker, Ken	(DB)	Fordham	1970
Parnell, Fred	(T)	Colgale	1925-27
Parry, Owen	(T)	Baylor	1937-39
Paschal, Bill	(B)	Georgia Tech	1942-47
Paschka, Gordon	(G)	Minnesota	1947
Patterson, Don	(DB)	Georgia Tech	1980
Patterson, Elvis	(DB)	Kansas	1984-87
Patton, Bob	(T)	Clemson	1952
Patton, Jim	(DB)	Mississippi	1955-66
Peay, Francis	(T)	Missouri	1966-67
Pederson, Winifield	(T)	Minnesota	1941-45
Pelfrey, Ray	(B)	Kentucky St.	1953
Perdue, Willard	(E)	Duke	1944
Perez, Mike	(QB)	San Jose State	1991
Perkins, Johnny	(WR)	Abilene Christian	1977-83
Perretta, Ralph	(C)	Purdue	1980
Perry, Leon	(RB)	Mississippi	1980-82
Pesonen, Dick	(DB)	Minn. (Duluth)	1962-64
Peterson, Marty	(T)	Pennsylvania	1987
Petrilas, William	(E)	No College	1944-45
Petigrew, Gary	(DT)	Stanford	1974
Petty, Jack	(G)	Rutgers	1926-28
Peviani, Bob	(G)	USC	1953
Phillips, Ewell	(G)	Okla. Baptist	1936-37
Piccolo, Bill	(C)	Canisius	1943-45
Pierce, Aaron	(TE)	Washington	1992-93
Pietrzak, Jim	(DT)	Eastern Michigan	1974-78
Pipkin, Joyce	(E)	Arkansas	1948
Pisarcik, Joe	(QB)	New Mexico St.	1977-79
Pittman, Danny	(WR)	Wyoming	1980-83
Plansky, Tony	(B)	Georgetown	1928-29
Plum, Milt	(QB)	Penn State	1969
Podoley, Jim	(B)	Central Mich.	1962
Poole, Barney	(E)	Mississippi	1954-55
Poole, Jim	(E)	Mississippi	1937-41, 46
Poole, Ray	(E)	Mississippi	1947-52
Porter, Rob	(DB)	Holy Cross	1987
Post, Bob	(DB)	Kings Point	1967
Potteiger, Earl	(B)	Ursinus	1926-28
Powell, Andre	(LB)	Penn State	1993
Powell, Dick	(E)	Davis-Elkins	1931
Powers, Clyde	(DB)	Oklahoma	1974-77
Pough, Ernie	(WR)	Texas Southern	1978
Prestel, Jim	(DT)	Idaho	1966
Price, Eddie	(FB)	Tulane	1950-55
Principe, Dominic	(B)	Fordham	1940-42
Pritchard, Bosh	(B)	VMI	1951
Pritko, Steve	(E)	Villanova	1943
Prokop, Joe	(P)	Cal Poly Pomona	1992
Pugh, Marion	(QB)	Texas A&M	1941, 45

Q

Quatse, Jess	(T)	Pitt	1935

R

Rader, Dave	(QB)	Tulsa	1979
Ragazzo, Phil	(T)	Western Reserve	1945-47
Ramona, Joe	(G)	Santa Clara	1953
Rapacz, John	(C)	Oklahoma	1950-54
Rasheed, Kenyon	(FB)	Oklahoma	1993
Raymond, Corey	(S)	LSU	1992-93
Reagan, Frank	(B)	Penn	1941, 46-48
Reasons, Gary	(LB)	NW Louisiana St.	1984-91
Reece, Beasley	(DB)	North Texas St.	1977-83
Reed, Henry	(DE)	Weber State	1971-74
Reed, Mark	(QB)	Moorehead St.	1982
Reed, Max	(C)	Bucknell	1928
Reed, Smith	(B)	Alcorn A&M	1965-66
Reese, Henry	(C)	Temple	1933-34
Rehage, Steve	(S)	Louisiana State	1987
Rehder, Tom	(T)	Notre Dame	1990
Reynolds, Ed	(LB)	Virginia	1992
Reynolds, Owen	(E)	Georgia	1925
Rhenquist, Milt	(C)	Bethany	1931
Rhodes, Ray	(WR)	Tulsa	1974-79
Rice, J	(B)	No College	1929
Rich, Herb	(B)	Vanderbilt	1954-56
Richards, Elvin	(B)	Simpson	1933-39
Riesenberg, Doug	(T)	California	1987-93
Riley, Lee	(DB)	Detroit	1960
Rivers, Nate	(RB)	So. Carolina State	1980
Rizzo, Jack	(RB)	Lehigh	1973
Roberts, Gene	(B)	Chattanooga	1947-50
Roberts, Tom	(T)	DePaul	1943
Roberts, William	(T)	Ohio State	1984-93
Robinson, Jimmy	(WR)	Georgia Tech	1976-79
Robinson, Stacy	(WR)	No. Dakota State	1985-90
Robustelli, Andy	(DE)	Arnold	1956-64
Rodriguez, Ruben	(P)	Arizona	1992
Roland, Johnny	(RB)	Missouri	1973
Roller, Dave	(DT)	Kentucky	1971
Roman, George	(T)	Western Reserve	1950
Rooney, Cobb	(B)	Colorado	1925
Rosatti, Roman	(T)	Michigan	1928
Rose, Roy	(E)	Tennessee	1936
Rote, Kyle	(E)	SMU	1951-61
Rouson, Lee	(RB)	Colorado	1985-90
Rovinski, Tony	(B)	Holy Cross	1933
Rowe, Harmon	(B)	San Francisco	1950-52
Royston, Ed	(G)	Wake Forest	1948-49
Rossell, Fay	(B)	Lafayette	1933
Rucker, Reggie	(WR)	Boston U	1971
Rutledge, Jeff	(QB)	Alabama	1982-88

S

Saalfeld, Kelly	(C)	Nebraska	1980
Sally, Jerome	(DT)	Missouri	1982-86
Salschieder, John	(B)	St. Thomas	1949
Sanchez, John	(T)	San Francisco	1949-50

Name	Pos.	College	Years
Sarausky, Tony	(B)	Fordham	1935-37
Sark, Harvey	(G)	Phillips	1931
Satenstein, Bernie	(G)	NYU	1933
Scales, Dwight	(WR)	Grambling	1979
Schichtle. Henry	(QB)	Wichita	1964
Schmeelk, Gary	(T)	Manhattan	1942
Schmidt, Bob	(T)	Minnesota	1959-60
Schmit, Bob	(LB)	Nebraska	1975-76
Schnelker, Bob	(E)	Bowling Green	1954-60
Schnellbacher, Otto	(B)	Kansas	1950-51
Scholtz, Bob	(C-T)	Notre Dame	1965-66
Schubert, Eric	(K)	Pittsburgh	1985
Schuene, Paul	(G)	Wisconsin	1928
Schuler, Bill	(T)	Yale	1947-48
Schwab, Ray	(B)	Oklahoma City	1931
Scott, George	(B)	Miami, (Ohio)	1959
Scott, Joe	(B)	San Francisco	1948-53
Scott, Malcolm	(TE)	LSU	1983
Scott, Tom	(LB)	Virginia	1959-64
Sczurek, Stan	(LB)	Purdue	1966
Sedbrook, Len	(B)	Oklahoma City	1929-31
Seick, Earl	(G)	Manhattan	1942-43
Seitz, Warren	(WR)	Missouri	1987
Selfridge, Andy	(LB)	Virginia	1974-77
Shaffer, Leland	(QB)	Kansas St.	1935-43, 45
Shaw, Dennis	(QB)	San Diego State	1976
Shaw, George	(QB)	Oregon	1959-60
Shaw, Pete	(DB)	Northwestern	1982-84
Shaw, Rickey	(LB)	Oklahoma St.	1988-89
Shay, Jerry	(CT)	Purdue	1970-71
Shediosky, Ed	(B)	Tulsa	1945
Sherrard, Mike	(WR)	UCLA	1993
Sherrod, Horace	(E)	Tennessee	1952
Sherwin, Tim	(TE)	Boston College	1988
Shiner, Dick	(QB)	Maryland	1970
Shipp, Bill	(T)	Alabama	1954
Shirk, Gary	(TE)	Morehead State	1976-82
Shofner, Del	(E)	Baylor	1961-67
Shy, Les	(RB)	Long Beach St.	1970
Siegel, Jules	(B)	Northwestern	1948
Silas, Sam	(DT)	So. Illinois	1968
Simmons, Roy	(G)	Georgia Tech	1977-80
Simms, Bob	(E)	Rutgers	1960-62
Simms, Phil	(QB)	Morehead State	1979-93
Simonson, Dave	(T)	U. of Minn	1975
Simpson, Al	(T)	Colorado State	1975-76
Singer, Walter	(E)	Syracuse	1935-37
Sinnott, John	(T)	Brown	1980
Singletary, Bill	(LB)	Temple	1974
Sisley, Brian	(NT)	So. Dakota State	1987
Sivell, Ralph	(G)	Auburn	1944-45
Skladany, Leo	(E)	Pittsburgh	1950
Skorupan, John	(LB)	Penn State	1978-80
Slaby, Lou	(LB)	Pittsburgh	1964-65
Small, Eldridge	(DB)	Texas A&I	1972-74
Small, George	(DT)	No. Carolina A&T	1980
Smith, Doug	(S)	Ohio State	1987
Smith, Jeff	(LB)	USC	1966-67
Smith, Jeff	(TE)	Tennessee	1993
Smith, Joey	(WR)	Louisville	1991-92
Smith, Richard	(G)	Notre Dame	1930-31
Smith, Torin	(DE)	Hampton Univ.	1987
Smith, Willis	(B)	Idaho	1934-35
Smith, Zeke	(G)	Auburn	1961-62
Snead, Norm	(QB)	Wake Forest	1972-74, 76
Snyder, Gerry	(B)	Maryland	1929
Soar, Hank	(B)	Providence	1937-44, 46
Sohn, Ben	(G)	USC	1941
Sparks, Phillipi	(CB)	Arizona State	1992-93
Spencer, Willie	(RB)	No College	1977-78
Spinks, Jack	(G)	Alcorn A&M	1956-57
Springer, Harold	(E)	Oklahoma St.	1945
Stafford, Harrison	(B)	Texas	1934
Stahlman, Dick	(E)	DePaul	1927
Staten, Randy	(DE)	Minnesota	1967
Stein, Sam	(E)	No College	1931
Steinfeld, Al	(C)	C W Post	1983
Stenn, Paul	(T)	Villanova	1942
Stevens, Ted	(C)	Brown	1926
Stienke, Jim	(DB)	Southwest Texas St.	1974-77
Stits, Billy	(DB)	UCLA	1959-61
Stokes, Tm	(T)	Oregon	1981
Strada, John	(TE)	William Jewell	1974
Strahan, Michael	(DE)	Texas Southern	1993
Stribling, Bill	(E)	Mississippi	1951-53
Strong, Ken	(B)	NYU	1933-35, 39-47
Stroud, Jack	(G-T)	Tennessee	1953-64
Stuckey, Henry	(DB)	Missouri	1975-76
Stynchula, Andy	(D-E)	Penn State	1964-65
Sulaitis, Joe	(B)	No College	1943-53
Summerall, Pat	(D-E)	Arkansas	1958-61
Summerell, Carl	(QB)	East Carolina	1974-75
Sutherin, Don	(B)	Ohio State	1959
Sutton Ed	(B)	North Carolina	1960-61
Sutton Frank	(T)	Jackson State	1987
Svare, Harland	(LB)	Washington St.	1955-60
Svoboda, Bill	(LB)	Tulane	1954-59
Swain, Bill	(LB)	Oregon State	1965-67
Swiacki, Bill	(E)	Columbia	1948-50
Swartwoudt, Gregg	(T)	North Dakota	1987
Szczecko, Joe	(DT)	Northwestern	1969

T

Name	Pos.	College	Years
Tabor, Phil	(DT)	Oklahoma	1979-82
Taibi, Joe	(DE)	Idaho	1987
Taffoni, Joe	(T)	Tennessee-Martin	1972-73
Tarkenton, Fran	(QB)	Georgia	1967-71
Tarrant, Bob	(E)	Kansas St. Teachers	1936
Tate, David	(S)	Colorado	1993
Tate, John	(LB)	Jackson State	1976
Tautolo, John	(OG)	UCLA	1982-83
Taylor, Billy	(RB)	Texas Tech	1978-80
Taylor, Bob	(DE)	Maryland St.	1963-64
Taylor, Lawrence	(LB)	North Carolina	1981-93
Thigpen, Tommy	(LB	North Carolina	1993
Thomas, Aaron	(E)	Oregon State	1962-70
Thomas, Bob	(K)	Notre Dame	1986
Thomas, George	(B)	Oklahoma	1952
Thome, Chris	(C)	Minnesota	1992
Thompson, James	(WR)	Memphis State	1978
Thompson, Reyna	(CB)	Baylor	1989-92
Thompson, Rocky	(RB)	West Texas St.	1971-73
Thompson, Warren	(LB)	Oklahoma State	1987
Thornton, George	(DE)	Alabama	1993
Thorpe, Jim	(B)	Carlisle	1925
Thurlow, Steve	(B)	Stanford	1964-66
Tidwell, Travis	(QB)	Auburn	1950-51
Tierney, Leo	(C)	Georgia Tech	1978
Tillman, Lewis	(RB)	Jackson State	1989-93
Timberlake, Bob	(QB)	Michigan	1965
Tipton, Dave	(DE)	Stanford	1971-73
Tittle, Y A	(QB)	LSU	1961-64
Tobin, George	(G)	Notre Dame	1947
Tobin, Steve	(C)	Minnesota	1980
Tomaini, Army	(T)	Catawba	1945
Tomlin, Tom	(G)	Syracuse	1925
Toogood, Charlie	(DT)	Nebraska	1958
Tootie, Jeff	(LB)	San Francisco St.	1987
Topp, Bob	(E)	Michigan	1954-56
Torrey, Bob	(RB)	Penn State	1979
Treadaway, John	(T)	Hardon-Simmons	1947-48
Treadwell, David	(PK)	Clemson	1993
Triplett, Bill	(HB)	Miami (Ohio)	1967
Triplett, Mel	(FB)	Toledo	1955-60
Trocolor. Bob	(B)	Alabama	1942-44
Tucker, Bob	(TE)	Bloomsburg St.	1970-76
Tuggle, John	(RB)	California	1983-85
Tunnell, Emlen	(DB)	Iowa	1948-58
Turbert, Francis	(B)	Morris Harvey	1943
Turner, Kevin	(LB)	Pacific	1980
Turner, J. T.	(DT)	Duke	1977-83
Turner, Odessa	(WR)	NW LouisianaSt.	1987-91
Tunle, Orville	(G)	Oklahoma City	1937-41
Tyler, Maurice	(DB)	Morgan State	1978
Tyler, Pete	(B)	Hardin-Simmons	1938

U

Name	Pos.	College	Years
Umont, Frank	(T)	No College	1943-45
Umphrey, Rich	(C)	Colorado	1982-84
Underwood, Olen	(LB)	Texas	1965
Urch, Scott	(T)	Virginia	1987

V

Name	Pos.	College	Years
Van Horn, Doug	(G)	Ohio State	1968-79
Vanoy, Vernon	(DT)	Kansas	1971
Van Pelt, Brad	(LB)	Michigan State	1973-83
Vargo, Larry	(LB)	Detroit	1966-67
Visnic, Larry	(G)	St. Benedict	1943-45
Vokaty, Otto	(B)	Heidelberg	1932
Volk, Rick	(DB)	Michigan	1976
Vosberg, Don	(E)	Marquette	1941
Voss, Walter	(E)	Detroit	1926

W

Name	Pos.	College	Years
Wafer, Carl	(DT)	Tennessee St.	1974
Walbridge, Lymen	(G)	Fordham	1925
Walker, Mickey	(G)	Michigan St	1961-65
Wallace, Roger	(WR)	Bowling Green	1976
Walls, Bill	(E)	TCU	1937-43
Walls, Everson	(DB)	Grambling	1990-92
Walton, Joe	(E)	Pittsburgh	1961-63
Walton, Wayne	(G)	Abilene Christian	1971
Walton, Whip	(LB)	San Diego State	1980
Warren, Vince	(WR)	San Diego State	1986
Watkins, Larry	(RB)	Alcorn A&M	1975-77
Watts, Ted	(CB)	Texas Tech	1985
Washington, Gene	(WR)	Georgia	1979
Washington, John	(DE)	Oklahoma St.	1986-92
Weaver, Larry	(B)	Fullerton	1955
Webb, Allen	(DB)	Arnold	1961-65
Webber, Howard	(E)	Kansas State	1926
Webster, Alex	(B)	No. Carolina St	1955-64
Weinmeister, Arnie	(T)	Washington	1950-53
Weisacosky, Ed	(LB)	Miami (Fla.)	1967
Weiss, John	(E)	No College	1944-47
Welch, Herb	(S)	UCLA	1985-88
Wells, Harold	(LB)	Purdue	1969
Wells, Joel	(B)	Clemson	1961
Wells, Kent	(DT)	Nebraska	1990
Wells, Mike	(QB)	Illinois	1975
Wellborn, Joe	(C)	Texas A&M	1966-67
Wesley, Cecil	(C)	Alabama	1928
West, Stan	(G)	Oklahoma	1955
Weston, Jef1	(DT)	Notre Dame	1979-82
Westoupal, Joe	(C)	Nebraska	1929-30
Wheelwright, Ernie	(B)	So. Illinois	1964-65
White, Adrian	(S)	Florida	1987-89
White, Art	(G)	Alabama	1937-39, 45
White, Jim	(T)	Notre Dame	1945-50
White, Freeman	(E-LB)	Nebraska	1966-69
White, Marsh	(RB)	Arkansas	1975-77
White, Phil	(E)	Oklahoma	1925-27
White, Robb	(DE)	South Dakota	1988-89
White, Sheldon	(CB)	Miami (Ohio)	1988-89
Whittington, Mike	(LB)	Notre Dame	1980-83
Whitmore, David	(DB)	Stephen Austin	1990
Wilberg, Oscar	(E)	Nebraska Wesleyan	1930
Widmer, Corey	(LB)	Montana St.	1992-93
Widseth, Ed	(T)	Minnesota	1937-40
Wietecha, Ray	(C)	Northwestern	1953-62
Wilkins, Dick	(E)	Oregon	1954
Wilkinson, Bob	(E)	UCLA	1951-52
Williams, Brian	(C-G)	Minnesota	1989-93
Williams, Byron	(WR)	Texas-Arlington	1983-85
Williams, Ellery	(E)	Santa Clara	1950
Williams, Frank	(B)	Utah State	1948
Williams, Joe	(G)	Lafayette	1925-26
Williams, Perry	(DB)	No. Carolina St.	1984-93
Williams, Van	(RB)	East Tenn. State	1987
Williams, Willie	(B)	Grambling	1965, 67-73
Williamson, Ernie	(T)	North Carolina	1948
Willis, Ken	(K)	Kentucky	1992
Wilson, Butch	(E)	Alabama	1968-69
Wilson, Fay	(B)	Texas A&M	1927-32
Windauer, Bill	(DT)	Iowa	1975
Winter, Bill	(LB)	St. Olaf	1962-64
Winters, Frank	(C)	Western Illinois	1989
Wolfe, Hugh	(B)	Texas	1938
Wood, Gary	(QB)	Cornell	1964-66, 68-69
Woodward, Dick	(C)	Iowa	1950-51, 53
Woolfolk, Butch	(RB)	Michigan	1982-84
Woolford, Gary	(S)	Florida State	1980
Word, Roscoe	(DB)	Jackson State	1976
Wright, Mike	(DE)	Washington St.	1992
Wright, Steve	(T)	Alabama	1968-69
Wyan Kervin	(LB)	Maryland	1980
Wycoff, Doug	(B)	Georgia Tech	1927-31
Wynne, Harry	(E)	Arkansas	1945

Y

Name	Pos.	College	Years
Yarbrough, James	(S)	Murray State	1987
Yeager, Howard	(B)	Santa Barbara	1940-44
Yelvington, Dick	(T)	Georgia	1952-57
Younce, Len	(G)	Oregon State	1941-48
Young, Dave	(TE)	Purdue	1981
Young, Willie	(T)	Grambling	1966-75
Youso, Frank	(T)	Minnesota	1958-60
Yowarsky, Walt	(E)	Kentucky	1955-57

Z

Name	Pos.	College	Years
Zapustas, Joe	(E)	Fordham	1933
Zeno, Coleman	(WR)	Grambling	1971
Zofko, Mickey	(RB)	Auburn	1974
Zyntell, Jim	(G)	Holy Cross	1933